PENGUIN BOOKS

11

SEVEN ONE-ACT PLAYS

BERNARD SHAW

SEVEN ONE-ACT PLAYS

BERNARD SHAW

★

OVERRULED

THE MAN OF DESTINY

HOW HE LIED TO HER HUSBAND

PASSION, POISON, AND PETRIFACTION

THE DARK LADY OF THE SONNETS

THE ADMIRABLE BASHVILLE

VILLAGE WOOING

Foreword by

R. Martin Browne

★

PENGUIN BOOKS

BALTIMORE · MARYLAND

This edition first published 1958
Reprinted 1966
Penguin Books Inc.
3300 Clipper Mill Road, Baltimore 11, Maryland

Library of Congress Catalog
Card Number 58-10107

Printed in the United States of America

CONTENTS

FOREWORD

BERNARD SHAW never published his one-act plays in a single volume. To some of them he wrote full Prefaces, to others short notes of introduction, and all these are reproduced here. There is nothing to be added to his own inimitable comments on each play: but a few words on the character of the whole collection as it appears here may not be out of place.

All the plays but one date from before the first World War. (Shaw wrote a few more short plays, not included, during that War.) This was the period when *pièces d'occasion* were still frequently demanded. Some were needed to fill out a bill where the main play was on the short side and the patrons wanted their money's worth. The modern audience is satisfied, it seems, with two hours of playing time and will even accept less without complaint: but the audience of fifty years ago did not regard that as a full evening's entertainment. Other pieces were written at the instance of a leading actor who wanted to show off a particular aspect of his skill: and none was better able than Shaw to provide him with material for this purpose. Others again were created to grace a charitable occasion or to plead a cause.

Looked at one by one, therefore, these plays naturally appear slight: but apart from their continued usefulness to performers, especially the great band of amateurs who have created a new theatre of the one-act play, they give collectively a good quick impression of the range and versatility of Shaw's genius. The earliest is also the longest. Shaw describes *The Man of Destiny* (1895) as "hardly more than a *bravura* piece to display the virtuosity of the two principal characters," and this is fair enough. But the style of the writing demands of the actors not only brilliance of characterisation and polish of manner but also that athletic suppleness and vitality of speech on which Shaw was accustomed to insist. Nowadays one seldom hears the Shavian rhythms as he created them, for the naturalistic actor has not developed the breath-control and agility of inflection to deliver his long and subtly articulated phrases without breaking them up. A masterly performance of Shaw's Napoleon could still give the almost operatic pleasure for which he designed it.

The little sex comedies, *How He Lied to Her Husband* (1904) and *Overruled* (1912), also demand style in playing, and amply repay the actor's skill. Though the ideas behind these have become so familiar as to be no longer important in themselves, the fun is as good as ever and the structure of the comedy is firm and sound. *Village Wooing,* which can be classed with them as a comedy of the sexes, is in other ways very different. It is an old man's writing, created in 1933 to mitigate the tedium of convalescence on a world cruise. The theme is that of *Man and Superman,* but it is treated, not in the jewel-hard manner of 1911 but in a much more relaxed and warmer vein. Well played, it can give an audience an intimate pleasure rarely gained from Shaw, for the two characters – especially the man in whom Shaw is clearly seeing himself – are unusually free to be human beings.

Shaw once said, a few years after he wrote *Village Wooing,* that he had come to find the theatre was no longer of interest compared to the opera and the circus. But in truth he had always had the clown in his nature. He loved exaggeration, whether of comedy or tragedy. This side of his work has little appeal at present but its appeal will certainly return. The two examples here, *Passion, Poison and Petrifaction* (a 'tragedy' written for a charity in 1915) and *The Admirable Bashville* (from a novel of Shaw's own, 1909) serve well to keep actors in training and audiences aware of the medium. The latter play is also Shaw's skilfully clownish challenge to the early Shakespeare, and proves that he had a considerable command of blank verse, as he had an inimitable command of the English language.

The Dark Lady pleads the cause – always dear to Shaw's heart – of the National Theatre. No better plea has yet been made, though the play was written in 1910. The English persist in going their haphazard way, in the theatre even more than in the other arts, and the answer to the plea for a National Theatre is at the moment merely dusty. But the dust will be blown off, later or perhaps sooner: and when that happens Shaw's little play will be found to speak the right words in the right order.

1958 E. MARTIN BROWNE

THE MAN OF DESTINY

The Man of Destiny was first produced at the Grand Theatre, Croydon, on 1 July 1897, with the following cast:

NAPOLEON	*Murray Carson*
A LIEUTENANT	*E. H. Kelly*
GIUSEPPE	*Horace Hodges*
A STRANGE LADY	*Florence West*

THE MAN OF DESTINY

The twelfth of May, 1796, in north Italy, at Tavazzano, on the road from Lodi to Milan. The afternoon sun is blazing serenely over the plains of Lombardy, treating the Alps with respect and the anthills with indulgence, neither disgusted by the basking of the swine in the villages nor hurt by its cool reception in the churches, but ruthlessly disdainful of two hordes of mischievous insects which are the French and Austrian armies. Two days before, at Lodi, the Austrians tried to prevent the French from crossing the river by the narrow bridge there; but the French, commanded by a general aged 27, Napoleon Bonaparte, who does not respect the rules of war, rushed the fireswept bridge, supported by a tremendous cannonade in which the young general assisted with his own hands. Cannonading is his technical specialty: he has been trained in the artillery under the old régime, and made perfect in the military arts of shirking his duties, swindling the paymaster over travelling expenses, and dignifying war with the noise and smoke of cannon, as depicted in all military portraits. He is, however, an original observer, and has perceived, for the first time since the invention of gunpowder, that a cannon ball, if it strikes a man, will kill him. To a thorough grasp of this remarkable discovery he adds a highly evolved faculty for physical geography and for the calculation of times and distances. He has prodigious powers of work, and a clear realistic knowledge of human nature in public affairs, having seen it exhaustively tested in that department during the French Revolution. He is imaginative without illusions, and creative without religion, loyalty, patriotism, or any of the common ideals. Not that he is incapable of these ideals: on the contrary, he has swallowed them all in his boyhood, and now, having a keen dramatic faculty, is extremely clever at playing upon them by the arts of the actor and stage manager. Withal, he is no spoiled child. Poverty, ill-luck, the shifts of impecuni-

ous shabby-gentility, repeated failure as a would-be author, humiliation as a rebuffed time server, reproof and punishment as an incompetent and dishonest officer, an escape from dismissal from the service so narrow that if the emigration of the nobles had not raised the value of even the most rascally lieutenant to the famine price of a general he would have been swept contemptuously from the army: these trials have ground his conceit out of him, and forced him to be self-sufficient and to understand that to such men as he is the world will give nothing that he cannot take from it by force. In this the world is not free from cowardice and folly; for Napoleon, as a merciless cannonader of political rubbish, is making himself useful: indeed, it is even now impossible to live in England without sometimes feeling how much that country lost in not being conquered by him as well as by Julius Cæsar.

However, on this May afternoon in 1796, *it is early days with him. He has but recently been promoted general, partly by using his wife to seduce the Directory* (*then governing France*)*; partly by the scarcity of officers caused by the emigration as aforesaid; partly by his faculty of knowing a country, with all its roads, rivers, hills, and valleys, as he knows the palm of his hand; and largely by that new faith of his in the efficacy of firing cannons at people. His army is, as to discipline, in a state which has so greatly shocked some modern writers before whom the following story has been enacted, that they, impressed with the later glory of "L'Empereur," have altogether refused to credit it. But Napoleon is not L'Empereur yet: his men call him Le Petit Caporal, as he is still in the stage of gaining influence over them by displays of pluck. He is not in a position to force his will on them in orthodox military fashion by the cat o' nine tails. The French Revolution, which has escaped suppression solely through the monarchy's habit of being at least four years in arrear with its soldiers in the matter of pay, has substituted for that habit, as far as possible, the habit of not paying at all, except in promises and patriotic flatteries which are not compatible with martial law of the Prussian type. Napoleon has therefore approached the Alps in command of men without money, in* *rags, and consequently indisposed to stand much discipline, especially from upstart generals. This circumstance, which would have embarrassed an idealist soldier, has been worth a thousand cannon to Napoleon. He has said to his army "You have patriotism and courage; but you have no money, no clothes, and hardly anything to eat. In Italy there are all these things, and glory as well, to be gained by a devoted army led by a general who regards loot as the natural right of the soldier. I am such a general. En avant, mes enfants!" The result has entirely justified him. The army conquers Italy as the locusts conquered Cyprus. They fight all day and march all night, covering impossible distances and appearing in incredible places, not because every soldier carries a field marshal's baton in his knapsack, but because he hopes to carry at least half a dozen silver forks there next day.*

It must be understood, by the way, that the French army does not make war on the Italians. It is there to rescue them from the tyranny of their Austrian conquerors, and confer republican institutions on them; so that in incidentally looting them it merely makes free with the property of its friends, who ought to be grateful to it, and perhaps would be if ingratitude were not the proverbial failing of their country. The Austrians, whom it fights, are a thoroughly respectable regular army, well disciplined, commanded by gentlemen versed in orthodox campaigning: at the head of them Beaulieu, practising the classic art of war under orders from Vienna, and getting horribly beaten by Napoleon, who acts on his own responsibility in defiance of professional precedents or orders from Paris. Even when the Austrians win a battle, all that is necessary is to wait until their routine obliges them to return to their quarters for afternoon tea, so to speak, and win it back again from them: a course pursued later on with brilliant success at Marengo. On the whole, with his foe handicapped by Austrian statesmanship, classic generalship, and the exigencies of the aristocratic social structure of Viennese society, Napoleon finds it possible to be irresistible without working heroic miracles. The world, however, likes miracles and heroes, and is quite incapable of conceiving the action of such forces as academic militarism or Viennese drawing-roomism. Hence it has already begun to manufacture "L'Empereur," and thus to make it difficult for the romanticists of a hundred years later to credit the hitherto unrecorded little scene now in question at Tavazzano.

The best quarters in Tavazzano are at a little inn, the first house reached by travellers passing through the place from Milan to Lodi. It stands in a vineyard; and its principal room, a pleasant refuge from the summer heat, is open so widely at the back to this vineyard that it is almost a large veranda. The bolder children, much excited by the alarums and excursions of the past few days, and by an irruption of French troops at six o'clock, know that the French commander has quartered himself in this room, and are divided between a craving to peep in at the front windows, and a mortal dread of the sentinel, a young gentleman-soldier who, having no natural moustache, has had a most ferocious one painted on his face with boot blacking by his sergeant. As his heavy uniform, like all the uniforms of that day, is designed for parade without the least reference to his health or comfort, he perspires profusely in the sun; and his painted moustache has run in little streaks down his chin and round his neck, except where it has dried in stiff japanned flakes and had its sweeping outline chipped off in grotesque little bays and headlands, making him unspeakably ridiculous in the eye of History a hundred years later, but monstrous and horrible to the contemporary north Italian infant, to whom nothing would seem more natural than that he should relieve the monotony of his guard by pitchforking a stray child up on his bayonet, and eating it uncooked. Nevertheless one girl of bad character, in whom an instinct of privilege with soldiers is already stirring, does peep in at the safest window for a moment before a glance and a clink from the sentinel sends her flying. Most of what she sees she has seen before: the vineyard at the back, with the old winepress and a cart among the vines; the door close on her right leading to the street entry; the landlord's best sideboard, now in full action for dinner, further back on the same side; the fireplace on the other side with a couch near it; another door, leading to the inner rooms, between it and the vineyard; and the table in the middle set out with a repast of Milanese risotto, cheese, grapes, bread, olives, and a big wickered flask of red wine.

The landlord, Giuseppe Grandi, she knows well. He is a swarthy vivacious shrewdly cheerful black-curled bullet headed grinning little innkeeper of 40. Naturally an excellent host, he is in the highest spirits this evening at his good fortune in having as his guest the French commander to protect him against the license of the troops. He actually sports a pair of gold earrings which would otherwise have been hidden carefully under the winepress with his little equipment of silver plate.

Napoleon, sitting facing her on the further side of the table, she sees for the first time. He is working hard, partly at his meal, which he has discovered how to dispatch in ten minutes by attacking all the courses simultaneously (this practice is the beginning of his downfall), and partly at a military map on which he from time to time marks the position of the forces by taking a grapeskin from his mouth and planting it on the map with his thumb like a wafer. There is no revolutionary untidiness about his dress or person; but his elbow has displaced most of the dishes and glasses; and his long hair trails into the risotto when he forgets it and leans more intently over the map.

GIUSEPPE. Will your excellency—

NAPOLEON [*intent on his map, but cramming himself mechanically with his left hand*] Dont talk. I'm busy.

GIUSEPPE [*with perfect goodhumor*] Excellency: I obey.

NAPOLEON. Some red ink.

GIUSEPPE. Alas! excellency, there is none.

NAPOLEON [*with Corsican facetiousness*] Kill something and bring me its blood.

GIUSEPPE [*grinning*] There is nothing but your excellency's horse, the sentinel, the lady upstairs, and my wife.

NAPOLEON. Kill your wife.

GIUSEPPE. Willingly, your excellency; but unhappily I am not strong enough. She would kill me.

NAPOLEON. That will do equally well.

GIUSEPPE. Your excellency does me too much honor. [*Stretching his hand towards the flask*] Perhaps some wine will answer your excellency's purpose.

NAPOLEON [*hastily protecting the flask, and becoming quite serious*] Wine! No: that would be waste. You are all the same: waste! waste! waste! [*He marks the map with gravy, using his fork as a pen*]. Clear away. [*He finishes his wine; pushes back his chair; and uses his napkin, stretching his legs and leaning back, but still frowning and thinking*].

GIUSEPPE [*clearing the table and removing the things to a tray on the sideboard*] Every man to his trade, excellency. We innkeepers have plenty of cheap wine: we think nothing of spilling it. You great generals have plenty of cheap blood: you think nothing of spilling it. Is it not so, excellency?

NAPOLEON. Blood costs nothing: wine costs money. [*He rises and goes to the fireplace*].

GIUSEPPE. They say you are careful of everything except human life, excellency.

NAPOLEON. Human life, my friend, is the only thing that takes care of itself. [*He throws himself at his ease on the couch*].

GIUSEPPE [*admiring him*] Ah, excellency, what fools we all are beside you! If I could only find out the secret of your success!

NAPOLEON. You would make yourself Emperor of Italy, eh?

GIUSEPPE. Too troublesome, excellency: I leave all that to you. Besides, what would become of my inn if I were Emperor? See how you enjoy looking on at me whilst I keep the inn for you and wait on you! Well, I shall enjoy looking on at you whilst you become Emperor of Europe, and govern the country for me. [*As he chatters, he takes the cloth off deftly without removing the map, and finally takes the corners in his hands and the middle in his mouth, to fold it up*].

NAPOLEON. Emperor of Europe, eh? Why only Europe?

GIUSEPPE. Why, indeed? Emperor of the world, excellency! Why not? [*He folds and rolls up the cloth, emphasizing his phrase by the steps of the process*]. One man is like another [*fold*]: one country is like another [*fold*]: one battle is like another. [*At the last fold, he slaps the cloth on the table and deftly rolls it up, adding, by way of peroration*] Conquer one: conquer all. [*He takes the cloth to the sideboard, and puts it in a drawer*].

NAPOLEON. And govern for all; fight for all; be everybody's servant under cover of being everybody's master. Giuseppe.

GIUSEPPE [*at the sideboard*] Excellency?

NAPOLEON. I forbid you to talk to me about myself.

GIUSEPPE [*coming to the foot of the couch*] Pardon. Your excellency is so unlike other great men. It is the subject they like best.

NAPOLEON. Well, talk to me about the subject they like next best, whatever that may be.

GIUSEPPE [*unabashed*] Willingly, your excellency. Has your excellency by any chance caught a glimpse of the lady upstairs?

NAPOLEON [*sitting up promptly*] How old is she?

GIUSEPPE. The right age, excellency.

NAPOLEON. Do you mean seventeen or thirty?

GIUSEPPE. Thirty, excellency.

NAPOLEON. Goodlooking?

GIUSEPPE. I cannot see with your excellency's eyes: every man must judge that for himself. In my opinion, excellency, a fine figure of a lady. [*Slyly*] Shall I lay the table for her collation here?

NAPOLEON [*brusquely, rising*] No: lay nothing here until the officer for whom I am waiting comes back. [*He looks at his watch, and takes to walking to and fro between the fireplace and the vineyard*].

GIUSEPPE [*with conviction*] Excellency: believe me, he has been captured by the accursed Austrians. He dare not keep you waiting if he were at liberty.

NAPOLEON [*turning at the edge of the shadow of the veranda*] Giuseppe: if that turns out to be true, it will put me into such a temper that nothing short of hanging you and your whole household, including the lady upstairs, will satisfy me.

GIUSEPPE. We are all cheerfully at your excellency's disposal, except the lady. I cannot answer for her; but no lady could resist you, General.

NAPOLEON [*sourly, resuming his march*] Hm! You will never be hanged. There is no satisfaction in hanging a man who does not object to it.

GIUSEPPE [*sympathetically*] Not the least in the world, excellency: is there? [*Napoleon again looks at his watch, evidently growing anxious*]. Ah, one can see that you are a great man, General: you know how to wait. If it were a corporal now, or a sub-lieutenant, at the end of three minutes he would be swearing, fuming, threatening, pulling the house about our ears.

NAPOLEON. Giuseppe: your flatteries are insufferable. Go and talk outside. [*He sits down again at the table, with his jaws in his hands, and his elbows propped on the map, poring over it with a troubled expression*].

GIUSEPPE. Willingly, your excellency. You shall not be disturbed. [*He takes up the tray and prepares to withdraw*].

NAPOLEON. The moment he comes back, send him to me.

GIUSEPPE. Instantaneously, your excellency.

A LADY'S VOICE [*calling from some distant part of the inn*] Giusep-pe! [*The voice is very musical, and the two final notes make an ascending interval*].

NAPOLEON [*startled*] Who's that?

GIUSEPPE. The lady, excellency.

NAPOLEON. The lady upstairs?

GIUSEPPE. Yes, excellency. The strange lady.

NAPOLEON. Strange? Where does she come from?

GIUSEPPE [*with a shrug*] Who knows? She arrived here just before your excellency in a hired carriage belonging to the Golden Eagle at Borghetto. By herself, excellency. No servants. A dressing bag and a trunk: that is all. The postillion says she left a horse at the Golden Eagle. A charger, with military trappings.

NAPOLEON. A woman with a charger! French or Austrian?

GIUSEPPE. French, excellency.

NAPOLEON. Her husband's charger, no doubt. Killed at Lodi, poor fellow.

THE LADY'S VOICE [*the two final notes now making a peremptory descending interval*] Giuseppe!

NAPOLEON [*rising to listen*] Thats not the voice of a woman whose husband was killed yesterday.

GIUSEPPE. Husbands are not always regretted, excellency. [*Calling*] Coming, lady, coming. [*He makes for the inner door*].

NAPOLEON [*arresting him with a strong hand on his shoulder*] Stop. Let her come.

VOICE. Giuseppe!! [*impatiently*].

GIUSEPPE. Let me go, excellency. It is my point of honor as an innkeeper to come when I am called. I appeal to you as a soldier.

A MAN'S VOICE [*outside, at the inn door, shouting*] Here, someone. Hollo! Landlord! Where are you? [*Somebody raps vigorously with a whip handle on a bench in the passage*].

NAPOLEON [*suddenly becoming the commanding officer again and throwing Giuseppe off*] My man at last. [*Pointing to the inner door*] Go. Attend to your business: the lady is calling you. [*He goes to the fireplace and stands with his back to it with a determined military air*].

GIUSEPPE [*with bated breath, snatching up his tray*] Certainly, excellency. [*He hurries out by the inner door*].

THE MAN'S VOICE [*impatiently*] Are you all asleep here?

The other door is kicked rudely open. A dusty sub-lieutenant bursts into the room. He is a tall chuckle-headed young man of 24, with the complexion and style of a man of rank, and a self-assurance on that ground which the French Revolution has failed to shake in the smallest degree. He has a thick silly lip, an eager credulous eye, an obstinate nose, and a loud confident voice.

A young man without fear, without reverence, without imagination, without sense, hopelessly insusceptible to the Napoleonic or any other idea, stupendously egotistical, eminently qualified to rush in where angels fear to tread, yet of a vigorous babbling vitality which bustles him into the thick of things. He is just now boiling with vexation, attributable by a superficial observer to his impatience at not being promptly attended to by the staff of the inn, but in which a more discerning eye can perceive a certain moral depth, indicating a more permanent and momentous grievance. On seeing Napoleon, he is sufficiently taken aback to check himself and salute; but he does not betray by his manner any of that prophetic consciousness of Marengo and Austerlitz, Waterloo and St Helena, or the Napoleonic pictures of Delaroche and Meissonier, which later ages expect from him.

NAPOLEON [*watch in hand*] Well, sir, you have come at last. Your instructions were that I should arrive here at six, and find you waiting for me with my mail from Paris and with despatches. It is now twenty minutes to eight. You were sent on this service as a hard rider with the fastest horse in the camp. You arrive a hundred minutes late, on foot. Where is your horse?

THE LIEUTENANT [*moodily pulling off his gloves and dashing them with his cap and whip on the table*] Ah! where indeed? Thats just what I should like to know, General. [*With emotion*] You dont know how fond I was of that horse.

NAPOLEON [*angrily sarcastic*] Indeed! [*With sudden misgiving*] Where are the letters and despatches?

THE LIEUTENANT [*importantly, rather pleased than otherwise at having some remarkable news*] I dont know.

NAPOLEON [*unable to believe his ears*] You dont know!

LIEUTENANT. No more than you do, General. Now I suppose I shall be court-martialled. Well, I dont mind being court-martialled; but [*with solemn determination*] I tell you, General, if ever I catch that innocent looking youth,

I'll spoil his beauty, the slimy little liar! I'll make a picture of him. I'll—

NAPOLEON [*advancing from the hearth to the table*] What innocent looking youth? Pull yourself together, sir, will you; and give an account of yourself.

LIEUTENANT [*facing him at the opposite side of the table, leaning on it with his fists*] Oh, I'm all right, General: I'm perfectly ready to give an account of myself. I shall make the court-martial thoroughly understand that the fault was not mine. Advantage has been taken of the better side of my nature; and I'm not ashamed of it. But with all respect to you as my commanding officer, General, I say again that if ever I set eyes on that son of Satan, I'll—

NAPOLEON [*angrily*] So you said before.

LIEUTENANT [*drawing himself upright*] I say it again. Just wait until I catch him. Just wait: thats all. [*He folds his arms resolutely, and breathes hard, with compressed lips*].

NAPOLEON. I am waiting, sir. For your explanation.

LIEUTENANT [*confidently*] Youll change your tone, General, when you hear what has happened to me.

NAPOLEON. Nothing has happened to you, sir: you are alive and not disabled. Where are the papers entrusted to you?

LIEUTENANT. Nothing happened to me! Nothing!! He swore eternal brotherhood with me. Was that nothing? He said my eyes reminded him of his sister's eyes. Was that nothing? He cried—actually cried—over the story of my separation from Angelica. Was that nothing? He paid for both bottles of wine, though he only ate bread and grapes himself. Perhaps you call that nothing. He gave me his pistols and his horse and his despatches—most important despatches—and let me go away with them. [*Triumphantly, seeing that he has reduced Napoleon to blank stupefaction*] Was that nothing?

NAPOLEON [*enfeebled by astonishment*] What did he do that for?

LIEUTENANT [*as if the reason were obvious*] To shew his confidence in me, of course. [*Napoleon's jaw does not ex-*

actly drop; but its hinges become nerveless]. And I was worthy of his confidence: I brought them all back honorably. But would you believe it? when I trusted him with my pistols, and my horse, and my despatches—

NAPOLEON. What the devil did you do that for?

LIEUTENANT. I'm telling you: to shew my confidence in him. And he betrayed it! abused it! never came back again! The thief! the swindler! the heartless treacherous little blackguard! You call that nothing, I suppose. But look here, General: [*again resorting to the table with his fists for greater emphasis*] you may put up with this outrage from the Austrians if you like; but speaking for myself personally, I tell you that if ever I catch—

NAPOLEON [*turning on his heel in disgust and irritably resuming his march to and fro*] Yes: you have said that more than once already.

LIEUTENANT [*excitedly*] More than once! I'll say it fifty times; and whats more, I'll do it. Youll see, General. I'll shew my confidence in him, so I will. I'll—

NAPOLEON. Yes, yes, sir: no doubt you will. What kind of man was he?

LIEUTENANT. Well, I should think you ought to be able to tell from his conduct the kind of man he was.

NAPOLEON. Psha! What was he like?

LIEUTENANT. Like! He was like—well, you ought to have just seen the fellow: that will give you a notion of what he was like. He wont be like it five minutes after I catch him; for I tell you that if ever—

NAPOLEON [*shouting furiously for the innkeeper*] Giuseppe! [*To the Lieutenant, out of all patience*] Hold your tongue, sir, if you can.

LIEUTENANT [*plaintively*] I warn you it's no use trying to put the blame on me. How was I to know the sort of fellow he was? [*He takes a chair from between the sideboard and the outer door; places it near the table; and sits down*]. If you only knew how hungry and tired I am, youd have more consideration.

GIUSEPPE [*returning*] What is it, excellency?

NAPOLEON [*struggling with his temper*] Take this—this officer. Feed him; and put him to bed, if necessary. When he is in his right mind again, find out what has happened to him and bring me word. [*To the Lieutenant*] Consider yourself under arrest, sir.

LIEUTENANT [*with sulky stiffness*] I was prepared for that. It takes a gentleman to understand a gentleman. [*He throws his sword on the table*].

GIUSEPPE [*with sympathetic concern*] Have you been attacked by the Austrians, lieutenant? Dear! dear! dear!

LIEUTENANT [*contemptuously*] Attacked! I could have broken his back between my finger and thumb. I wish I had, now. No: it was by appealing to the better side of my nature: thats what I cant get over. He said he'd never met a man he liked so much as me. He put his handkerchief round my neck because a gnat bit me, and my stock was chafing it. Look! [*He pulls a handkerchief from his stock. Giuseppe takes it and examines it*].

GIUSEPPE [*to Napoleon*] A lady's handkerchief, excellency. [*He smells it*]. Perfumed.

NAPOLEON. Eh? [*He takes it and looks at it attentively*]. Hm! [*He smells it*]. Ha! [*He walks thoughtfully across the room, looking at the handkerchief, which he finally sticks in the breast of his coat*].

LIEUTENANT. Good enough for him, anyhow. I noticed that he had a woman's hands when he touched my neck, with his coaxing fawning ways, the mean effeminate little hound. [*Lowering his voice with thrilling intensity*] But mark my words, General. If ever—

THE LADY'S VOICE [*outside, as before*] Giuseppe!

LIEUTENANT [*petrified*] What was that?

GIUSEPPE. Only a lady upstairs, lieutenant, calling me.

LIEUTENANT. Lady!

VOICE. Giuseppe, Giuseppe: where are you?

LIEUTENANT [*murderously*] Give me that sword. [*He snatches up the sword and draws it*].

GIUSEPPE [*rushing forward and seizing his right arm*] What

are you thinking of, lieutenant? It's a lady: dont you hear? It's a woman's voice.

LIEUTENANT. It's his voice, I tell you. Let me go. [*He breaks away, and rushes to the edge of the veranda, where he posts himself, sword in hand, watching the door like a cat watching a mousehole*].

It opens; and the Strange Lady steps in. She is tall and extraordinarily graceful, with a delicately intelligent, apprehensive, questioning face: perception in the brow, sensitiveness in the nostrils, character in the chin: all keen, refined, and original. She is very feminine, but by no means weak: the lithe tender figure is hung on a strong frame: the hands and feet, neck and shoulders, are useful vigorous members, of full size in proportion to her stature, which perceptibly exceeds that of Napoleon and the innkeeper, and leaves her at no disadvantage with the lieutenant. Only, her elegance and radiant charm keep the secret of her size and strength. She is not, judging by her dress, an admirer of the latest fashions of the Directory; or perhaps she uses up her old dresses for travelling. At all events she wears no jacket with extravagant lappels, no Greco-Tallien sham chiton, nothing, indeed, that the Princesse de Lamballe might not have worn. Her dress of flowered silk is long waisted, with a Watteau pleat behind, but with the paniers reduced to mere rudiments, as she is too tall for them. It is cut low in the neck, where it is eked out by a creamy fichu. She is fair, with golden brown hair and grey eyes.

She enters with the self-possession of a woman accustomed to the privileges of rank and beauty. The innkeeper, who has excellent natural manners, is highly appreciative of her. Napoleon is smitten self-conscious. His color deepens: he becomes stiffer and less at ease than before. She is advancing in an infinitely well bred manner to pay her respects to him when the lieutenant pounces on her and seizes her right wrist. As she recognizes him, she becomes deadly pale. There is no mistaking her expression: a revelation of some fatal error, utterly unexpected, has suddenly appalled her in the midst of tranquillity, security, and victory. The next moment a wave of angry color rushes up from beneath the creamy fichu and drowns her whole face. One can see that she is blushing all over her body. Even the lieutenant, ordinarily incapable of observation, can see a thing when it is painted red for him. Interpreting the blush as the involuntary confession of black deceit confronted with its victim, he addresses her in a loud crow of retributive triumph.

LIEUTENANT. So Ive got you, my lad. So youve disguised yourself, have you? [*In a voice of thunder, releasing her wrist*] Take off that skirt.

GIUSEPPE [*remonstrating*] Oh, lieutenant!

LADY [*affrighted, but highly indignant at his having dared to touch her*] Gentlemen: I appeal to you. [*To Napoleon*] You, sir, are an officer: a general. You will protect me, will you not?

LIEUTENANT. Never you mind him, General. Leave me to deal with him.

NAPOLEON. With him! With whom, sir? Why do you treat this lady in such a fashion?

LIEUTENANT. Lady! He's a man! the man I shewed my confidence in. [*Raising his sword*] Here, you—

LADY [*running behind Napoleon and in her agitation clasping to her breast the arm which he extends before her as a fortification*] Oh, thank you, General. Keep him away.

NAPOLEON. Nonsense, sir. This is certainly a lady [*she suddenly drops his arm and blushes again*]; and you are under arrest. Put down your sword, sir, instantly.

LIEUTENANT. General: I tell you he's an Austrian spy. He passed himself off on me as one of General Masséna's staff this afternoon; and now he's passing himself off on you as a woman. Am I to believe my own eyes or not?

LADY. General: it must be my brother. He is on General Masséna's staff. He is very like me.

LIEUTENANT [*his mind giving way*] Do you mean to say that youre not your brother, but your sister? the sister who was so like me? who had my beautiful blue eyes? It's a lie: your eyes are not like mine: theyre exactly like your own.

NAPOLEON [*with contained exasperation*] Lieutenant: will you obey my orders and leave the room, since you are convinced at last that this is no gentleman?

LIEUTENANT. Gentleman! I should think not. No gentleman would have abused my confid—

NAPOLEON [*out of all patience*] That will do, sir: do you hear? Will you leave the room? I order you to leave the room.

LADY. Oh pray let me go instead.

NAPOLEON [*drily*] Excuse me, madam. With all possible respect for your brother, I do not yet understand what an officer on General Masséna's staff wants with my letters. I have some questions to put to you.

GIUSEPPE [*discreetly*] Come, lieutenant. [*He opens the door*].

LIEUTENANT. I'm off. General: take warning by me: be on your guard against the better side of your nature. [*To the lady*] Madam: my apologies. I thought you were the same person, only of the opposite sex; and that naturally misled me.

LADY [*recovering her good humor*] It was not your fault, was it? I'm so glad youre not angry with me any longer, lieutenant. [*She offers her hand*].

LIEUTENANT [*bending gallantly to kiss it*] Oh, madam, not the lea—[*Checking himself and looking at it*] You have your brother's hand. And the same sort of ring!

LADY [*sweetly*] We are twins.

LIEUTENANT. That accounts for it. [*He kisses her hand*]. A thousand pardons. I didnt mind about the despatches at all: thats more the General's affair than mine: it was the abuse of my confidence through the better side of my nature. [*Taking his cap, gloves, and whip from the table and going*] Youll excuse my leaving you, General, I hope. Very sorry, I'm sure. [*He talks himself out of the room. Giuseppe follows him and shuts the door*].

NAPOLEON [*looking after them with concentrated irritation*] Idiot!

The Strange Lady smiles sympathetically. He comes frowning down the room between the table and the fireplace, all his awkwardness gone now that he is alone with her.

LADY. How can I thank you, General, for your protection?

NAPOLEON [*turning on her suddenly*] My despatches: come! [*He puts out his hand for them*].

LADY. General! [*She involuntarily puts her hands on her fichu as if to protect something there*].

NAPOLEON. You tricked that blockhead out of them. You disguised yourself as a man. I want my despatches. They are there in the bosom of your dress, under your hands.

LADY [*quickly removing her hands*] Oh, how unkindly you are speaking to me! [*She takes her handkerchief from her fichu*] You frighten me. [*She touches her eyes as if to wipe away a tear*].

NAPOLEON. I see you dont know me, madam, or you would save yourself the trouble of pretending to cry.

LADY [*producing an effect of smiling through her tears*] Yes, I do know you. You are the famous General Buonaparte. [*She gives the name a marked Italian pronunciation: Bwawna-parr-te*].

NAPOLEON [*angrily, with the French pronunciation*] Bonaparte, Madam, Bonaparte. The papers, if you please.

LADY. But I assure you—[*He snatches the handkerchief rudely*]. General! [*indignantly*].

NAPOLEON [*taking the other handkerchief from his breast*] You lent one of your handkerchiefs to my lieutenant when you robbed him. [*He looks at the two handkerchiefs*]. They match one another. [*He smells them*]. The same scent. [*He flings them down on the table*]. I am waiting for my despatches. I shall take them, if necessary, with as little ceremony as I took the handkerchief.

LADY [*in dignified reproof*] General: do you threaten women?

NAPOLEON [*bluntly*] Yes.

LADY [*disconcerted, trying to gain time*] But I dont understand. I—

NAPOLEON. You understand perfectly. You came here because your Austrian employers calculated that I was six leagues away. I am always to be found where my enemies dont expect me. You have walked into the lion's den. Come! you are a brave woman. Be a sensible one: I have no time to waste. The papers. [*He advances a step ominously*].

LADY [*breaking down in the childish rage of impotence, and throwing herself in tears on the chair left beside the table by the lieutenant*] *I* brave! How little you know! I have spent the day in an agony of fear. I have a pain here from the tightening of my heart at every suspicious look, every threatening movement. Do you think everyone is as brave as you? Oh, why will not you brave people do the brave things? Why do you leave them to us, who have no courage at all? I'm not brave: I shrink from violence: danger makes me miserable.

NAPOLEON [*interested*] Then why have you thrust yourself into danger?

LADY. Because there is no other way: I can trust nobody else. And now it is all useless: all because of you, who have no fear because you have no heart, no feeling, no—[*She breaks off, and throws herself on her knees*]. Ah, General, let me go: let me go without asking any questions. You shall have your despatches and letters: I swear it.

NAPOLEON [*holding out his hand*] Yes: I am waiting for them.

She gasps, daunted by his ruthless promptitude into despair of moving him by cajolery. She looks up perplexedly at him, racking her brains for some device to outwit him. He meets her regard inflexibly.

LADY [*rising at last with a quiet little sigh*] I will get them for you. They are in my room. [*She turns to the door*].

NAPOLEON. I shall accompany you, madam.

LADY [*drawing herself up with a noble air of offended deli-*

cacy] I cannot permit you, General, to enter my chamber.

NAPOLEON. Then you shall stay here, madam, whilst I have your chamber searched for my papers.

LADY [*spitefully, openly giving up her plan*] You may save yourself the trouble. They are not there.

NAPOLEON. No: I have already told you where they are [*pointing to her breast*].

LADY [*with pretty piteousness*] General: I only want to keep one little private letter. Only one. Let me have it.

NAPOLEON [*cold and stern*] Is that a reasonable demand, madam?

LADY [*encouraged by his not refusing point-blank*] No; but that is why you must grant it. Are your own demands reasonable? thousands of lives for the sake of your victories, your ambitions, your destiny! And what I ask is such a little thing. And I am only a weak woman, and you a brave man. [*She looks at him with her eyes full of tender pleading, and is about to kneel to him again*].

NAPOLEON [*brusquely*] Get up, get up. [*He turns moodily away and takes a turn across the room, pausing for a moment to say, over his shoulder*] Youre talking nonsense; and you know it. [*She sits down submissively on the couch. When he turns and sees her despair, he feels that his victory is complete, and that he may now indulge in a little play with his victim. He comes back and sits beside her. She looks alarmed and moves a little away from him; but a ray of rallying hope beams from her eye. He begins like a man enjoying some secret joke*]. How do you know I am a brave man?

LADY [*amazed*] You! General Buonaparte [*Italian pronunciation*].

NAPOLEON. Yes, I, General Bonaparte [*emphasizing the French pronunciation*].

LADY. Oh, how can you ask such a question? you! who stood only two days ago at the bridge at Lodi, with the air full of death, fighting a duel with cannons across the river! [*Shuddering*]. Oh, you do brave things.

NAPOLEON. So do you.

LADY. I! [*With a sudden odd thought*] Oh! Are you a coward?

NAPOLEON [*laughing grimly and slapping his knees*] That is the one question you must never ask a soldier. The sergeant asks after the recruit's height, his age, his wind, his limb, but never after his courage.

LADY [*as if she had found it no laughing matter*] Ah, you can laugh at fear. Then you dont know what fear is.

NAPOLEON. Tell me this. Suppose you could have got that letter by coming to me over the bridge at Lodi the day before yesterday! Suppose there had been no other way, and that this was a sure way—if only you escaped the cannon! [*She shudders and covers her eyes for a moment with her hands*]. Would you have been afraid?

LADY. Oh, horribly afraid, agonizingly afraid. [*She presses her hands on her heart*]. It hurts only to imagine it.

NAPOLEON [*inflexibly*] Would you have come for the despatches?

LADY [*overcome by the imagined horror*] Dont ask me. I must have come.

NAPOLEON. Why?

LADY. Because I must. Because there would have been no other way.

NAPOLEON [*with conviction*] Because you would have wanted my letter enough to bear your fear. [*He rises suddenly, and deliberately poses for an oration*]. There is only one universal passion: fear. Of all the thousand qualities a man may have, the only one you will find as certainly in the youngest drummer boy in my army as in me, is fear. It is fear that makes men fight: it is indifference that makes them run away: fear is the mainspring of war. Fear! I know fear well, better than you, better than any woman. I once saw a regiment of good Swiss soldiers massacred by a mob in Paris because I was afraid to interfere: I felt myself a coward to the tips of my toes as I looked on at it. Seven months ago I revenged my shame by pounding that mob to death with cannon balls. Well, what of that? Has fear ever held a man back from anything he really wanted—or a woman either? Never. Come with me; and I will shew you twenty thousand cowards who will risk death every day for the price of a glass of brandy. And do you think there are no women in the army, braver than the men, though their lives are worth more? Psha! I think nothing of your fear or your bravery. If you had had to come across to me at Lodi, you would not have been afraid: once on the bridge, every other feeling would have gone down before the necessity—the necessity—for making your way to my side and getting what you wanted.

And now, suppose you had done all this! suppose you had come safely out with that letter in your hand, knowing that when the hour came, your fear had tightened, not your heart, but your grip of your own purpose! that it had ceased to be fear, and had become strength, penetration, vigilance, iron resolution! how would you answer then if you were asked whether you were a coward?

LADY [*rising*] Ah, you are a hero, a real hero.

NAPOLEON. Pooh! there's no such thing as a real hero. [*He strolls about the room, making light of her enthusiasm, but by no means displeased with himself for having evoked it*].

LADY. Ah yes, there is. There is a difference between what you call my bravery and yours. You wanted to win the battle of Lodi for yourself and not for anyone else, didnt you?

NAPOLEON. Of course. [*Suddenly recollecting himself*] Stop: no [*He pulls himself piously together, and says, like a man conducting a religious service*] I am only the servant of the French republic, following humbly in the footsteps of the heroes of classical antiquity. I win battles for humanity: for my country, not for myself.

LADY [*disappointed*] Oh, then you are only a womanish hero after all. [*She sits down again, all her enthusiasm gone*].

NAPOLEON [*greatly astonished*] Womanish!

LADY [*listlessly*] Yes, like me. [*With deep melancholy*] Do you think that if I wanted those despatches only for myself,

I dare venture into a battle for them? No: if that were all, I should not have the courage to ask to see you at your hotel, even. My courage is mere slavishness: it is of no use to me for my own purposes. It is only through love, through pity, through the instinct to save and protect someone else, that I can do the things that terrify me.

NAPOLEON [*contemptuously*] Pshaw! [*He turns slightingly away from her*].

LADY. Aha! now you see that I'm not really brave. [*Relapsing into petulant listlessness*] But what right have you to despise me if you only win your battles for others? for your country! through patriotism! That is what I call womanish: it is so like a Frenchman!

NAPOLEON [*furiously*] I am no Frenchman.

LADY [*innocently*] I thought you said you won the battle of Lodi for your country, General Bu— shall I pronounce it in Italian or French?

NAPOLEON. You are presuming on my patience, madam. I was born a French subject, but not in France.

LADY [*affecting a marked access of interest in him*] You were not born a subject at all, I think.

NAPOLEON [*greatly pleased*] Eh? Eh? You think not.

LADY. I am sure of it.

NAPOLEON. Well, well, perhaps not. [*The self-complacency of his assent catches his own ear. He stops short, reddening. Then, composing himself into a solemn attitude, modelled on the heroes of classical antiquity, he takes a high moral tone*]. But we must not live for ourselves alone, little one. Never forget that we should always think of others, and work for others, and lead and govern them for their own good. Self-sacrifice is the foundation of all true nobility of character.

LADY [*again relaxing her attitude with a sigh*] Ah, it is easy to see that you have never tried it, General.

NAPOLEON [*indignantly, forgetting all about Brutus and Scipio*] What do you mean by that speech, madam?

LADY. Havnt you noticed that people always exaggerate

the value of the things they havnt got? The poor think they need nothing but riches to be quite happy and good. Everybody worships truth, purity, unselfishness, for the same reason: because they have no experience of them. Oh, if they only knew!

NAPOLEON [*with angry derision*] If they only knew! Pray do you know?

LADY. Yes. I had the misfortune to be born good. [*Glancing up at him for a moment*] And it is a misfortune, I can tell you, General. I really am truthful and unselfish and all the rest of it; and it's nothing but cowardice; want of character; want of being really, strongly, positively oneself.

NAPOLEON. Ha? [*turning to her quickly with a flash of strong interest*].

LADY [*earnestly, with rising enthusiasm*] What is the secret of your power? Only that you believe in yourself. You can fight and conquer for yourself and for nobody else. You are not afraid of your own destiny. You teach us what we all might be if we had the will and courage; and that [*suddenly sinking on her knees before him*] is why we all begin to worship you. [*She kisses his hands*].

NAPOLEON [*embarrassed*] Tut! tut! Pray rise, madam.

LADY. Do not refuse my homage: it is your right. You will be Emperor of France—

NAPOLEON [*hurriedly*] Take care. Treason!

LADY [*insisting*] Yes, Emperor of France; then of Europe; perhaps of the world. I am only the first subject to swear allegiance. [*Again kissing his hand*] My Emperor!

NAPOLEON [*overcome, raising her*] Pray! pray! No, no: this is folly. Come: be calm, be calm. [*Petting her*] There! there! my girl.

LADY [*struggling with happy tears*] Yes, I know it is an impertinence in me to tell you what you must know far better than I do. But you are not angry with me, are you?

NAPOLEON. Angry! No, no: not a bit, not a bit. Come: you are a very clever and sensible and interesting woman. [*He pats her on the cheek*], Shall we be friends?

LADY [*enraptured*] Your friend! You will let me be your friend! Oh! [*She offers him both her hands with a radiant smile*]. You see: I shew my confidence in you.

This incautious echo of the lieutenant undoes her. Napoleon starts: his eyes flash: he utters a yell of rage.

NAPOLEON. What!!!

LADY. What's the matter?

NAPOLEON. Shew your confidence in me! So that I may shew my confidence in you in return by letting you give me the slip with the despatches, eh? Ah, Dalila, Dalila, you have been trying your tricks on me; and I have been as gross a gull as my jackass of a lieutenant. [*Menacingly*] Come: the despatches. Quick: I am not to be trifled with now.

LADY [*flying round the couch*] General—

NAPOLEON. Quick, I tell you. [*He passes swiftly up the middle of the room and intercepts her as she makes for the vineyard*].

LADY [*at bay, confronting him and giving way to her temper*] You dare address me in that tone.

NAPOLEON. Dare!

LADY. Yes, dare. Who are you that you should presume to speak to me in that coarse way. Oh, the vile, vulgar Corsican adventurer comes out in you very easily.

NAPOLEON [*beside himself*] You she devil! [*Savagely*] Once more, and only once, will you give me those papers or shall I tear them from you?—by force!

LADY. Tear them from me: by force!

As he glares at her like a tiger about to spring, she crosses her arms on her breast in the attitude of a martyr. The gesture and pose instantly awaken his theatrical instinct: he forgets his rage in the desire to shew her that in acting, too, she has met her match. He keeps her a moment in suspense; then suddenly clears up his countenance; puts his hands behind him with provoking coolness; looks at her up and down a couple of times; takes a pinch of snuff; wipes his fingers carefully and puts up his handkerchief, her heroic pose becoming more and more ridiculous all the time.

NAPOLEON [*at last*] Well?

LADY [*disconcerted, but with her arms still crossed devotedly*] Well: what are you going to do?

NAPOLEON. Spoil your attitude.

LADY. You brute! [*Abandoning the attitude, she comes to the end of the couch, where she turns with her back to it, leaning against it and facing him with her hands behind her*].

NAPOLEON. Ah, thats better. Now listen to me. I like you. Whats more, I value your respect.

LADY. You value what you have not got, then.

NAPOLEON. I shall have it presently. Now attend to me. Suppose I were to allow myself to be abashed by the respect due to your sex, your beauty, your heroism, and all the rest of it! Suppose I, with nothing but such sentimental stuff to stand between these muscles of mine and those papers which you have about you, and which I want and mean to have! suppose I, with the prize within my grasp, were to falter and sneak away with my hands empty; or, what would be worse, cover up my weakness by playing the magnanimous hero, and sparing you the violence I dared not use! would you not despise me from the depths of your woman's soul? Would any woman be such a fool? Well, Bonaparte can rise to the situation and act like a woman when it is necessary. Do you understand?

The lady, without speaking, stands upright, and takes a packet of papers from her bosom. For a moment she has an intense impulse to dash them in his face. But her good breeding cuts her off from any vulgar method of relief. She hands them to him politely, only averting her head. The moment he takes them, she hurries across to the other side of the room; sits down; and covers her face with her hands.

NAPOLEON [*gloating over the papers*] Aha! Thats right. Thats right. [*Before he opens them, he looks at her and says*] Excuse me. [*He sees that she is hiding her face*]. Very angry with me, eh? [*He unties the packet, the seal of which is already broken, and puts it on the table to examine its contents*].

LADY [*quietly, taking down her hands and shewing that she is not crying, but only thinking*] No. You were right. But I am sorry for you.

NAPOLEON [*pausing in the act of taking the uppermost paper from the packet*] Sorry for me! Why?

LADY. I am going to see you lose your honor.

NAPOLEON. Hm! Nothing worse than that? [*He takes up the paper*].

LADY. And your happiness.

NAPOLEON. Happiness! Happiness is the most tedious thing in the world to me. Should I be what I am if I cared for happiness? Anything else?

LADY. Nothing.

NAPOLEON. Good.

LADY. Except that you will cut a very foolish figure in the eyes of France.

NAPOLEON [*quickly*] What? [*The hand unfolding the paper involuntarily stops. The lady looks at him enigmatically, in tranquil silence. He throws the letter down and breaks out into a torrent of scolding*]. What do you mean? Eh? Are you at your tricks again? Do you think I dont know what these papers contain? I'll tell you. First, my information as to Beaulieu's retreat. There are only two things he can do —leather-brained idiot that he is!—shut himself up in Mantua or violate the neutrality of Venice by taking Peschiera. You are one of old Leatherbrain's spies: he has discovered that he has been betrayed, and has sent you to intercept the information at all hazards. As if that could save him from me, the old fool! The other papers are only my private letters from Paris, of which you know nothing.

LADY [*prompt and businesslike*] General: let us make a fair division. Take the information your spies have sent you about the Austrian army; and give me the Paris correspondence. That will content me.

NAPOLEON [*his breath taken away by the coolness of the proposal*] A fair di— [*he gasps*]. It seems to me, madam, that you have come to regard my letters as your own property, of which I am trying to rob you.

LADY [*earnestly*] No: on my honor I ask for no letter of yours: not a word that has been written by you or to you. That packet contains a stolen letter: a letter written by a woman to a man: a man not her husband: a letter that means disgrace, infamy—

NAPOLEON. A love letter?

LADY [*bitter-sweetly*] What else but a love letter could stir up so much hate?

NAPOLEON. Why is it sent to me? To put the husband in my power, eh?

LADY. No, no: it can be of no use to you: I swear that it will cost you nothing to give it to me. It has been sent to you out of sheer malice: solely to injure the woman who wrote it.

NAPOLEON. Then why not send it to her husband instead of to me?

LADY [*completely taken aback*] Oh! [*Sinking back into the chair*] I—I dont know. [*She breaks down*].

NAPOLEON. Aha! I thought so: a little romance to get the papers back. Per Bacco, I cant help admiring you. I wish I could lie like that. It would save me a great deal of trouble.

LADY [*wringing her hands*] Oh, how *I* wish I really had told you some lie! You would have believed me then. The truth is the one thing nobody will believe.

NAPOLEON [*with coarse familiarity, treating her as if she were a vivandière*] Capital! Capital! [*He puts his hands behind him on the table, and lifts himself on to it, sitting with his arms akimbo and his legs wide apart*] Come: I am a true Corsican in my love for stories. But I could tell them better than you if I set my mind to it. Next time you are asked why a letter compromising a wife should not be sent to her husband, answer simply that the husband wouldnt read it. Do you suppose, you goose, that a man wants to be compelled by public opinion to make a scene, to fight a duel, to break up his household, to injure his career by a scandal, when he can avoid it all by taking care not to know?

LADY [*revolted*] Suppose that packet contained a letter about your own wife?

NAPOLEON [*offended, coming off the table*] You are impertinent, madam.

LADY [*humbly*] I beg your pardon. Cæsar's wife is above suspicion.

NAPOLEON [*with a deliberate assumption of superiority*] You have committed an indiscretion. I pardon you. In future, do not permit yourself to introduce real persons in your romances.

LADY [*politely ignoring a speech which is to her only a breach of good manners*] General: there really is a woman's letter there. [*Pointing to the packet*] Give it to me.

NAPOLEON [*with brute conciseness*] Why?

LADY. She is an old friend: we were at school together. She has written to me imploring me to prevent the letter falling into your hands.

NAPOLEON. Why has it been sent to me?

LADY. Because it compromises the director Barras.

NAPOLEON [*frowning, evidently startled*] Barras! [*Haughtily*] Take care, madam, The director Barras is my attached personal friend.

LADY [*nodding placidly*] Yes. You became friends through your wife.

NAPOLEON. Again! Have I not forbidden you to speak of my wife? [*She keeps looking curiously at him, taking no account of the rebuke. More and more irritated, he drops his haughty manner, of which he is himself somewhat impatient, and says suspiciously, lowering his voice*] Who is this woman with whom you sympathize so deeply?

LADY. Oh, General! How could I tell you that?

NAPOLEON [*ill humoredly, beginning to walk about again in angry perplexity*] Ay, ay: stand by one another. You are all the same, you women.

LADY [*indignantly*] We are not all the same, any more than

you are. Do you think that if *I* loved another man, I should pretend to go on loving my husband, or be afraid to tell him or all the world? But this woman is not made that way. She governs men by cheating them; and they like it, and let her govern them. [*She turns her back to him in disdain*].

NAPOLEON [*not attending to her*] Barras? Barras? [*Very threateningly, his face darkening*] Take care. Take care: do you hear? You may go too far.

LADY [*innocently turning her face to him*] Whats the matter?

NAPOLEON. What are you hinting at? Who is this woman?

LADY [*meeting his angry searching gaze with tranquil indifference as she sits looking up at him*] A vain, silly, extravagant creature, with a very able and ambitious husband who knows her through and through: knows that she has lied to him about her age, her income, her social position, about everything that silly women lie about: knows that she is incapable of fidelity to any principle or any person; and yet cannot help loving her—cannot help his man's instinct to make use of her for his own advancement with Barras.

NAPOLEON [*in a stealthy coldly furious whisper*] This is your revenge, you she cat, for having had to give me the letters.

LADY. Nonsense! Or do you mean that you are that sort of man?

NAPOLEON [*exasperated, clasps his hands behind him, his fingers twitching, and says, as he walks irritably away from her to the fireplace*] This woman will drive me out of my senses. [*To her*] Begone.

LADY [*seated immovably*] Not without that letter.

NAPOLEON. Begone, I tell you. [*Walking from the fireplace to the vineyard and back to the table*] You shall have no letter. I dont like you. Youre a detestable woman, and as ugly as Satan. I dont choose to be pestered by strange women. Be off. [*He turns his back on her. In quiet amusement, she leans her cheek on her hand and laughs at him. He turns again, angrily mocking her*]. Ha! ha! ha! What are you laughing at?

LADY. At you, General. I have often seen persons of your sex getting into a pet and behaving like children; but I never saw a really great man do it before.

NAPOLEON [*brutally, flinging the words in her face*] Psha! Flattery! Flattery! Coarse, impudent flattery!

LADY [*springing up with a bright flush in her cheeks*] Oh, you are too bad. Keep your letters. Read the story of your own dishonor in them; and much good may they do you. Good-bye. [*She goes indignantly towards the inner door*].

NAPOLEON. My own—! Stop. Come back. Come back, I order you. [*She proudly disregards his savagely peremptory tone and continues on her way to the door. He rushes at her; seizes her by the arm; and drags her back*]. Now, what do you mean? Explain. Explain. I tell you, or— [*threatening her. She looks at him with unflinching defiance*]. Rrrr! you obstinate devil, you. [*Throwing her arm away*] Why cant you answer a civil question?

LADY [*deeply offended by his violence*] Why do you ask me? You have the explanation.

NAPOLEON. Where?

LADY [*pointing to the letters on the table*] There. You have only to read it.

He snatches the packet up; hesitates; looks at her suspiciously; and throws it down again.

NAPOLEON. You seem to have forgotten your solicitude for the honor of your old friend.

LADY. I do not think she runs any risk now. She does not quite understand her husband.

NAPOLEON. I am to read the letter, then? [*He stretches out his hand as if to take up the packet again, with his eye on her*].

LADY. I do not see how you can very well avoid doing so now. [*He instantly withdraws his hand*]. Oh, dont be afraid. You will find many interesting things in it.

NAPOLEON. For instance?

LADY. For instance, a duel with Barras, a domestic scene, a broken household, a public scandal, a checked career, all sorts of things.

NAPOLEON. Hm! [*He looks at her; takes up the packet and looks at it, pursing his lips and balancing it in his hands; looks at her again; passes the packet into his left hand and puts it behind his back, raising his right to scratch the back of his head as he turns and goes up to the edge of the vineyard, where he stands for a moment looking out into the vines, deep in thought. The Lady watches him in silence, somewhat slightingly. Suddenly he turns and comes back again, full of force and decision*]. I grant your request, madam. Your courage and resolution deserve to succeed. Take the letters for which you have fought so well; and remember henceforth that you found the vile vulgar Corsican adventurer as generous to the vanquished after the battle as he was resolute in the face of the enemy before it. [*He offers her the packet*].

LADY [*without taking it, looking hard at him*] What are you at now, I wonder? [*He dashes the packet furiously to the floor*]. Aha! Ive spoilt that attitude, I think. [*She makes him a pretty mocking curtsey*].

NAPOLEON [*snatching it up again*] Will you take the letters and begone [*advancing and thrusting them upon her*]?

LADY [*escaping around the table*] No: I dont want your letters.

NAPOLEON. Ten minutes ago, nothing else would satisfy you.

LADY [*keeping the table carefully between them*] Ten minutes ago you had not insulted me beyond all bearing.

NAPOLEON. I— [*swallowing his spleen*] I apologize.

LADY [*coolly*] Thanks. [*With forced politeness he offers her the packet across the table. She retreats a step out of its reach and says*] But dont you want to know whether the Austrians are at Mantua or Peschiera?

NAPOLEON. I have already told you that I can conquer my enemies without the aid of spies, madam.

LADY. And the letter? dont you want to read that?

NAPOLEON. You have said that it is not addressed to me. I am not in the habit of reading other people's letters. [*He again offers the packet*].

LADY. In that case there can be no objection to your keeping it. All I wanted was to prevent your reading it. [*Cheerfully*] Good afternoon, General. [*She turns coolly towards the inner door*].

NAPOLEON [*angrily flinging the packet on the couch*] Heaven grant me patience! [*He goes determinedly to the door, and places himself before it*]. Have you any sense of personal danger? Or are you one of those women who like to be beaten black and blue?

LADY. Thank you, General: I have no doubt the sensation is very voluptuous; but I had rather not. I simply want to go home: thats all. I was wicked enough to steal your despatches; but you have got them back; and you have forgiven me, because [*delicately reproducing his rhetorical cadence*] you are as generous to the vanquished after the battle as you are resolute in the face of the enemy before it. Wont you say goodbye to me? [*She offers her hand sweetly*].

NAPOLEON [*repulsing the advance with a gesture of concentrated rage, and opening the door to call fiercely*] Giuseppe! [*Louder*] Giuseppe! [*He bangs the door to, and comes to the middle of the room. The lady goes a little way into the vineyard to avoid him*].

GIUSEPPE [*appearing at the door*] Excellency?

NAPOLEON. Where is that fool?

GIUSEPPE. He has had a good dinner, according to your instructions, excellency, and is now doing me the honor to gamble with me to pass the time.

NAPOLEON. Send him here. Bring him here. Come with him. [*Giuseppe, with unruffled readiness, hurries off. Napoleon turns curtly to the lady, saying*] I must trouble you to remain some moments longer, madam. [*He comes to the couch*].

She comes from the vineyard along the opposite side of the room to the sideboard, and posts herself there, leaning against it, watching him. He takes the packet from the couch and deliberately buttons it carefully into his breast pocket, looking at her meanwhile with an expression which suggests that she will soon find out the meaning of his proceedings, and will not like it. Nothing more is said until the Lieutenant arrives followed by Giuseppe, who stands modestly in attendance at the table. The Lieutenant, without cap, sword, or gloves, and much improved in temper and spirits by his meal, chooses the lady's side of the room, and waits, much at his ease, for Napoleon to begin.

NAPOLEON. Lieutenant.

LIEUTENANT [*encouragingly*] General.

NAPOLEON. I cannot persuade this lady to give me much information; but there can be no doubt that the man who tricked you out of your charge was, as she admitted to you, her brother.

LIEUTENANT [*triumphantly*] What did I tell you, General! What did I tell you!

NAPOLEON. You must find that man. Your honor is at stake; and the fate of the campaign, the destiny of France, of Europe, of humanity, perhaps, may depend on the information those despatches contain.

LIEUTENANT. Yes, I suppose they really are rather serious [*as if this had hardly occurred to him before*].

NAPOLEON [*energetically*] They are so serious, sir, that if you do not recover them, you will be degraded in the presence of your regiment.

LIEUTENANT. Whew! The regiment wont like that, I can tell you.

NAPOLEON. Personally I am sorry for you. I would willingly hush up the affair if it were possible. But I shall be called to account for not acting on the despatches. I shall have to prove to all the world that I never received them, no matter what the consequences may be to you. I am sorry; but you see that I cannot help myself.

LIEUTENANT [*goodnaturedly*] Oh, dont take it to heart, General: it's really very good of you. Never mind what happens to me: I shall scrape through somehow; and we'll beat the Austrians for you, despatches or no despatches. I hope you wont insist on my starting off on a wild goose chase after the fellow now. I havnt a notion where to look for him.

GIUSEPPE [*deferentially*] You forget, Lieutenant: he has your horse.

LIEUTENANT [*starting*] I forgot that. [*Resolutely*] I'll go after him, General: I'll find that horse if it's alive anywhere in Italy. And I shant forget the despatches: never fear. Giuseppe: go and saddle one of those mangy old post-horses of yours while I get my cap and sword and things. Quick march. Off with you [*bustling him*].

GIUSEPPE. Instantly, Lieutenant, instantly. [*He disappears in the vineyard, where the light is now reddening with the sunset*].

LIEUTENANT [*looking about him on his way to the inner door*] By the way, General, did I give you my sword or did I not? Oh, I remember now. [*Fretfully*] It's all that nonsense about putting a man under arrest: one never knows where to find—[*he talks himself out of the room*].

LADY [*still at the sideboard*] What does all this mean, General?

NAPOLEON. He will not find your brother.

LADY. Of course not. Theres no such person.

NAPOLEON. The despatches will be irrecoverably lost.

LADY. Nonsense! They are inside your coat.

NAPOLEON. You will find it hard, I think, to prove that wild statement. [*The lady starts. He adds, with clinching emphasis*] Those papers are lost.

LADY [*anxiously, advancing to the corner of the table*] And that unfortunate young man's career will be sacrificed?

NAPOLEON. His career! The fellow is not worth the gunpowder it would cost to have him shot. [*He turns contemptuously and goes to the hearth, where he stands with his back to her*].

LADY [*wistfully*] You are very hard. Men and women are nothing to you but things to be used, even if they are broken in the use.

NAPOLEON [*turning on her*] Which of us has broken this

fellow? I or you? Who tricked him out of the despatches? Did you think of his career then?

LADY [*conscience-stricken*] Oh, I never thought of that. It was wicked of me; but I couldnt help it, could I? How else could I have got the papers? [*Supplicating*] General: you will save him from disgrace.

NAPOLEON [*laughing sourly*] Save him yourself, since you are so clever: it was you who ruined him. [*With savage intensity*] I hate a bad soldier.

He goes out determinedly through the vineyard. She follows him a few steps with an appealing gesture, but is interrupted by the return of the Lieutenant, gloved and capped, with his sword on, ready for the road. He is crossing to the outer door when she intercepts him.

LADY. Lieutenant.

LIEUTENANT [*importantly*] You mustnt delay me, you know. Duty, madam, duty.

LADY [*imploringly*] Oh, sir, what are you going to do to my poor brother?

LIEUTENANT. Are you very fond of him?

LADY. I should die if anything happened to him. You must spare him. [*The Lieutenant shakes his head gloomily*]. Yes, yes: you must: you shall: he is not fit to die. Listen to me. If I tell you where to find him—if I undertake to place him in your hands a prisoner, to be delivered up by you to General Bonaparte—will you promise me on your honor as an officer and a gentleman not to fight with him or treat him unkindly in any way?

LIEUTENANT. But suppose he attacks me. He has my pistols.

LADY. He is too great a coward.

LIEUTENANT. I dont feel so sure about that. He's capable of anything.

LADY. If he attacks you, or resists you in any way, I release you from your promise.

LIEUTENANT. My promise! I didnt mean to promise. Look here: youre as bad as he is: youve taken an advantage of me through the better side of my nature. What about my horse?

LADY. It is part of the bargain that you are to have your horse and pistols back.

LIEUTENANT. Honor bright?

LADY. Honor bright. [*She offers her hand*].

LIEUTENANT [*taking it and holding it*] All right: I'll be as gentle as a lamb with him. His sister's a very pretty woman. [*He attempts to kiss her*].

LADY [*slipping away from him*] Oh, Lieutenant! You forget: your career is at stake—the destiny of Europe—of humanity.

LIEUTENANT. Oh, bother the destiny of humanity! [*Making for her*] Only a kiss.

LADY [*retreating round the table*] Not until you have regained your honor as an officer. Remember: you have not captured my brother yet.

LIEUTENANT [*seductively*] Youll tell me where he is, wont you?

LADY. I have only to send him a certain signal; and he will be here in quarter of an hour.

LIEUTENANT. He's not far off, then.

LADY. No: quite close. Wait here for him: when he gets my message he will come here at once and surrender himself to you. You understand?

LIEUTENANT [*intellectually overtaxed*] Well, it's a little complicated; but I daresay it will be all right.

LADY. And now, whilst youre waiting, dont you think you had better make terms with the General?

LIEUTENANT. Oh, look here: this is getting frightfully complicated. What terms?

LADY. Make him promise that if you catch my brother he will consider that you have cleared your character as a soldier. He will promise anything you ask on that condition.

LIEUTENANT. Thats not a bad idea. Thank you: I think I'll try it.

LADY. Do. And mind, above all things, dont let him see how clever you are.

LIEUTENANT. I understand. He'd be jealous.

LADY. Dont tell him anything except that you are resolved to capture my brother or perish in the attempt. He wont believe you. Then you will produce my brother—

LIEUTENANT [*interrupting as he masters the plot*] And have the laugh at him! I say: what a jolly clever woman you are! [*Shouting*] Giuseppe!

LADY. Sh! Not a word to Giuseppe about me. [*She puts her finger on her lips. He does the same. They look at one another warningly. Then, with a ravishing smile, she changes the gesture into wafting him a kiss, and runs out through the inner door. Electrified, he bursts into a volley of chuckles*].

Giuseppe comes back by the outer door.

GIUSEPPE. The horse is ready, Lieutenant.

LIEUTENANT. I'm not going just yet. Go and find the General and tell him I want to speak to him.

GIUSEPPE [*shaking his head*] That will never do, Lieutenant.

LIEUTENANT. Why not?

GIUSEPPE. In this wicked world a general may send for a lieutenant; but a lieutenant must not send for a general.

LIEUTENANT. Oh, you think he wouldnt like it. Well, perhaps youre right: one has to be awfully particular about that sort of thing now we're a republic.

Napoleon reappears, advancing from the vineyard, buttoning the breast of his coat, pale and full of gnawing thoughts.

GIUSEPPE [*unconscious of Napoleon's approach*] Quite true, Lieutenant, quite true. You are all like innkeepers now in France: you have to be polite to everybody.

NAPOLEON [*putting his hand on Giuseppe's shoulder*] And that destroys the whole value of politeness, eh?

LIEUTENANT. The very man I wanted! See here, General: suppose I catch that fellow for you!

NAPOLEON [*with ironical gravity*] You will not catch him, my friend.

LIEUTENANT. Aha! you think so; but youll see. Just wait.

Only, if I do catch him and hand him over to you, will you cry quits? Will you drop all this about degrading me in the presence of my regiment? Not that *I* mind, you know; but still no regiment likes to have all the other regiments laughing at it.

NAPOLEON [*a cold ray of humor striking pallidly across his gloom*] What shall we do with this officer, Giuseppe? Everything he says is wrong.

GIUSEPPE [*promptly*] Make him a general, excellency; and then everything he says will be right.

LIEUTENANT [*crowing*] Haw-aw! [*He throws himself ecstatically on the couch to enjoy the joke*].

NAPOLEON [*laughing and pinching Giuseppe's ear*]: You are thrown away in this inn, Giuseppe. [*He sits down and places Giuseppe before him like a schoolmaster with a pupil*]. Shall I take you away with me and make a man of you?

GIUSEPPE [*shaking his head rapidly and repeatedly*] No no no no no no no. All my life long people have wanted to make a man of me. When I was a boy, our good priest wanted to make a man of me by teaching me to read and write. Then the organist at Melegnano wanted to make a man of me by teaching me to read music. The recruiting sergeant would have made a man of me if I had been a few inches taller. But it always meant making me work; and I am too lazy for that, thank Heaven! So I taught myself to cook and became an innkeeper; and now I keep servants to do the work, and have nothing to do myself except talk, which suits me perfectly.

NAPOLEON [*looking at him thoughtfully*] You are satisfied?

GIUSEPPE [*with cheerful conviction*] Quite, excellency.

NAPOLEON. And you have no devouring devil inside you who must be fed with action and victory: gorged with them night and day: who makes you pay, with the sweat of your brain and body, weeks of Herculean toil for ten minutes of enjoyment: who is at once your slave and your tyrant, your genius and your doom: who brings you a crown in one hand and the oar of a galley slave in the other: who shews you all the kingdoms of the earth and offers to make you their master on condition that you become their servant! have you nothing of that in you?

GIUSEPPE. Nothing of it! Oh, I assure you, excellency, my devouring devil is far worse than that. He offers me no crowns and kingdoms: he expects to get everything for nothing: sausages! omelettes! grapes! cheese! polenta! wine! three times a day, excellency: nothing less will content him.

LIEUTENANT. Come: drop it, Giuseppe: you're making me feel hungry again.

Giuseppe, with an apologetic shrug, retires from the conversation.

NAPOLEON [*turning to the Lieutenant with sardonic politeness*] I hope *I* have not been making you feel ambitious.

LIEUTENANT. Not at all: I dont fly so high. Besides, I'm better as I am: men like me are wanted in the army just now. The fact is, the Revolution was all very well for civilians; but it wont work in the army. You know what soldiers are, General: they will have men of family for their officers. A subaltern must be a gentleman, because he's so much in contact with the men. But a general, or even a colonel, may be any sort of riff-raff if he understands his job well enough. A lieutenant is a gentleman: all the rest is chance. Why, who do you suppose won the battle of Lodi? I'll tell you. My horse did.

NAPOLEON [*rising*] Your folly is carrying you too far, sir. Take care.

LIEUTENANT. Not a bit of it. You remember all that red-hot cannonade cross the river: the Austrians blazing away at you to keep you from crossing, and you blazing away at them to keep them from setting the bridge on fire? Did you notice where I was then?

NAPOLEON. I am sorry. I am afraid I was rather occupied at the moment.

GIUSEPPE [*with eager admiration*] They say you jumped off your horse and worked the big guns with your own hands, General.

LIEUTENANT. That was a mistake: an officer should never let himself down to the level of his men. [*Napoleon looks at him dangerously, and begins to walk tigerishly to and fro*]. But you might have been firing away at the Austrians still if we cavalry fellows hadnt found the ford and got across and turned old Beaulieu's flank for you. You know you didnt dare give the order to charge the bridge until you saw us on the other side. Consequently, I say that whoever found that ford won the battle of Lodi. Well, who found it? I was the first man to cross; and I know. It was my horse that found it. [*With conviction, as he rises from the couch*] That horse is the true conqueror of the Austrians.

NAPOLEON [*passionately*] You idiot: I'll have you shot for losing those despatches: I'll have you blown from the mouth of a cannon: nothing less could make any impression on you. [*Baying at him*] Do you hear? Do you understand?

A French officer enters unobserved, carrying his sheathed sabre in his hand.

LIEUTENANT [*unabashed*] If I dont capture him, General. Remember the if.

NAPOLEON. If!! Ass: there is no such man.

THE OFFICER [*suddenly stepping between them and speaking in the unmistakeable voice of the Strange Lady*] Lieutenant: I am your prisoner. [*She offers him her sabre*].

Napoleon gazes at her for a moment thunderstruck; then seizes her by the wrist and drags her roughly to him, looking closely and fiercely at her to satisfy himself as to her identity; for it now begins to darken rapidly into night, the red glow over the vineyard giving way to clear starlight.

NAPOLEON. Pah! [*He flings her hand away with an exclamation of disgust, and turns his back on them with his hand in his breast, his brow lowering, and his toes twitching*].

LIEUTENANT [*triumphantly, taking the sabre*] No such man! eh, General? [*To the Lady*] I say: wheres my horse?

LADY. Safe at Borghetto, waiting for you, Lieutenant.

NAPOLEON [*turning on them*] Where are the despatches?

LADY. You would never guess. They are in the most unlikely place in the world. Did you meet my sister here, any of you?

LIEUTENANT. Yes. Very nice woman. She's wonderfully like you: but of course she's better-looking

LADY [*mysteriously*] Well, do you know that she is a witch?

GIUSEPPE [*in terror, crossing himself*] Oh, no, no, no. It is not safe to jest about such things. I cannot have it in my house, excellency.

LIEUTENANT. Yes, drop it. Youre my prisoner, you know. Of course I dont believe in any such rubbish; but still it's not a proper subject for joking.

LADY. But this is very serious. My sister has bewitched the General. [*Giuseppe and the lieutenant recoil from Napoleon*]. General: open your coat: you will find the despatches in the breast of it. [*She puts her hand quickly on his breast*]. Yes: there they are: I can feel them. Eh? [*She looks up into his face half coaxingly, half mockingly*]. Will you allow me, General? [*She takes a button as if to unbutton his coat, and pauses for permission*].

NAPOLEON [*inscrutably*] If you dare.

LADY. Thank you. [*She opens his coat and takes out the despatches*]. There! [*To Giuseppe, shewing him the despatches*] See!

GIUSEPPE [*flying to the outer door*] No, in heaven's name! They're bewitched.

LADY [*turning to the lieutenant*] Here, Lieutenant: you are not afraid of them.

LIEUTENANT [*retreating*] Keep off. [*Seizing the hilt of the sabre*] Keep off, I tell you.

LADY [*to Napoleon*] They belong to you, General. Take them.

GIUSEPPE. Dont touch them, excellency. Have nothing to do with them.

LIEUTENANT. Be careful, General: be careful.

GIUSEPPE. Burn them. And burn the witch too.

LADY [*to Napoleon*] Shall I burn them?

NAPOLEON [*thoughtfully*] Yes, burn them. Giuseppe: go and fetch a light.

GIUSEPPE [*trembling and stammering*] Do you mean go alone? in the dark? with a witch in the house?

NAPOLEON. Psha! Youre a poltroon. [*To the lieutenant*] Oblige me by going, Lieutenant.

LIEUTENANT [*remonstrating*] Oh, I say, General! No, look here, you know: nobody can say I'm a coward after Lodi. But to ask me to go into the dark by myself without a candle after such an awful conversation is a little too much. How would you like to do it yourself?

NAPOLEON [*irritably*] You refuse to obey my order?

LIEUTENANT [*resolutely*] Yes I do. It's not reasonable. But I'll tell you what I'll do. If Giuseppe goes, I'll go with him and protect him.

NAPOLEON [*to Giuseppe*] There! will that satisfy you? Be off, both of you.

GIUSEPPE [*humbly, his lips trembling*] W-willingly, your excellency. [*He goes reluctantly towards the inner door*]. Heaven protect me! [*To the lieutenant*] After you, Lieutenant.

LIEUTENANT. You'd better go first: I dont know the way.

GIUSEPPE. You cant miss it. Besides [*imploringly, laying his hand on his sleeve*] I am only a poor innkeeper: you are a man of family.

LIEUTENANT. Theres something in that. Here: you neednt be in such a fright. Take my arm. [*Giuseppe does so*]. Thats the way. [*They go out, arm in arm*].

It is now starry night. The lady throws the packet on the table and seats herself at her ease on the couch, enjoying the sensation of freedom from petticoats.

LADY. Well, General: Ive beaten you.

NAPOLEON [*walking about*] You are guilty of indelicacy: of unwomanliness. Is that costume proper?

LADY. It seems to me much the same as yours.

NAPOLEON. Psha! I blush for you.

LADY [*naïvely*] Yes: soldiers blush so easily. [*He growls and turns away. She looks mischievously at him, balancing the despatches in her hand*]. Wouldnt you like to read these before theyre burnt, General? You must be dying with curiosity. Take a peep. [*She throws the packet on the table, and turns her face away from it*]. I wont look.

NAPOLEON. I have no curiosity whatever, madam. But since you are evidently burning to read them, I give you leave to do so.

LADY. Oh, Ive read them already.

NAPOLEON [*starting*] What!

LADY. I read them the first thing after I rode away on that poor lieutenant's horse. So you see I know whats in them; and you dont.

NAPOLEON. Excuse me: I read them when I was out there in the vineyard ten minutes ago.

LADY. Oh! [*Jumping up*] Oh, General: Ive not beaten you after all. I do admire you so. [*He laughs and pats her cheek*]. This time, really and truly without shamming, I do you homage [*kissing his hand*].

NAPOLEON [*quickly withdrawing it*] Brr! Dont do that. No more witchcraft.

LADY. I want to say something to you; only you would misunderstand it.

NAPOLEON. Need that stop you?

LADY. Well, it is this. I adore a man who is not afraid to be mean and selfish.

NAPOLEON [*indignantly*] I am neither mean nor selfish.

LADY. Oh, you dont appreciate yourself. Besides, I dont really mean meanness and selfishness.

NAPOLEON. Thank you. I thought perhaps you did.

LADY. Well, of course I do. But what I mean is a certain strong simplicity about you.

NAPOLEON. Thats better.

LADY. You didnt want to read the letters; but you were curious about what was in them. So you went into the garden and read them when no one was looking, and then came back and pretended you hadnt. Thats the meanest thing I ever knew any man do; but it exactly fulfilled your purpose; and so you wernt a bit afraid or ashamed to do it.

NAPOLEON [*abruptly*] Where did you pick up all these vulgar scruples? this [*with contemptuous emphasis*] conscience of yours? I took you for a lady: an aristocrat. Was your grandfather a shopkeeper, pray?

LADY. No: he was an Englishman.

NAPOLEON. That accounts for it. The English are a nation of shopkeepers. Now I understand why youve beaten me.

LADY. Oh, I havent beaten you. And I'm not English.

NAPOLEON. Yes you are: English to the backbone. Listen to me: I will explain the English to you.

LADY [*eagerly*] Do. [*With a lively air of anticipating an intellectual treat, she sits down on the couch and composes herself to listen to him. Secure of his audience, he at once nerves himself for a performance. He considers a little before he begins; so as to fix her attention by a moment of suspense. His style is at first modelled on Talma's in Corneille's Cinna; but it is somewhat lost in the darkness, and Talma presently gives way to Napoleon, the voice coming through the gloom with startling intensity*].

NAPOLEON. There are three sorts of people in the world: the low people, the middle people, and the high people. The low people and the high people are alike in one thing: they have no scruples, no morality. The low are beneath morality, the high above it. I am not afraid of either of them; for the low are unscrupulous without knowledge, so that they make an idol of me; whilst the high are unscrupulous without purpose, so that they go down before my will. Look you: I shall go over all the mobs and all the courts of Europe as a plough goes over a field. It is the middle people who are dangerous: they have both knowledge and purpose. But they, too, have their weak point. They are full of scruples: chained hand and foot by their morality and respectability.

LADY. Then you will beat the English; for all shopkeepers are middle people.

NAPOLEON. No, because the English are a race apart. No Englishman is too low to have scruples: no Englishman is high enough to be free from their tyranny. But every Englishman is born with a certain miraculous power that makes him master of the world. When he wants a thing, he never tells himself that he wants it. He waits patiently until there comes into his mind, no one knows how, a burning conviction that it is his moral and religious duty to conquer those who possess the thing he wants. Then he becomes irresistible. Like the aristocrat, he does what pleases him and grabs what he covets: like the shopkeeper, he pursues his purpose with the industry and steadfastness that come from strong religious conviction and deep sense of moral responsibility. He is never at a loss for an effective moral attitude. As the great champion of freedom and national independence, he conquers and annexes half the world, and calls it Colonization. When he wants a new market for his adulterated Manchester goods, he sends a missionary to teach the natives the Gospel of Peace. The natives kill the missionary: he flies to arms in defence of Christianity; fights for it; conquers for it; and takes the market as a reward from heaven. In defence of his island shores, he puts a chaplain on board his ship; nails a flag with a cross on it to his top-gallant mast; and sails to the ends of the earth, sinking, burning, and destroying all who dispute the empire of the seas with him. He boasts that a slave is free the moment his foot touches British soil; and he sells the children of his poor at six years of age to work under the lash in his factories for sixteen hours a day. He makes two revolutions, and then declares war on our one in the name of law and order. There is nothing so bad or so good that you will not find Englishmen doing it; but you will never find an Englishman in the wrong. He does everything on principle. He fights you on patriotic principles; he robs you on business principles; he enslaves you on imperial principles; he bullies you on manly principles; he supports his king on loyal principles and cuts off his king's head on republican principles. His watchword is always Duty; and he never forgets that the nation which lets its duty get on the opposite side to its interest is lost. He—

LADY. W-w-w-w-w-wh! Do stop a moment. I want to know how you make me out to be English at this rate.

NAPOLEON [*dropping his rhetorical style*] It's plain enough. You wanted some letters that belonged to me. You have spent the morning in stealing them: yes, stealing them, by highway robbery. And you have spent the afternoon in putting me in the wrong about them: in assuming that it was *I* who wanted to steal your letters: in explaining that it all came about through my meanness and selfishness, and your goodness, your devotion, your self-sacrifice. Thats English.

LADY. Nonsense! I am sure I am not a bit English. The English are a very stupid people.

NAPOLEON. Yes, too stupid sometimes to know when theyre beaten. But I grant that your brains are not English. You see, though your grandfather was an Englishman, your grandmother was—what? A Frenchwoman?

LADY. Oh no. An Irishwoman.

NAPOLEON [*quickly*] Irish! [*Thoughtfully*] Yes: I forgot the Irish. An English army led by an Irish general: that might be a match for a French army led by an Italian general. [*He pauses, and adds, half jestingly, half moodily*] At all events, you have beaten me; and what beats a man first will beat him last. [*He goes meditatively into the moonlit vineyard and looks up*].

She steals out after him. She ventures to rest her hand on his shoulder, overcome by the beauty of the night and emboldened by its obscurity.

LADY [*softly*] What are you looking at?

NAPOLEON [*pointing up*] My star.

LADY. You believe in that?

NAPOLEON. I do.

They look at it for a moment, she leaning a little on his shoulder.

LADY. Do you know that the English say that a man's star is not complete without a woman's garter?

NAPOLEON [*scandalized: abruptly shaking her off and coming back into the room*]: Pah! The hypocrites! If the French said that, how they would hold up their hands in pious horror! [*He goes to the inner door and holds it open, shouting*] Hallo! Giuseppe! Wheres that light, man? [*He comes between the table and the sideboard, and moves the second chair to the table, beside his own*]. We have still to burn the letter. [*He takes up the packet*].

Giuseppe comes back, pale and still trembling, carrying in one hand a branched candlestick with a couple of candles alight, and a broad snuffers tray in the other.

GIUSEPPE [*piteously, as he places the light on the table*] Excellency: what were you looking up at just now? Out there! [*He points across his shoulder to the vineyard, but is afraid to look round*].

NAPOLEON [*unfolding the packet*] What is that to you?

GIUSEPPE. Because the witch is gone: vanished; and no one saw her go out.

LADY [*coming behind him from the vineyard*] We were watching her riding up to the moon on your broomstick, Giuseppe. You will never see her again.

GIUSEPPE. Gesu Maria! [*He crosses himself and hurries out*].

NAPOLEON [*throwing down the letters in a heap on the table*] Now! [*He sits down at the table in the chair which he has just placed*].

LADY. Yes; but you know you have THE letter in your pocket. [*He smiles; takes a letter from his pocket; and tosses it on top of the heap. She holds it up and looks at him, saying*] About Cæsar's wife.

NAPOLEON. Cæsar's wife is above suspicion. Burn it.

LADY [*taking up the snuffers and holding the letter to the candle flame with it*] I wonder would Cæsar's wife be above suspicion if she saw us here together!

NAPOLEON [*echoing her, with his elbows on the table and*

his cheeks on his hands, looking at the letter] I wonder!

The Strange Lady puts the letter down alight on the snuffers tray, and sits down beside Napoleon, in the same attitude, elbows on table, cheeks on hands, watching it burn. When it is burnt, they simultaneously turn their eyes and look at one another. The curtain steals down and hides them.

HOW HE LIED TO HER HUSBAND

LIKE many other works of mine, this playlet is a *pièce d'occasion*. In 1905 it happened that the late Arnold Daly, who was then playing the part of Napoleon in The Man of Destiny in New York, found that whilst the play was too long to take a secondary place in the evening's performance, it was too short to suffice by itself. I therefore took advantage of four days continuous rain during a holiday in the north of Scotland to write How He Lied To Her Husband for Daly. In his hands, it served its turn very effectively.

Trifling as it is, I print it as a sample of what can be done with even the most hackneyed stage framework by filling it in with an observed touch of actual humanity instead of with doctrinaire romanticism. Nothing in the theatre is staler than the situation of husband, wife, and lover, or the fun of knockabout farce. I have taken both, and got an original play out of them, as anybody else can if only he will look about him for his material instead of plagiarizing Othello and the thousand plays that have proceeded on Othello's romantic assumptions and false point of honor.

How He Lied to Her Husband was first produced at the Berkeley Lyceum Theatre, New York, on 26 September 1904, with the following cast:

HER LOVER (APJOHN) *Arnold Daly*

HER HUSBAND (BOMPAS) *Dodson Mitchell*

HERSELF (AURORA BOMPAS) *Selene Johnson*

HOW HE LIED TO HER HUSBAND

It is eight o'clock in the evening. The curtains are drawn and the lamps lighted in the drawing room of Her flat in Cromwell Road. Her lover, a beautiful youth of eighteen, in evening dress and cape, with a bunch of flowers and an opera hat in his hands, comes in alone. The door is near the corner; and as he appears in the doorway, he has the fireplace on the nearest wall to his right, and the grand piano along the opposite wall to his left. Near the fireplace a small ornamental table has on it a hand mirror, a fan, a pair of long white gloves, and a little white woollen cloud to wrap a woman's head in. On the other side of the room, near the piano, is a broad, square, softly upholstered stool. The room is furnished in the most approved South Kensington fashion: that is, it is as like a shop window as possible, and is intended to demonstrate the social position and spending powers of its owners, and not in the least to make them comfortable.

He is, be it repeated, a very beautiful youth, moving as in a dream, walking as on air. He puts his flowers down carefully on the table beside the fan; takes off his cape, and, as there is no room on the table for it, takes it to the piano; puts his hat on the cape; crosses to the hearth; looks at his watch; puts it up again; notices the things on the table; lights up as if he saw heaven opening before him; goes to the table and takes the cloud in both hands, nestling his nose into its softness and kissing it; kisses the gloves one after another; kisses the fan; gasps a long shuddering sigh of ecstasy; sits down on the stool and presses his hands to his eyes to shut out reality and dream a little; takes his hands down and shakes his head with a little smile of rebuke for his folly; catches sight of a speck of dust on his shoes and hastily and carefully brushes it off with his handkerchief; rises and takes the hand mirror from the table to make sure of his tie with the gravest anxiety; and is looking at his watch again when She comes in, much flustered. As she is dressed for the theatre; has spoilt, petted ways; and wears many diamonds, she has an air of being a young and beautiful woman; but as a matter of hard fact, she is, dress and pretensions apart, a very ordinary South Kensington female of about thirty seven, hopelessly inferior in physical and spiritual distinction to the beautiful youth, who hastily puts down the mirror as she enters.

HE [*kissing her hand*] At last!

SHE. Henry: something dreadful has happened.

HE. Whats the matter?

SHE. I have lost your poems.

HE. They were unworthy of you. I will write you some more.

SHE: No, thank you. Never any more poems for me. Oh, how could I have been so mad! so rash! so imprudent!

HE. Thank Heaven for your madness, your rashness, your imprudence!

SHE [*impatiently*] Oh, be sensible, Henry. Cant you see what a terrible thing this is for me? Suppose anybody finds these poems! what will they think?

HE. They will think that a man once loved a woman more devotedly than ever man loved woman before. But they will not know what man it was.

SHE. What good is that to me if everybody will know what woman it was?

HE. But how will they know?

SHE. How will they know! Why, my name is all over them: my silly, unhappy name. Oh, if I had only been christened Mary Jane, or Gladys Muriel, or Beatrice, or Francesca, or Guinevere, or something quite common! But Aurora! Aurora! I'm the only Aurora in London; and everybody knows it. I believe I'm the only Aurora in the world. And it's so horribly easy to rhyme to it! Oh, Henry, why didnt you try to restrain your feelings a little in common consideration for me? Why didnt you write with some little reserve?

HE. Write poems to you with reserve! You ask me that!

SHE [*with perfunctory tenderness*] Yes, dear, of course it was very nice of you; and I know it was my own fault as much as yours. I ought to have noticed that your verses ought never to have been addressed to a married woman.

HE. Ah, how I wish they had been addressed to an unmarried woman! how I wish they had!

SHE. Indeed you have no right to wish anything of the sort. They are quite unfit for anybody but a married woman. Thats just the difficulty. What will my sisters-in-law think of them?

HE [*painfully jarred*] Have you got sisters-in-law?

SHE. Yes, of course I have. Do you suppose I am an angel?

HE [*biting his lips*] I do. Heaven help me, I do—or I did—or [*he almost chokes a sob*].

SHE [*softening and putting her hand caressingly on his shoulder*] Listen to me, dear. It's very nice of you to live with me in a dream, and to love me, and so on; but I cant help my husband having disagreeable relatives, can I?

HE [*brightening up*] Ah, of course they are your husband's relatives: I forgot that. Forgive me, Aurora. [*He takes her hand from his shoulder and kisses it. She sits down on the stool. He remains near the table, with his back to it, smiling fatuously down at her*].

SHE. The fact is, Teddy's got nothing but relatives. He has eight sisters and six half-sisters, and ever so many brothers —but I dont mind his brothers. Now if you only knew the least little thing about the world, Henry, youd know that in a large family, though the sisters quarrel with one another like mad all the time, yet let one of the brothers marry, and they all turn on their unfortunate sister-in-law and devote the rest of their lives with perfect unanimity to persuading him that his wife is unworthy of him. They can do it to her very face without her knowing it, because they always have a lot of stupid low family jokes that nobody understands but themselves. Half the time you cant tell what theyre talking about: it just drives you wild. There ought to be a law against a man's sister ever entering his house after he's married. I'm as certain as that I'm sitting here that Georgina stole those poems out of my workbox.

HE. She will not understand them, I think.

SHE. Oh, wont she! She'll understand them only too well. She'll understand more harm than ever was in them: nasty vulgar-minded cat!

HE [*going to her*] Oh dont, dont think of people in that way. Dont think of her at all. [*He takes her hand and sits down on the carpet at her feet*]. Aurora: do you remember the evening when I sat here at your feet and read you those poems for the first time?

SHE. I shouldnt have let you: I see that now. When I think of Georgina sitting there at Teddy's feet and reading them to him for the first time, I feel I shall just go distracted.

HE. Yes, you are right. It will be a profanation.

SHE. Oh, I dont care about the profanation; but what will Teddy think? what will he do? [*Suddenly throwing his head away from her knee*] You dont seem to think a bit about Teddy. [*She jumps up, more and more agitated*].

HE [*supine on the floor; for she has thrown him off his balance*] To me Teddy is nothing, and Georgina less than nothing.

SHE. Youll soon find out how much less than nothing she is. If you think a woman cant do any harm because she's only a scandalmongering dowdy ragbag, youre greatly mistaken. [*She flounces about the room. He gets up slowly and dusts his hands. Suddenly she runs to him and throws herself into his arms*]. Henry: help me. Find a way out of this for me; and I'll bless you as long as you live. Oh, how wretched I am! [*She sobs on his breast*].

HE. And oh! how happy I am!

SHE [*whisking herself abruptly away*] Dont be selfish.

HE [*humbly*] Yes: I deserve that. I think if I were going to the stake with you, I should still be so happy with you that I should forget your danger as utterly as my own.

SHE [*relenting and patting his hand fondly*] Oh, you are a dear darling boy, Henry; but [*throwing his hand away fretfully*] youre no use. I want somebody to tell me what to do.

HE [*with quiet conviction*] Your heart will tell you at the right time. I have thought deeply over this; and I know what we two must do, sooner or later.

SHE. No, Henry. I will do nothing improper, nothing dishonorable. [*She sits down plump on the stool and looks inflexible*].

HE. If you did, you would no longer be Aurora. Our course is perfectly simple, perfectly straightforward, perfectly stainless and true. We love one another. I am not ashamed of that: I am ready to go out and proclaim it to all London as simply as I will declare it to your husband when you see—as you soon will see— that this is the only way honorable enough for your feet to tread. Let us go out together to our own house, this evening, without concealment and without shame. Remember! we owe something to your husband. We are his guests here: he is an honorable man: he has been kind to us: he has perhaps loved you as well as his prosaic nature and his sordid commercial environment permitted. We owe it to him in all honor not to let him learn the truth from the lips of a scandalmonger. Let us go to him now quietly, hand in hand; bid him farewell; and walk out of the house without concealment or subterfuge, freely and honestly, in full honor and self-respect.

SHE [*staring at him*] And where shall we go to?

HE. We shall not depart by a hair's breadth from the ordinary natural current of our lives. We were going to the theatre when the loss of the poems compelled us to take action at once. We shall go to the theatre still; but we shall leave your diamonds here; for we cannot afford diamonds, and do not need them.

SHE [*fretfully*] I have told you already that I hate diamonds; only Teddy insists on hanging me all over with them. You need not preach simplicity to me.

HE. I never thought of doing so, dearest: I know that these trivialities are nothing to you. What was I saying?—oh yes. Instead of coming back here from the theatre, you will come with me to my home—now and henceforth our home —and in due course of time, when you are divorced, we shall go through whatever idle legal ceremony you may desire. *I* attach no importance to the law: my love was not created in me by the law, nor can it be bound or loosed by it. That is simple enough, and sweet enough, is it not? [*He takes the flowers from the table*]. Here are flowers for you: I have the tickets: we will ask your husband to lend us the carriage to shew that there is no malice, no grudge, between us. Come!

SHE. Do you mean to say that you propose that we should walk right bang up to Teddy and tell him we're going away together?

HE. Yes. What can be simpler?

SHE. And do you think for a moment he'd stand it? He'd just kill you.

HE [*coming to a sudden stop and speaking with considerable confidence*] You dont understand these things, my darling: how could you? I have followed the Greek ideal and not neglected the culture of my body. Like all poets I have a passion for pugilism. Your husband would make a tolerable second-rate heavy weight if he were in training and ten years younger. As it is, he could, if strung up to a great effort by a burst of passion, give a good account of himself for perhaps fifteen seconds. But I am active enough to keep out of his reach for fifteen seconds; and after that I should be simply all over him.

SHE [*rising and coming to him in consternation*] What do you mean by all over him?

HE [*gently*] Dont ask me, dearest. At all events, I swear to you that you need not be anxious about me.

SHE. And what about Teddy? Do you mean to tell me that you are going to beat Teddy before my face like a brutal prizefighter?

HE. All this alarm is needless, dearest. Believe me, nothing will happen. Your husband knows that I am capable of defending myself. Under such circumstances nothing ever does happen. And of course *I* shall do nothing. The man who once loved you is sacred to me.

SHE [*suspiciously*] Doesnt he love me still? Has he told you anything?

HE. No, no. [*He takes her tenderly in his arms*]. Dearest, dearest: how agitated you are! how unlike yourself! All these worries belong to the lower plane. Come up with me to the higher one. The heights, the solitudes, the soul world!

SHE [*avoiding his gaze*] No: stop: it's no use, Mr Apjohn.

HE [*recoiling*] Mr Apjohn!!!

SHE. Excuse me: I meant Henry, of course.

HE. How could you even think of me as Mr Apjohn? I never think of you as Mrs Bompas: it is always Aurora, Aurora, Auro—

SHE. Yes, yes: thats all very well, Mr Apjohn [*he is about to interrupt again: but she wont have it*] no: it's no use: Ive suddenly begun to think of you as Mr Apjohn; and it's ridiculous to go on calling you Henry. I thought you were only a boy, a child, a dreamer. I thought you would be too much afraid to do anything. And now you want to beat Teddy and to break up my home and disgrace me and make a horrible scandal in the papers. It's cruel, unmanly, cowardly.

HE [*with grave wonder*] Are you afraid?

SHE. Oh, of course I'm afraid. So would you be if you had any common sense. [*She goes to the hearth, turning her back to him, and puts one tapping foot on the fender*].

HE [*watching her with great gravity*] Perfect love casteth out fear. That is why I am not afraid. Mrs Bompas: you do not love me.

SHE [*turning to him with a gasp of relief*] Oh, thank you, thank you! You really can be very nice, Henry.

HE. Why do you thank me?

SHE [*coming prettily to him from the fireplace*] For calling me Mrs Bompas again. I feel now that you are going to be reasonable and behave like a gentleman. [*He drops on the stool; covers his face with his hands; and groans*]. Whats the matter?

HE. Once or twice in my life I have dreamed that I was

exquisitely happy and blessed. But oh! the misgiving at the first stir of consciousness! the stab of reality! the prison walls of the bedroom! the bitter, bitter disappointment of waking! And this time! oh, this time I thought I was awake.

SHE. Listen to me, Henry: we really havnt time for all that sort of flapdoodle now. [*He starts to his feet as if she had pulled a trigger and straightened him by the release of a powerful spring, and goes past her with set teeth to the little table*]. Oh, take care: you nearly hit me in the chin with the top of your head.

HE [*with fierce politeness*] I beg your pardon. What is it you want me to do? I am at your service. I am ready to behave like a gentleman if you will be kind enough to explain exactly how.

SHE [*a little frightened*] Thank you, Henry: I was sure you would. Youre not angry with me, are you?

HE. Go on. Go on quickly. Give me something to think about, or I will—I will—[*he suddenly snatches up her fan and is about to break it in his clenched fist*].

SHE [*running forward and catching at the fan, with loud lamentation*] Dont break my fan—no, dont. [*He slowly relaxes his grip of it as she draws it anxiously out of his hands*]. No, really, thats a stupid trick: I dont like that. Youve no right to do that. [*She opens the fan, and finds that the sticks are disconnected*]. Oh, how could you be so inconsiderate?

HE. I beg your pardon. I will buy you a new one.

SHE [*querulously*] You will never be able to match it. And it was a particular favorite of mine.

HE [*shortly*] Then you will have to do without it: thats all.

SHE. Thats not a very nice thing to say after breaking my pet fan, I think.

HE. If you knew how near I was to breaking Teddy's pet wife and presenting him with the pieces, you would be thankful that you are alive instead of—of—of howling about fiveshillings-worth of ivory. Damn your fan!

SHE. Oh! Dont you dare swear in my presence. One would think you were my husband.

HE [*again collapsing on the stool*] This is some horrible dream. What has become of you? You are not my Aurora.

SHE. Oh, well, if you come to that, what has become of you? Do you think I would ever have encouraged you if I had known you were such a little devil?

HE. Dont drag me down—dont—dont. Help me to find the way back to the heights.

SHE [*kneeling beside him and pleading*] If you would only be reasonable, Henry. If you would only remember that I am on the brink of ruin, and not go on calmly saying it's all quite simple.

HE. It seems so to me.

SHE [*jumping up distractedly*] If you say that again I shall do something I'll be sorry for. Here we are, standing on the edge of a frightful precipice. No doubt it's quite simple to go over and have done with it. But cant you suggest anything more agreeable?

HE. I can suggest nothing now. A chill black darkness has fallen: I can see nothing but the ruins of our dream. [*He rises with a deep sigh*].

SHE. Cant you? Well, I can. I can see Georgina rubbing those poems into Teddy. [*Facing him determinedly*] And I tell you, Henry Apjohn, that you got me into this mess; and you must get me out of it again.

HE [*polite and hopeless*] All I can say is that I am entirely at your service. What do you wish me to do?

SHE. Do you know anybody else named Aurora?

HE. No.

SHE. Theres no use in saying No in that frozen pigheaded way. You must know some Aurora or other somewhere.

HE. You said you were the only Aurora in the world. And [*lifting his clasped fists with a sudden return of his emotion*] oh God! you were the only Aurora in the world for me. [*He turns away from her, hiding his face*].

SHE [*petting him*] Yes, yes, dear: of course. It's very nice of you; and I appreciate it: indeed I do; but it's not seasonable just at present. Now just listen to me. I suppose you know all those poems by heart.

HE. Yes, by heart. [*Raising his head and looking at her with a sudden suspicion*] Dont you?

SHE. Well, I never can remember verses; and besides, Ive been so busy that Ive not had time to read them all; though I intend to the very first moment I can get: I promise you that most faithfully, Henry. But now try and remember very particularly. Does the name of Bompas occur in any of the poems?

HE [*indignantly*] No.

SHE. Youre quite sure?

HE. Of course I am quite sure. How could I use such a name in a poem?

SHE. Well, I dont see why not. It rhymes to rumpus, which seems appropriate enough at present, goodness knows! However, youre a poet, and you ought to know.

HE. What does it matter—now?

SHE. It matters a lot, I can tell you. If theres nothing about Bompas in the poems, we can say that they were written to some other Aurora, and that you shewed them to me because my name was Aurora too. So youve got to invent another Aurora for the occasion.

HE [*very coldly*] Oh, if you wish me to tell a lie—

SHE. Surely, as a man of honor—as a gentleman, you wouldnt tell the truth: would you?

HE. Very well. You have broken my spirit and desecrated my dreams. I will lie and protest and stand on my honor: oh, I will play the gentleman, never fear.

SHE. Yes, put it all on me, of course. Dont be mean, Henry.

HE [*rousing himself with an effort*] You are quite right, Mrs Bompas: I beg your pardon. You must excuse my temper. I am having growing pains, I think.

SHE. Growing pains!

HE. The process of growing from romantic boyhood into cynical maturity usually takes fifteen years. When it is compressed into fifteen minutes, the pace is too fast; and growing pains are the result.

SHE. Oh, is this a time for cleverness? It's settled, isnt it, that youre going to be nice and good, and that youll brazen it out to Teddy that you have some other Aurora?

HE. Yes: I'm capable of anything now. I should not have told him the truth by halves; and now I will not lie by halves. I'll wallow in the honor of a gentleman.

SHE. Dearest boy, I knew you would. I—Sh! [*She rushes to the door, and holds it ajar, listening breathlessly*].

HE. What is it?

SHE [*white with apprehension*] It's Teddy: I hear him tapping the new barometer. He cant have anything serious on his mind or he wouldnt do that. Perhaps Georgina hasnt said anything. [*She steals back to the hearth*]. Try and look as if there was nothing the matter. Give me my gloves, quick. [*He hands them to her. She pulls on one hastily and begins buttoning it with ostentatious unconcern*]. Go further away from me, quick. [*He walks doggedly away from her until the piano prevents his going farther*]. If I button my glove, and you were to hum a tune, dont you think that—

HE. The tableau would be complete in its guiltiness. For Heaven's sake, Mrs Bompas, let that glove alone: you look like a pickpocket.

Her husband comes in: a robust, thicknecked, well groomed city man, with a strong chin but a blithering eye and credulous mouth. He has a momentous air, but shews no sign of displeasure: rather the contrary.

HER HUSBAND. Hallo! I thought you two were at the theatre.

SHE. I felt anxious about you, Teddy. Why didnt you come home to dinner?

HER HUSBAND. I got a message from Georgina. She wanted me to go to her.

SHE. Poor dear Georgina! I'm sorry I havnt been able to call on her this last week. I hope theres nothing the matter with her.

HER HUSBAND. Nothing, except anxiety for my welfare—and yours. [*She steals a terrified look at Henry*]. By the way, Apjohn, I should like a word with you this evening, if Aurora can spare you for a moment.

HE [*formally*] I am at your service.

HER HUSBAND. No hurry. After the theatre will do.

HE. We have decided not to go.

HER HUSBAND. Indeed! Well, then, shall we adjourn to my snuggery?

SHE. You neednt move. I shall go and lock up my diamonds since I'm not going to the theatre. Give me my things.

HER HUSBAND [*as he hands her the cloud and the mirror*] Well, we shall have more room here.

HE [*looking about him and shaking his shoulders loose*] I think I should prefer plenty of room.

HER HUSBAND. So, if it's not disturbing you, Rory—?

SHE. Not at all. [*She goes out*].

When the two men are alone together, Bompas deliberately takes the poems from his breast pocket; looks at them reflectively; then looks at Henry, mutely inviting his attention. Henry refuses to understand, doing his best to look unconcerned.

HER HUSBAND. Do these manuscripts seem at all familiar to you, may I ask?

HE. Manuscripts?

HER HUSBAND. Yes. Would you like to look at them a little closer? [*He proffers them under Henry's nose*].

HE [*as with a sudden illumination of glad surprise*] Why, these are my poems!

HER HUSBAND. So I gather.

HE. What a shame! Mrs Bompas has shewn them to you! You must think me an utter ass. I wrote them years ago after reading Swinburne's Songs Before Sunrise. Nothing would do me then but I must reel off a set of Songs to the Sunrise. Aurora, you know: the rosy fingered Aurora. Theyre all about Aurora. When Mrs Bompas told me her name was Aurora, I couldnt resist the temptation to lend them to her to read. But I didnt bargain for your unsympathetic eyes.

HER HUSBAND [*grinning*] Apjohn: thats really very ready of you. You are cut out for literature; and the day will come when Rory and I will be proud to have you about the house. I have heard far thinner stories from much older men.

HE [*with an air of great surprise*] Do you mean to imply that you dont believe me?

HER HUSBAND. Do you expect me to believe you?

HE. Why not? I dont understand.

HER HUSBAND. Come! Dont underrate your own cleverness, Apjohn. I think you understand pretty well.

HE. I assure you I am quite at a loss. Can you not be a little more explicit?

HER HUSBAND. Dont overdo it, old chap. However, I will just be so far explicit as to say that if you think these poems read as if they were addressed, not to a live woman, but to a shivering cold time of day at which you were never out of bed in your life, you hardly do justice to your own literary powers—which I admire and appreciate, mind you, as much as any man. Come! own up. You wrote those poems to my wife. [*An internal struggle prevents Henry from answering*]. Of course you did. [*He throws the poems on the table; and goes to the hearthrug, where he plants himself solidly, chuckling a little and waiting for the next move*].

HE [*formally and carefully*] Mr Bompas: I pledge you my word you are mistaken. I need not tell you that Mrs Bompas is a lady of stainless honor, who has never cast an unworthy thought on me. The fact that she has shewn you my poems—

HER HUSBAND. Thats not a fact. I came by them without her knowledge. She didnt shew them to me.

HE. Does not that prove their perfect innocence? She would have shewn them to you at once if she had taken your quite unfounded view of them.

HER HUSBAND [*shaken*] Apjohn: play fair. Dont abuse your intellectual gifts. Do you really mean that I am making a fool of myself?

HE [*earnestly*] Believe me, you are. I assure you, on my honor as a gentleman, that I have never had the slightest feeling for Mrs Bompas beyond the ordinary esteem and regard of a pleasant acquaintance.

HER HUSBAND [*shortly, shewing ill humor for the first time*] Oh! Indeed! [*He leaves his hearth and begins to approach Henry slowly, looking him up and down with growing resentment*].

HE [*hastening to improve the impression made by his mendacity*] I should never have dreamt of writing poems to her. The thing is absurd.

HER HUSBAND [*reddening ominously*] Why is it absurd?

HE [*shrugging his shoulders*] Well, it happens that I do not admire Mrs Bompas—in that way.

HER HUSBAND [*breaking out in Henry's face*] Let me tell you that Mrs Bompas has been admired by better men than you, you soapy headed little puppy, you.

HE [*much taken aback*] There is no need to insult me like this. I assure you, on my honor as a—

HER HUSBAND [*too angry to tolerate a reply, and boring Henry more and more towards the piano*] You dont admire Mrs Bompas! You would never dream of writing poems to Mrs Bompas! My wife's not good enough for you, isnt she? [*Fiercely*] Who are you, pray, that you should be so jolly superior?

HE. Mr Bompas: I can make allowances for your jealousy—

HER HUSBAND. Jealousy! do you suppose I'm jealous of you? No, nor of ten like you. But if you think I'll stand here and let you insult my wife in her own house, youre mistaken.

HE [*very uncomfortable with his back against the piano and Teddy standing over him threateningly*] How can I convince you? Be reasonable. I tell you my relations with Mrs Bompas are relations of perfect coldness—of indifference—

HER HUSBAND [*scornfully*] Say it again: say it again. Youre proud of it, arnt you? Yah! youre not worth kicking.

Henry suddenly executes the feat known to pugilists as slipping, and changes sides with Teddy, who is now between Henry and the piano.

HE. Look here: I'm not going to stand this.

HER HUSBAND. Oh, you have some blood in your body after all! Good job!

HE. This is ridiculous. I assure you Mrs Bompas is quite—

HER HUSBAND. What is Mrs Bompas to you, I'd like to know. I'll tell you what Mrs Bompas is. She's the smartest woman in the smartest set in South Kensington, and the handsomest, and the cleverest, and the most fetching to experienced men who know a good thing when they see it, whatever she may be to conceited penny-a-lining puppies who think nothing good enough for them. It's admitted by the best people; and not to know it argues yourself unknown. Three of our first actor-managers have offered her a hundred a week if she'll go on the stage when they start a repertory theatre; and I think they know what theyre about as well as you. The only member of the present Cabinet that you might call a handsome man has neglected the business of the country to dance with her, though he dont belong to our set as a regular thing. One of the first professional poets in Bedford Park wrote a sonnet to her, worth all your amateur trash. At Ascot last season the eldest son of a duke excused himself from calling on me on the ground that his feelings for Mrs Bompas were not consistent with his duty to me as host; and it did him honor and me too. But [*with gathering fury*] she isnt good enough for you, it seems. You regard her with coldness, with indifference; and you have the cool cheek to tell me so to my face. For two pins I'd flatten your nose in to teach you manners. Introducing a fine woman to you is casting pearls before swine [*yelling at him*] before SWINE! d'ye hear?

HE [*with a deplorable lack of polish*] You call me a swine again and I'll land you one on the chin thatll make your head sing for a week.

HER HUSBAND [*exploding*] What!

He charges at Henry with bull-like fury. Henry places himself on guard in the manner of a well taught boxer, and gets away smartly, but unfortunately forgets the stool which is just behind him. He falls backwards over it, unintentionally pushing it against the shins of Bompas, who falls forward over it. Mrs Bompas, with a scream, rushes into the room between the sprawling champions, and sits down on the floor in order to get her right arm round her husband's neck.

SHE. You shant, Teddy: you shant. You will be killed: he is a prizefighter.

HER HUSBAND [*vengefully*] I'll prizefight him. [*He struggles vainly to free himself from her embrace*].

SHE. Henry: dont let him fight you. Promise me that you wont.

HE [*ruefully*] I have got a most frightful bump on the back of my head. [*He tries to rise*].

SHE [*reaching out her left hand to seize his coat tail, and pulling him down again, whilst keeping fast hold of Teddy with the other hand*] Not until you have promised: not until you both have promised. [*Teddy tries to rise: she pulls him back again*]. Teddy: you promise, dont you? Yes, yes. Be good: you promise.

HER HUSBAND. I wont, unless he takes it back.

SHE. He will: he does. You take it back, Henry?—yes.

HE [*savagely*] Yes. I take it back. [*She lets go his coat. He gets up. So does Teddy*]. I take it all back, all, without reserve.

SHE [*on the carpet*] Is nobody going to help me up? [*They each take a hand and pull her up*]. Now wont you shake hands and be good?

HE [*recklessly*] I shall do nothing of the sort. I have steeped myself in lies for your sake; and the only reward I get is a lump on the back of my head the size of an apple. Now I will go back to the straight path.

SHE. Henry: for Heaven's sake—

HE. It's no use. Your husband is a fool and a brute—

HER HUSBAND. Whats that you say?

HE. I say you are a fool and a brute; and if youll step outside with me I'll say it again. [*Teddy begins to take off his coat for combat*]. Those poems were written to your wife, every word of them, and to nobody else. [*The scowl clears away from Bompas's countenance. Radiant, he replaces his coat*]. I wrote them because I loved her. I thought her the most beautiful woman in the world, and I told her so over and over again. I adored her: do you hear? I told her that you were a sordid commercial chump, utterly unworthy of her, and so you are.

HER HUSBAND [*so gratified, he can hardly believe his ears*] You dont mean it!

HE. Yes, I do mean it, and a lot more too. I asked Mrs Bompas to walk out of the house with me—to leave you—to get divorced from you and marry me. I begged and implored her to do it this very night. It was her refusal that ended everything between us. [*Looking very disparagingly at him*] What she can see in you, goodness only knows!

HER HUSBAND [*beaming with remorse*] My dear chap, why didnt you say so before? I apologize. Come! dont bear malice: shake hands. Make him shake hands, Rory.

SHE. For my sake, Henry. After all, he's my husband. Forgive him. Take his hand. [*Henry, dazed, lets her take his hand and place it in Teddy's*].

HER HUSBAND [*shaking it heartily*] Youve got to own that none of your literary heroines can touch my Rory. [*He turns to her and claps her with fond pride on the shoulders*]. Eh, Rory? They cant resist you: none of em. Never knew a man yet that could hold out three days.

SHE. Dont be foolish, Teddy. I hope you were not really hurt, Henry. [*She feels the back of his head. He flinches*]. Oh, poor boy, what a bump! I must get some vinegar and brown paper. [*She goes to the bell and rings*].

HER HUSBAND. Will you do me a great favor, Apjohn. I hardly like to ask; but it would be a real kindness to us both.

HE. What can I do?

HER HUSBAND [*taking up the poems*] Well, may I get these printed? It shall be done in the best style. The finest paper, sumptuous binding, everything first class. Theyre beautiful poems. I should like to shew them about a bit.

SHE [*running back from the bell, delighted with the idea, and coming between them*] Oh Henry, if you wouldnt mind?

HE. Oh, *I* dont mind. I am past minding anything.

HER HUSBAND. What shall we call the volume? To Aurora, or something like that, eh?

HE. I should call it How He Lied to Her Husband.

PASSION, POISON, AND PETRIFACTION

OR

THE FATAL GAZOGENE

A BRIEF TRAGEDY FOR BARNS AND BOOTHS

THIS tragedy was written at the request of Mr Cyril Maude, under whose direction it was performed repeatedly, with colossal success, in a booth in Regent's Park, for the benefit of The Actors' Orphanage, on the 14th July 1905, by Miss Irene Vanbrugh, Miss Nancy Price, Mr G. P. Huntley, Mr Cyril Maude, Mr Eric Lewis, Mr Arthur Williams, and Mr Lennox Pawle.

As it is extremely difficult to find an actor capable of eating a real ceiling, it will be found convenient in performance to substitute the tops of old wedding cakes for bits of plaster. There is but little difference in material between the two substances; but the taste of the wedding cake is considered more agreeable by many people.

The orchestra should consist of at least a harp, a drum, and a pair of cymbals, these instruments being the most useful in enhancing the stage effect.

The landlord may with equal propriety be a landlady, if that arrangement be better suited to the resources of the company.

As the Bill Bailey song has not proved immortal, any equally appropriate ditty of the moment may be substituted.

Passion, Poison, and Petrifaction was first produced at the *Theatre Royal* at the Theatrical Garden Party, Regent's Park, London, on 14 July 1905, with the following cast:

LADY MAGNESIA FITZTOLLEMACHE	*Irene Vanbrugh*
PHYLLIS (HER MAID)	*Nancy Price*
GEORGE FITZTOLLEMACHE	*Eric Lewis*
ADOLPHUS BASTABLE	*Cyril Maude*
LANDLORD	*Lennox Pawle*
POLICE CONSTABLE	*Arthur Williams*
DOCTOR	*G. P. Huntley*
CHOIR OF INVISIBLE ANGELS	*Messrs. Mason, Tucker, Mancy & Humphreys*

PASSION, POISON, AND PETRIFACTION

OR

THE FATAL GAZOGENE

In a bed-sitting room in a fashionable quarter of London a lady sits at her dressing-table, with her maid combing her hair. It is late; and the electric lamps are glowing. Apparently the room is bedless; but there stands against the opposite wall to that at which the dressing-table is placed a piece of furniture that suggests a bookcase without carrying conviction. On the same side is a chest of drawers of that disastrous kind which, recalcitrant to the opener until she is provoked to violence, then suddenly come wholly out and defy all her efforts to fit them in again. Opposite this chest of drawers, on the lady's side of the room, is a cupboard. The presence of a row of gentleman's boots beside the chest of drawers proclaims that the lady is married. Her own boots are beside the cupboard. The third wall is pierced midway by the door, above which is a cuckoo clock. Near the door a pedestal bears a portrait bust of the lady in plaster. There is a fan on the dressing-table, a hatbox and rug strap on the chest of drawers, an umbrella and a bootjack against the wall near the bed. The general impression is one of brightness, beauty, and social ambition, damped by somewhat inadequate means. A certain air of theatricality is produced by the fact that though the room is rectangular it has only three walls. Not a sound is heard except the overture and the crackling of the lady's hair as the maid's brush draws electric sparks from it in the dry air of the London midsummer.

The cuckoo clock strikes sixteen.

THE LADY. How much did the clock strike, Phyllis?

PHYLLIS. Sixteen, my lady.

THE LADY. That means eleven o'clock, does it not?

PHYLLIS. Eleven at night, my lady. In the morning it means half-past two; so if you hear it strike sixteen during your slumbers, do not rise.

THE LADY. I will not, Phyllis. Phyllis: I am weary. I will go to bed. Prepare my couch.

Phyllis crosses the room to the bookcase and touches a button. The front of the bookcase falls out with a crash and becomes a bed. A roll of distant thunder echoes the crash.

PHYLLIS [*shuddering*] It is a terrible night. Heaven help all poor mariners at sea! My master is late. I trust nothing has happened to him. Your bed is ready, my lady.

THE LADY. Thank you, Phyllis. [*She rises and approaches the bed*]. Goodnight.

PHYLLIS. Will your ladyship not undress?

THE LADY. Not tonight, Phyllis. [*Glancing through where the fourth wall is missing*] Not under the circumstances.

PHYLLIS [*impulsively throwing herself on her knees by her mistress's side, and clasping her round the waist*] Oh, my beloved mistress, I know not why or how; but I feel that I shall never see you alive again. There is murder in the air. [*Thunder*]. Hark!

THE LADY. Strange! As I sat there methought I heard angels singing, Oh, wont you come home, Bill Bailey? Why should angels call me Bill Bailey? My name is Magnesia Fitztollemache.

PHYLLIS [*emphasizing the title*] Lady Magnesia Fitztollemache.

LADY MAGNESIA. In case we should never again meet in this world, let us take a last farewell.

PHYLLIS [*embracing her with tears*] My poor murdered angel mistress!

LADY MAGNESIA. In case we should meet again, call me at half-past eleven.

PHYLLIS. I will, I will.

Phyllis withdraws, overcome by emotion. Lady Mag-

nesia switches off the electric light, and immediately hears the angels quite distinctly. They sing Bill Bailey so sweetly that she can attend to nothing else, and forgets to remove even her boots as she draws the coverlet over herself and sinks to sleep, lulled by celestial harmony. A white radiance plays on her pillow, and lights up her beautiful face. But the thunder growls again; and a lurid red glow concentrates itself on the door, which is presently flung open, revealing a saturnine figure in evening dress, partially concealed by a crimson cloak. As he steals towards the bed the unnatural glare in his eyes and the broad-bladed dagger nervously gripped in his right hand bode ill for the sleeping lady. Providentially she sneezes on the very brink of eternity; and the tension of the murderer's nerves is such that he bolts precipitately under the bed at the sudden and startling Atscha! *A dull, heavy, rhythmic thumping—the beating of his heart—betrays his whereabouts. Soon he emerges cautiously and raises his head above the bed coverlet level.*

THE MURDERER. I can no longer cower here listening to the agonized thumpings of my own heart. She but snoze in her sleep. I'll do't. [*He again raises the dagger. The angels sing again. He cowers*]. What is this? Has that tune reached Heaven?

LADY MAGNESIA [*waking and sitting up*] My husband! [*All the colors of the rainbow chase one another up his face with ghastly brilliancy*]. Why do you change color? And what on earth are you doing with that dagger?

FITZ [*affecting unconcern, but unhinged*] It is a present for you: a present from mother. Pretty, isnt it? [*He displays it fatuously*].

LADY MAGNESIA. But she promised me a fish slice.

FITZ. This is a combination fish slice and dagger. One day you have salmon for dinner. The next you have a murder to commit. See?

LADY MAGNESIA. My sweet mother-in-law! [*Someone*

knocks at the door]. That is Adolphus's knock. [*Fitz's face turns a dazzling green*]. What has happened to your complexion? You have turned green. Now I think of it, you always do when Adolphus is mentioned. Arnt you going to let him in?

FITZ. Certainly not. [*He goes to the door*]. Adolphus: you cannot enter. My wife is undressed and in bed.

LADY MAGNESIA [*rising*] I am not. Come in, Adolphus. [*She switches on the electric light*].

ADOLPHUS [*without*] Something most important has happened. I must come in for a moment.

FITZ [*calling to Adolphus*] Something important happened? What is it?

ADOLPHUS [*without*] My new clothes have come home.

FITZ. He says his new clothes have come home.

LADY MAGNESIA [*running to the door and opening it*] Oh, come in, come in. Let me see.

Adolphus Bastable enters. He is in evening dress, made in the latest fashion, with the right half of the coat and the left half of the trousers yellow and the other halves black. His silver-spangled waistcoat has a crimson handkerchief stuck between it and his shirt front.

ADOLPHUS. What do you think of it?

LADY MAGNESIA. It is a dream! a creation! [*She turns him about to admire him*].

ADOLPHUS [*proudly*] I shall never be mistaken for a waiter again.

FITZ. A drink, Adolphus?

ADOLPHUS. Thanks.

Fitztollemache goes to the cupboard and takes out a tray with tumblers and a bottle of whisky. He puts them on the dressing-table.

FITZ. Is the gazogene full?

LADY MAGNESIA. Yes: you put in the powders yourself today.

FITZ [*sardonically*] So I did. The special powders! Ha! ha! ha! ha! ha! [*His face is again strangely variegated*].

LADY MAGNESIA. Your complexion is really going to pieces. Why do you laugh in that silly way at nothing?

FITZ. Nothing! Ha, ha! Nothing! Ha, ha, ha!

ADOLPHUS. I hope, Mr. Fitztollemache, you are not laughing at my clothes. I warn you that I am an Englishman. You may laugh at my manners, at my brains, at my national institutions; but if you laugh at my clothes, one of us must die.

Thunder.

FITZ. I laughed but at the irony of Fate. [*He takes a gazogene from the cupboard*].

ADOLPHUS [*satisfied*] Oh, that! Oh, yes, of course!

FITZ. Let us drown all unkindness in a loving cup. [*He puts the gazogene on the floor in the middle of the room*]. Pardon the absence of a table: we found it in the way and pawned it. [*He takes the whisky bottle from the dressing-table*].

LADY MAGNESIA. We picnic at home now. It is delightful.

She takes three tumblers from the dressing-table and sits on the floor, presiding over the gazogene, with Fitz and Adolphus squatting on her left and right respectively. Fitz pours whisky into the tumblers.

FITZ [*as Magnesia is about to squirt soda into his tumbler*] Stay! No soda for me. Let Adolphus have it all—all. I will take mine neat.

LADY MAGNESIA [*proffering tumbler to Adolphus*] Pledge me, Adolphus.

FITZ. Kiss the cup, Magnesia. Pledge her, man. Drink deep.

ADOLPHUS. To Magnesia!

FITZ. To Magnesia! [*The two men drink*] It is done. [*Scrambling to his feet*] Adolphus: you have but ten minutes to live—if so long.

ADOLPHUS. What mean you?

MAGNESIA [*rising*] My mind misgives me. I have a strange feeling here [*touching her heart*].

ADOLPHUS. So have I, but lower down [*touching his stomach*]. That gazogene is disagreeing with me.

FITZ. It was poisoned!

Sensation.

ADOLPHUS [*rising*] Help! Police!

FITZ. Dastard! you would appeal to the law! Can you not die like a gentleman?

ADOLPHUS. But so young! when I have only worn my new clothes once.

MAGNESIA. It is too horrible. [*To Fitz*] Fiend! what drove you to this wicked deed?

FITZ. Jealousy. You admired his clothes: you did not admire mine.

ADOLPHUS. My clothes [*his face lights up with heavenly radiance*]! Have I indeed been found worthy to be the first clothes-martyr? Welcome, death! Hark! angels call me. [*The celestial choir again raises its favorite chant. He listens with a rapt expression. Suddenly the angels sing out of tune; and the radiance on the poisoned man's face turns a sickly green*]. Yah—ah! Oh—ahoo! The gazogene is disagreeing extremely. Oh! [*He throws himself on the bed, writhing*].

MAGNESIA [*to Fitz*] Monster: what have you done? [*She points to the distorted figure on the bed*]. That was once a Man, beautiful and glorious. What have you made of it? A writhing, agonized, miserable, moribund worm.

ADOLPHUS [*in a tone of the strongest remonstrance*] Oh, I say! Oh, come! No: look here, Magnesia! Really!

MAGNESIA. Oh, is this a time for petty vanity? Think of your misspent life—

ADOLPHUS [*much injured*] Whose misspent life?

MAGNESIA [*continuing relentlessly*] Look into your conscience: look into your stomach. [*Adolphus collapses in hideous spasms. She turns to Fitz*]. And this is your handiwork!

FITZ. Mine is a passionate nature, Magnesia. I must have your undivided love. I must have your love: do you hear? LOVE! LOVE!! LOVE!!! LOVE!!!! LOVE!!!!!

He raves, accompanied by a fresh paroxysm from the victim on the bed.

MAGNESIA [*with sudden resolution*] You shall have it.

FITZ [*enraptured*] Magnesia! I have recovered your love! Oh, how slight appears the sacrifice of this man compared to so glorious a reward! I would poison ten men without a thought of self to gain one smile from you.

ADOLPHUS [*in a broken voice*] Farewell, Magnesia: my last hour is at hand. Farewell, farewell, farewell!

MAGNESIA. At this supreme moment, George Fitztollemache, I solemnly dedicate to you all that I formerly dedicated to poor Adolphus.

ADOLPHUS. Oh, please not poor Adolphus yet. I still live, you know.

MAGNESIA. The vital spark but flashes before it vanishes. [*Adolphus groans*]. And now, Adolphus, take this last comfort from the unhappy Magnesia Fitztollemache. As I have dedicated to George all that I gave to you, so I will bury in your grave—or in your urn if you are cremated—all that I gave to him.

FITZ. I hardly follow this.

MAGNESIA. I will explain. George: hitherto I have given Adolphus all the romance of my nature—all my love—all my dreams—all my caresses. Henceforth they are yours!

FITZ. Angel!

MAGNESIA. Adolphus: forgive me if this pains you.

ADOLPHUS. Dont mention it. I hardly feel it. The gazogene is so much worse. [*Taken bad again*] Oh!

MAGNESIA. Peace, poor sufferer: there is still some balm. You are about to hear what I am going to dedicate to you.

ADOLPHUS. All I ask is a peppermint lozenge, for mercy's sake.

MAGNESIA. I have something far better than any lozenge: the devotion of a lifetime. Formerly it was George's. I kept his house, or rather, his lodgings. I mended his clothes. I darned his socks. I bought his food. I interviewed his creditors. I stood between him and the servants. I administered his domestic finances. When his hair needed cutting or his countenance was imperfectly washed, I pointed it out to him. The trouble that all this gave me made him prosaic in my eyes. Familiarity bred contempt. Now all that shall end. My husband shall be my hero, my lover, my perfect knight. He shall shield me from all care and trouble. He shall ask nothing in return but love—boundless, priceless, rapturous, soul-enthralling love, LOVE! LOVE!! LOVE!!! [*She raves and flings her arms about Fitz*]. And the duties I formerly discharged shall be replaced by the one supreme duty of duties: the duty of weeping at Adolphus's tomb.

FITZ [*reflectively*] My ownest, this sacrifice makes me feel that I have perhaps been a little selfish. I cannot help feeling that there is much to be said for the old arrangement. Why should Adolphus die for my sake?

ADOLPHUS. I am not dying for your sake, Fitz. I am dying because you poisoned me.

MAGNESIA. You do not fear to die, Adolphus, do you?

ADOLPHUS. N-n-no, I dont exactly fear to die. Still—

FITZ. Still, if an antidote—

ADOLPHUS [*bounding from the bed*] Antidote!

MAGNESIA [*with wild hope*] Antidote!

FITZ. If an antidote would not be too much of an anti-climax.

ADOLPHUS. Anti-climax be blowed! Do you think I am going to die to please the critics? Out with your antidote. Quick!

FITZ. The best antidote to the poison I have given you is lime, plenty of lime.

ADOLPHUS. Lime! You mock me! Do you think I carry lime about in my pockets?

FITZ. There is the plaster ceiling.

MAGNESIA. Yes, the ceiling. Saved, saved, saved!

All three frantically shy boots at the ceiling. Flakes of plaster rain down which Adolphus devours, at first ravenously, then with a marked falling off in relish.

MAGNESIA [*picking up a huge slice*] Take this, Adolphus: it is the largest. [*She crams it into his mouth*].

FITZ. Ha! a lump off the cornice! Try this.

ADOLPHUS [*desperately*] Stop! stop!

MAGNESIA. Do not stop. You will die. [*She tries to stuff him again*].

ADOLPHUS [*resolutely*] I prefer death.

MAGNESIA and FITZ [*throwing themselves on their knees on either side of him*] For our sakes, Adolphus, persevere.

ADOLPHUS. No: unless you can supply limo in liquid form, I must perish. Finish that ceiling I cannot and will not.

MAGNESIA. I have a thought—an inspiration. My bust. [*She snatches it from its pedestal and brings it to him*].

ADOLPHUS [*gazing fondly at it*] Can I resist it?

FITZ. Try the bun.

ADOLPHUS [*gnawing the knot of hair at the back of the bust's head: it makes him ill*] Yah, I cannot. I cannot. Not even your bust, Magnesia. Do not ask me. Let me die.

FITZ [*pressing the bust on him*] Force yourself to take a mouthful. Down with it, Adolphus!

ADOLPHUS. Useless. It would not stay down. Water! Some fluid! Ring for something to drink. [*He chokes*].

MAGNESIA. I will save you. [*She rushes to the bell and rings*].

Phyllis, in her night-gown, with her hair prettily made up into a chevaux de frise of crocuses with pink and yellow curl papers, rushes in straight to Magnesia.

PHYLLIS [*hysterically*] My beloved mistress, once more we meet. [*She sees Fitztollemache and screams*] Ah! ah! ah! A man! [*She sees Adolphus*] Men!! [*She flies; but Fitztollemache seizes her by the night-gown just as she is escaping*]. Unhand me, villain!

FITZ. This is no time for prudery, girl. Mr Bastable is dying.

PHYLLIS [*with concern*] Indeed, sir? I hope he will not think it unfeeling of me to appear at his deathbed in curl papers.

MAGNESIA. We know you have a good heart, Phyllis. Take this [*giving her the bust*]; dissolve it in a jug of hot water; and bring it back instantly. Mr Bastable's life depends on your haste.

PHYLLIS [*hesitating*] It do seem a pity, dont it, my lady, to spoil your lovely bust?

ADOLPHUS. Tush! This craze for fine art is beyond all

bounds. Off with you [*he pushes her out*]. Drink, drink, drink! My entrails are parched. Drink! [*he rushes deliriously to the gazogene*].

FITZ [*rushing after him*] Madman, you forget! It is poisoned!

ADOLPHUS. I dont care. Drink, drink! [*They wrestle madly for the gazogene. In the struggle they squirt all its contents away, mostly into one another's face. Adolphus at last flings Fitztollemache to the floor, and puts the spout into his mouth*]. Empty! empty! [*With a shriek of despair he collapses on the bed, clasping the gazogene like a baby, and weeping over it*].

FITZ [*aside to Magnesia*] Magnesia: I have always pretended not to notice it; but you keep a siphon for your private use in my hat-box.

MAGNESIA. I use it for washing old lace; but no matter: he shall have it. [*She produces a siphon from the hat-box, and offers a tumbler of soda-water to Adolphus*].

ADOLPHUS. Thanks, thanks, oh, thanks! [*He drinks. A terrific fizzing is heard. He starts up screaming*]. Help! help! The ceiling is effervescing! I am BURSTING! [*He wallows convulsively on the bed*].

FITZ. Quick! the rug strap! [*They pack him with blankets and strap him*]. Is that tight enough?

MAGNESIA [*anxiously*] Will you hold, do you think?

ADOLPHUS. The peril is past. The soda-water has gone flat.

MAGNESIA and FITZ. Thank heaven!

Phyllis returns with a washstand ewer, in which she has dissolved the bust.

MAGNESIA [*snatching it*] At last!

FITZ. You are saved. Drain it to the dregs.

Fitztollemache holds the lip of the ewer to Adolphus's mouth and gradually raises it until it stands upside down. Adolphus's efforts to swallow it are fearful, Phyllis thumping his back when he chokes, and Magnesia loosening the straps when he moans. At last, with a sigh of relief, he sinks back in the women's arms. Fitz shakes the empty ewer upside down like a potman shaking the froth out of a flagon.

ADOLPHUS. How inexpressibly soothing to the chest! A delicious numbness steals through all my members. I would sleep.

MAGNESIA
FITZ
PHYLLIS } [*whispering*] Let him sleep.

He sleeps. Celestial harps are heard; but their chords cease on the abrupt entrance of the landlord, a vulgar person in pyjamas.

THE LANDLORD. Eah! Eah! Wots this? Wots all this noise? Ah kin ennybody sleep through it? [*Looking at the floor and ceiling*] Ellow! wot you bin doin te maw ceilin?

FITZ. Silence, or leave the room. If you wake that man he dies.

THE LANDLORD. If e kin sleep through the noise you three mikes e kin sleep through ennythink.

MAGNESIA. Detestable vulgarian: your pronunciation jars on the finest chords of my nature. Begone!

THE LANDLORD [*looking at Adolphus*] Aw downt blieve eze esleep. Aw blieve eze dead. [*Calling*] Pleece! Pleece! Merder! [*A blue halo plays mysteriously on the door, which opens and reveals a policeman. Thunder*]. Eah, pleecmin: these three's bin an merdered this gent between em, an naw tore moy ahse dahn.

THE POLICEMAN [*offended*] Policeman, indeed! Wheres your manners?

FITZ. Officer—

THE POLICEMAN [*with distinguished consideration*] Sir?

FITZ. As between gentlemen—

THE POLICEMAN [*bowing*] Sir: to you.

FITZ [*bowing*] I may inform you that my friend had an acute attack of indigestion. No carbonate of soda being available, he swallowed a portion of this man's ceiling. [*Pointing to Adolphus*] Behold the result!

THE POLICEMAN. The ceiling was poisoned! Well, of all the artful—[*He collars the landlord*]. I arrest you for wilful murder.

THE LANDLORD [*appealing to the heavens*] Ow, is this

jestice! Ah could aw tell e wiz gowin te eat moy ceilin?

THE POLICEMAN [*releasing him*] True. The case is more complicated than I thought. [*He tries to lift Adolphus's arm but cannot*]. Stiff already.

THE LANDLORD [*trying to lift Adolphus's leg*] An' precious evvy. [*Feeling the calf*] Woy, eze gorn ez awd ez niles.

FITZ [*rushing to the bed*] What is this?

MAGNESIA. Oh, say not he is dead. Phyllis: fetch a doctor. [*Phyllis runs out. They all try to lift Adolphus; but he is perfectly stiff, and as heavy as lead*]. Rouse him. Shake him.

THE POLICEMAN [*exhausted*] Whew! Is he a man or a statue? [*Magnesia utters a piercing scream*]. Whats wrong, Miss?

MAGNESIA [*to Fitz*] Do you not see what has happened?

FITZ [*striking his forehead*] Horror on horror's head!

THE LANDLORD. Wotjemean?

MAGNESIA. The plaster has set inside him. The officer was right: he is indeed a living statue.

Magnesia flings herself on the stony breast of Adolphus. Fitztollemache buries his head in his hands; and his chest heaves convulsively. The policeman takes a small volume from his pocket and consults it.

THE POLICEMAN. This case is not provided for in my book of instructions. It dont seem no use trying artificial respiration, do it? [*To the landlord*] Here! lend a hand, you. We'd best take him and set him up in Trafalgar Square.

THE LANDLORD. Aushd pat im in the cestern an worsh it aht of im.

Phyllis comes back with a Doctor.

PHYLLIS. The medical man, my lady.

THE POLICEMAN. A poison case, sir.

THE DOCTOR. Do you mean to say that an unqualified person! a layman! has dared to administer poison in my district?

THE POLICEMAN [*raising Magnesia tenderly*] It looks like it. Hold up, my lady.

THE DOCTOR. Not a moment must be lost. The patient must be kept awake at all costs. Constant and violent motion is necessary.

He snatches Magnesia from the policeman, and rushes her about the room.

FITZ. Stop! That is not the poisoned person!

THE DOCTOR. It is you, then. Why did you not say so before?

He seizes Fitztollemache and rushes him about.

THE LANDLORD. Naow, naow, thet ynt im.

THE DOCTOR. What, you!

He pounces on the landlord and rushes him round.

THE LANDLORD. Eah! chack it. [*He trips the doctor up. Both fall*]. Jest owld this leoonatic, will you, Mister Horficer?

THE POLICEMAN [*dragging both of them to their feet*] Come out of it, will you. You must all come with me to the station.

Thunder.

MAGNESIA. What! In this frightful storm!

The hail patters noisily on the window.

PHYLLIS. I think it's raining.

The wind howls.

THE LANDLORD. It's thanderin and lawtnin.

FITZ. It's dangerous.

THE POLICEMAN [*drawing his baton and whistle*] If you wont come quietly, then—

He whistles. A fearful flash is followed by an appalling explosion of heaven's artillery. A thunderbolt enters the room, and strikes the helmet of the devoted constable, whence it is attracted to the waistcoat of the doctor by the lancet in his pocket. Finally it leaps with fearful force on the landlord, who, being of a gross and spongy nature, absorbs the electric fluid at the cost of his life. The others look on horror-stricken as the three victims, after reeling, jostling, cannoning through a ghastly quadrille, at last sink inanimate on the carpet.

MAGNESIA [*listening at the doctor's chest*] Dead!

FITZ [*kneeling by the landlord, and raising his hand, which drops with a thud*] Dead!

PHYLLIS [*seizing the looking-glass and holding it to the Policeman's lips*] Dead!

FITZ [*solemnly rising*] The copper attracted the lightning.

MAGNESIA [*rising*] After life's fitful fever they sleep well. Phyllis: sweep them up.

Phyllis replaces the looking-glass on the dressing-table; takes up the fan; and fans the policeman, who rolls away like a leaf before the wind to the wall. She disposes similarly of the landlord and doctor.

PHYLLIS. Will they be in your way if I leave them there until morning, my lady? Or shall I bring up the ashpan and take them away?

MAGNESIA. They will not disturb us. Goodnight, Phyllis.

PHYLLIS. Goodnight, my lady. Goodnight, sir.

She retires.

MAGNESIA. And now, husband, let us perform our last sad duty to our friend. He has become his own monument. Let us erect him. He is heavy; but love can do much.

FITZ. A little leverage will get him on his feet. Give me my umbrella.

MAGNESIA. True.

She hands him the umbrella, and takes up the boot-jack. They get them under Adolphus's back, and prize him up on his feet.

FITZ. Thats done it! Whew!

MAGNESIA [*kneeling at the left hand of the statue*] For ever and for ever, Adolphus.

FITZ [*kneeling at the right hand of the statue*] The rest is silence.

The Angels sing Bill Bailey. The statue raises its hands in an attitude of blessing, and turns its limelit face to heaven as the curtain falls. National Anthem.

ATTENDANTS [*in front*] All out for the next performance. Pass along, please, ladies and gentlemen: pass along.

THE DARK LADY OF THE SONNETS

The Dark Lady of the Sonnets was first produced at the Haymarket Theatre, London, on 24 November 1910, with the following cast:

THE WARDER	*Hugh B. Tabberer*
WILLIAM SHAKESPEAR	*Granville Barker*
QUEEN ELIZABETH	*Suzanne Sheldon*
THE DARK LADY	*Mona Limerick*

PREFACE TO THE DARK LADY OF THE SONNETS

How the Play came to be Written

I HAD better explain why, in this little *pièce d'occasion,* written for a performance in aid of the funds of the project of establishing a National Theatre as a memorial to Shakespear, I have identified the Dark Lady with Mistress Mary Fitton. First, let me say that I do not contend that the Dark Lady was Mary Fitton, because when the case in Mary's favor (or against her, if you please to consider that the Dark Lady was no better than she ought to have been) was complete, a portrait of Mary came to light and turned out to be that of a fair lady, not of a dark one. That settles the question, if the portrait is authentic, which I see no reason to doubt, and the lady's hair undyed, which is perhaps less certain. Shakespear rubbed in the lady's complexion in his sonnets mercilessly; for in his day black hair was as unpopular as red hair was in the early days of Queen Victoria. Any tinge lighter than raven black must be held fatal to the strongest claim to be the Dark Lady. And so, unless it can be shewn that Shakespear's sonnets exasperated Mary Fitton into dyeing her hair and getting painted in false colors, I must give up all pretence that my play is historical. The later suggestion of Mr Acheson that the Dark Lady, far from being a maid of honor, kept a tavern in Oxford, and was the mother of Davenant the poet, is the one I should have adopted had I wished to be up to date. Why, then, did I introduce the Dark Lady as Mistress Fitton?

Well, I had two reasons. The play was not to have been written by me at all, but by Dame Edith Lyttelton; and it was she who suggested a scene of jealousy between Queen Elizabeth and the Dark Lady at the expense of the unfortunate Bard. Now this, if the Dark Lady was a maid of honor, was quite easy. If she were a tavern landlady, it would have strained all probability. So I stuck to Mary Fitton. But I had another and more personal reason. I was, in a manner, present at the birth of the Fitton theory. Its parent and I had become acquainted; and he used to consult me on obscure passages in the sonnets, on which, as far as I can remember, I never succeeded in throwing the faintest light, at a time when nobody else thought my opinion, on that or any other subject, of the slightest importance. I thought it would be friendly to immortalize him, as the silly literary saying is, much as Shakespear immortalized Mr W. H., as he said he would, simply by writing about him.

Let me tell the story formally.

Thomas Tyler

Throughout the eighties at least, and probably for some years before, the British Museum reading room was used daily by a gentleman of such astonishing and crushing ugliness that no one who had once seen him could ever thereafter forget him. He was of fair complexion, rather golden red than sandy; aged between forty-five and sixty; and dressed in frock coat and tall hat of presentable but never new appearance. His figure was rectangular, waistless, neckless, ankleless, of middle height, looking shortish because, though he was not particularly stout, there was nothing slender about him. His ugliness was not unamiable: it was accidental, external, excrescential. Attached to his face from the left ear to the point of his chin was a monstrous goitre, which hung down to his collar bone, and was very inadequately balanced by a smaller one on his right eyelid. Nature's malice was so overdone in his case that it somehow failed to produce the effect of repulsion it seemed to have aimed at. When you first met Thomas Tyler you could think of nothing else but whether surgery could really do nothing for him. But after a very brief acquaintance you never thought of his disfigurements at all, and talked to him as you might to Romeo or Lovelace; only, so many people, especially women, would not risk the preliminary ordeal, that he remained a man apart and a bachelor all his days. I am not to be frightened or prejudiced by a tumor; and I struck up a cordial acquaintance with him, in the course of which he kept me pretty closely on the track of his work at the Museum, in which I was then, like himself, a daily reader.

He was by profession a man of letters of an uncommercial kind. He was a specialist in pessimism; had made a translation of Ecclesiastes of which eight copies a year were sold; and followed up the pessimism of Shakespear and Swift with keen interest. He delighted in a hideous conception which he called the theory of the cycles, according to which the history of mankind and the universe keeps eternally repeating itself without the slightest variation throughout all eternity; so that he had lived and died and had his goitre before and would live and die and have it again and again and again. He liked to believe that nothing that happened to him was completely novel: he was persuaded that he often had some recollection of its previous occurrence in the last cycle. He hunted out allusions to this favorite theory in his three favorite pessimists. He tried his hand occasionally at deciphering ancient inscriptions, reading them as people seem to read the stars, by discovering bears and bulls and swords and goats where, as it seems to me, no sane human being can see anything but stars higgledy-piggledy. Next to the translation of Ecclesiastes, his *magnum opus* was his work on Shakespear's Sonnets, in which he accepted a previous identification of Mr W. H., the "onlie begetter" of the sonnets, with the Earl of Pembroke (William Herbert), and promulgated his own identification of Mistress Mary Fitton with the Dark Lady. Whether he was right or wrong about the Dark Lady did not matter urgently to me: she might have been Maria Tompkins for all I cared. But Tyler would have it that she was Mary Fitton; and he tracked Mary down from the first of her marriages in her teens to her tomb in Cheshire, whither he made a pilgrimage and whence returned in triumph with a picture of her statue, and the news that he was convinced she was a dark lady by traces of paint still discernible.

In due course he published his edition of the Sonnets, with the evidence he had collected. He lent me a copy of the book, which I never returned. But I reviewed it in the Pall Mall Gazette on the 7th of January 1886, and thereby let loose the Fitton theory in a wider circle of readers than the book could reach. Then Tyler died, sinking unnoted like a stone in the sea. I observe that Mr Acheson, Mrs Davenant's champion, calls him Reverend. It may very well be that he got his knowledge of Hebrew in reading for the Church; and there was always something of the clergyman or the schoolmaster in his dress and air. Possibly he may actually have been ordained. But he never told me that or anything else about his affairs; and his black pessimism would have shot him violently out of any church at present established in the West. We never talked about affairs: we talked about Shakespear, and the Dark Lady, and Swift, and Koheleth, and the cycles, and the mysterious moments when a feeling came over us that this had happened to us before, and about the forgeries of the Pentateuch which were offered for sale to the British Museum, and about literature and things of the spirit generally. He always came to my desk at the Museum and spoke to me about something or other, no doubt finding that people who were keen on this sort of conversation were rather scarce. He remains a vivid spot of memory in the void of my forgetfulness, a quite considerable and dignified soul in a grotesquely disfigured body.

Frank Harris

To the review in the Pall Mall Gazette I attribute, rightly or wrongly, the introduction of Mary Fitton to Mr Frank Harris. My reason for this is that Mr Harris wrote a play about Shakespear and Mary Fitton; and when I, as a pious duty to Tyler's ghost, reminded the world that it was to Tyler we owed the Fitton theory, Frank Harris, who clearly had not a notion of what had first put Mary into his head, believed, I think, that I had invented Tyler expressly for his discomfiture; for the stress I laid on Tyler's claims must have seemed unaccountable and perhaps malicious on the assumption that he was to me a mere name among the thousands of names in the British Museum catalogue. Therefore I make it clear that I had and have personal reasons for remembering Tyler, and for regarding myself as in some sort charged with the duty of reminding the world of his work. I am sorry for his sake that Mary's portrait is fair, and that Mr W. H. has veered round again from Pembroke to Southampton; but even so his work was not wasted: it is by exhausting all the hypotheses that we reach the verifiable one; and after all, the wrong road always leads somewhere.

Frank Harris's play was written long before mine. I read it in manuscript before the Shakespear Memorial National Theatre was mooted; and if there is anything except the Fitton theory (which is Tyler's property) in my play which is also in Mr Harris's it was I who annexed it from him and not he from me. It does not matter anyhow, because this play of mine is a brief trifle, and full of manifest impossibilities at that; whilst Mr Harris's play is serious both in size, intention, and quality. But there could not in the nature of things be much resemblance, because Frank conceives Shakespear to have been a broken-hearted, melancholy, enormously sentimental person, whereas I am convinced that he was very like myself: in fact, if I had been born in 1556 instead of in 1856, I should have taken to blank verse and given Shakespear a harder run for his money than all the other Elizabethans put together. Yet the success of Frank Harris's book on Shakespear gave me great delight.

To those who know the literary world of London there was a sharp stroke of ironic comedy in the irresistible verdict in its favor. In critical literature there is one prize that is always open to competition, one blue ribbon that always carries the highest critical rank with it. To win, you must write the best book of your generation on Shakespear. It is felt on all sides that to do this a certain fastidious refinement, a delicacy of taste, a correctness of manner and tone, and high academic distinction in addition to the indispensable scholarship and literary reputation, are needed; and men who pretend to these qualifications are constantly looked to with a gentle expectation that presently they will achieve the great feat. Now if there is a man on earth who is the utter contrary of everything that this description implies; whose very existence is an insult to the ideal it realizes; whose eye disparages, whose resonant voice denounces, whose cold shoulder jostles every decency, every delicacy, every amenity, every dignity, every sweet usage of that quiet life of mutual admiration in which perfect Shakespearean appreciation is expected to arise, that man is Frank Harris. Here is one who is extraordinarily qualified, by a range of sympathy and understanding that extends from the ribaldry of a buccaneer to the shyest tendernesses of the most sensitive poetry, to be all things to all men, yet whose proud humor it is to be to every man, provided the man is eminent and pretentious, the champion of his enemies. To the Archbishop he is an atheist, to the atheist a Catholic mystic, to the Bismarckian Imperialist an Anacharsis Klootz, to Anacharsis Klootz a Washington, to Mrs Proudie a Don Juan, to Aspasia a John Knox: in short, to everyone his complement rather than his counterpart, his antagonist rather than his fellow-creature. Always provided, however, that the persons thus affronted are respectable persons. Sophie Perovskaia, who perished on the scaffold for blowing Alexander II to fragments, may perhaps have echoed Hamlet's

> Oh God, Horatio, what a wounded name—
> Things standing thus unknown—I leave behind!

but Frank Harris, in his Sonia, has rescued her from that injustice, and enshrined her among the saints. He has lifted the Chicago anarchists out of their infamy, and shewn that, compared with the Capitalism that killed them, they were heroes and martyrs. He has done this with the most unusual power of conviction. The story, as he tells it, inevitably and irresistibly displaces all the vulgar, mean, purblind, spiteful versions. There is a precise realism and an unsmiling, measured, determined sincerity which gives a strange dignity to the work of one whose fixed practice and ungovernable impulse it is to kick conventional dignity whenever he sees it.

Harris "durch Mitleid wissend"

Frank Harris is everything except a humorist, not, apparently, from stupidity, but because scorn overcomes humor in him. Nobody ever dreamt of reproaching Milton's Lucifer for not seeing the comic side of his fall; and nobody who has read Mr Harris's stories desires to have them lightened by chapters from the hand of Artemus Ward. Yet he knows the taste and the value of humor. He was one of the few men of letters who really appreciated Oscar Wilde, though he did not rally fiercely to Wilde's side until the world deserted Oscar in his ruin. I myself was present at a curious meeting between the two, when Harris, on the eve of the Queensberry trial, prophesied to Wilde with miraculous precision exactly what immediately afterwards happened to him, and warned him to leave the country. It was the first time within my knowledge that such a forecast proved true. Wilde, though under no illusion as to the folly of the quite unselfish suit-at-law he had been persuaded to begin, nevertheless so miscalculated the force of the social vengeance he was unloosing on himself that he fancied it could be stayed by putting up the editor of The Saturday Review (as Mr Harris then was) to declare that he considered Dorian Gray a highly moral book, which it certainly is. When Harris foretold him the truth, Wilde denounced him as a fainthearted friend who was failing him in his hour of need, and left the room in anger. Harris's idiosyncratic power of pity saved him from feeling or shewing the smallest resentment; and events presently proved to Wilde how insanely he had been advised in taking the action, and how accurately Harris had gauged the situation.

The same capacity for pity governs Harris's study of Shakespear, whom, as I have said, he pities too much; but that he is not insensible to humor is shewn not only by his appreciation of Wilde, but by the fact that the group of contributors who made his editorship of The Saturday Review so remarkable, and of whom I speak none the less highly because I happened to be one of them myself, were all, in their various ways, humorists.

"Sidney's Sister: Pembroke's Mother"

And now to return to Shakespear. Though Mr Harris followed Tyler in identifying Mary Fitton as the Dark Lady, and the Earl of Pembroke as the addressee of the other sonnets and the man who made love successfully to Shakespear's mistress, he very characteristically refuses to follow Tyler on one point, though for the life of me I cannot remember whether it was one of the surmises which Tyler published, or only one which he submitted to me to see what I would say about it, just as he used to submit difficult lines from the sonnets.

This surmise was that "Sidney's sister: Pembroke's mother" set Shakespear on to persuade Pembroke to marry, and that this was the explanation of those earlier sonnets which so persistently and unnaturally urged matrimony on Mr W. H. I take this to be one of the brightest of Tyler's ideas, because the persuasions in the sonnets are unaccountable and out of character unless they were offered to please somebody whom Shakespear desired to please, and who took a motherly interest in Pembroke. There is a further temptation in the theory for me. The most charming of all Shakespear's old women, indeed the most charming of all his women, young or old, is the Countess of Rousillon in All's Well That Ends Well. It has a certain individuality among them which suggests a portrait. Mr Harris will have it that all Shakespear's nice old women are drawn from his beloved mother; but I see no evidence whatever that Shakespear's mother was a particularly nice woman or that he was particularly fond of her. That she was a simple incarnation of extravagant maternal pride like the mother of Coriolanus in Plutarch, as Mr Harris asserts, I cannot believe: she is quite as likely to have borne her son a grudge for becoming "one of these harlotry players" and disgracing the Ardens. Anyhow, as a conjectural model for the Countess of Rousillon, I prefer that one of whom Jonson wrote

> Sidney's sister: Pembroke's mother:
> Death ere thou has slain another,
> Learned and fair and good as she,
> Time shall throw a dart at thee.

But Frank will not have her at any price, because his ideal

Shakespear is rather like a sailor in a melodrama; and a sailor in a melodrama must adore his mother. I do not at all belittle such sailors. They are the emblems of human generosity; but Shakespear was not an emblem; he was a man and the author of Hamlet, who had no illusions about his mother. In weak moments one almost wishes he had.

Shakespear's Social Standing

On the vexed question of Shakespear's social standing Mr Harris says that Shakespear "had not had the advantage of a middle-class training." I suggest that Shakespear missed this questionable advantage, not because he was socially too low to have attained to it, but because he conceived himself as belonging to the upper class from which our public school boys are now drawn. Let Mr Harris survey for a moment the field of contemporary journalism. He will see there some men who have the very characteristics from which he infers that Shakespear was at a social disadvantage through his lack of middle-class training. They are rowdy, ill-mannered, abusive, mischievous, fond of quoting obscene schoolboy anecdotes, adepts in that sort of blackmail which consists in mercilessly libelling and insulting every writer whose opinions are sufficiently heterodox to make it almost impossible for him to risk perhaps five years of a slender income by an appeal to a prejudiced orthodox jury; and they see nothing in all this cruel blackguardism but an uproariously jolly rag, although they are by no means without genuine literary ability, a love of letters, and even some artistic conscience. But he will find not one of the models of this type (I say nothing of mere imitators of it) below the rank that looks at the middle class, not humbly and enviously from below, but insolently from above. Mr Harris himself notes Shakespear's contempt for the tradesman and mechanic, and his incorrigible addiction to smutty jokes. He does us the public service of sweeping away the familiar plea of the Bardolatrous ignoramus, that Shakespear's coarseness was part of the manners of his time, putting his pen with precision on the one name, Spenser, that is necessary to expose such a libel on Elizabethan decency. There was nothing whatever to prevent Shakespear from being as decent as More was before him, or Bunyan after him, and as self-respecting as Raleigh or Sidney, except the tradition of his class, in which education or statesmanship may no doubt be acquired by those who have a turn for them, but in which insolence, derision, profligacy, obscene jesting, debt contracting, and rowdy mischievousness, give continual scandal to the pious, serious, industrious, solvent bourgeois. No other class is infatuated enough to believe that gentlemen are born and not made by a very elaborate process of culture. Even kings are taught and coached and drilled from their earliest boyhood to play their part. But the man of family (I am convinced that Shakespear took that view of himself) will plunge into society without a lesson in table manners, into politics without a lesson in history, into the city without a lesson in business, and into the army without a lesson in honor.

It has been said, with the object of proving Shakespear a laborer, that he could hardly write his name. Why? Because he "had not the advantage of a middle-class training." Shakespear himself tells us, through Hamlet, that gentlemen purposely wrote badly lest they should be mistaken for scriveners; but most of them, then as now, wrote badly because they could not write any better. In short, the whole range of Shakespear's foibles: the snobbishness, the naughtiness, the contempt for tradesmen and mechanics, the assumption that witty conversation can only mean smutty conversation, the flunkeyism towards social superiors and insolence towards social inferiors, the easy ways with servants which is seen not only between The Two Gentlemen of Verona and their valets, but in the affection and respect inspired by a great servant like Adam: all these are the characteristics of Eton and Harrow, not of the public elementary or private adventure school. They prove, as everything we know about Shakespear suggests, that he thought of the Shakespears and Ardens as families of consequence, and regarded himself as a gentleman under a cloud through his father's ill luck in business, and never for a moment as a man of the people. This is at once the explanation of and excuse for his snobbery. He was not a parvenu trying to cover his humble origin with a purchased coat of arms: he was a gentleman resuming what he conceived to be his natural position as soon as he gained the means to keep it up.

This Side Idolatry

There is another matter which I think Mr Harris should ponder. He says that Shakespear was but "little esteemed by his own generation." He even describes Jonson's description of his "little Latin and less Greek" as a sneer, whereas it occurs in an unmistakeably sincere eulogy of Shakespear, written after his death, and is clearly meant to heighten the impression of Shakespear's prodigious natural endowments by pointing out that they were not due to scholastic acquirements. Now there is a sense in which it is true enough that Shakespear was too little esteemed by his own generation, or, for the matter of that, by any subsequent generation. The bargees on the Regent's Canal do not chant Shakespear's verses as the gondoliers in Venice are said to chant the verses of Tasso (a practice which was suspended for some reason during my stay in Venice: at least no gondolier ever did it in my hearing). Shakespear is no more a popular author than Rodin is a popular sculptor or Richard Strauss a popular composer. But Shakespear was certainly not such a fool as to expect the Toms, Dicks, and Harrys of his time to be any more interested in dramatic poetry than Newton, later on, expected them to be interested in fluxions. And when we come to the question whether Shakespear missed that assurance which all great men have had from the more capable and susceptible members of their generation that they were great men, Ben Jonson's evidence disposes of so improbable a notion at once and for ever. "I loved the man," says Ben, "this side idolatry, as well as any." Now why in the name of common sense should he have made that qualification unless there had been, not only idolatry, but idolatry fulsome enough to irritate Jonson into an express disavowal of it? Jonson, the bricklayer, must have felt sore sometimes when Shakespear spoke and wrote of bricklayers as his inferiors. He must have felt it a little hard that being a better scholar, and perhaps a braver and tougher man physically than Shakespear, he was not so successful or so well liked. But in spite of this he praised Shakespear to the utmost stretch of his powers of eulogy: in fact, notwithstanding his disclaimer, he did not stop "this side idolatry." If, therefore, even Jonson felt himself forced to clear himself of extravagance and absurdity in his appreciation of Shakespear, there must have been many people about who idolized Shakespear as American ladies idolize Paderewski, and who carried Bardolatry, even in the Bard's own time, to an extent that threatened to make his reasonable admirers ridiculous.

Shakespear's Pessimism

I submit to Mr Harris that by ruling out this idolatry, and its possible effect in making Shakespear think that his public would stand anything from him, he has ruled out a far more plausible explanation of the faults of such a play as Timon of Athens than his theory that Shakespear's passion for the Dark Lady "cankered and took on proud flesh in him, and tortured him to nervous breakdown and madness." In Timon the intellectual bankruptcy is obvious enough: Shakespear tried once too often to make a play out of the cheap pessimism which is thrown into despair by a comparison of actual human nature with theoretical morality, actual law and administration with abstract justice, and so forth. But Shakespear's perception of the fact that all men, judged by the moral standard which they apply to others and by which they justify their punishment of others, are fools and scoundrels, does not date from the Dark Lady complication: he seems to have been born with it. If in The Comedy of Errors and A Midsummer Night's Dream the persons of the drama are not quite so ready for treachery and murder as Laertes and even Hamlet himself (not to mention the procession of ruffians who pass through the latest plays) it is certainly not because they have any more regard for law or religion. There is only one place in Shakespear's plays where the sense of shame is used as a human attribute; and that is where Hamlet is ashamed, not of anything he himself has done, but of his mother's relations with his uncle. This scene is an unnatural one: the son's reproaches to his mother, even the fact of his being able to discuss the subject with her, is more repulsive than her relations with her deceased husband's brother.

Here, too, Shakespear betrays for once his religious sense by making Hamlet, in his agony of shame, declare that his mother's conduct makes "sweet religion a rhapsody of words." But for that passage we might almost suppose that the feeling of Sunday morning in the country which Orlando describes so perfectly in As You Like It was the beginning and end of Shakespear's notion of religion. I say almost, because Isabella in Measure for Measure has religious charm, in spite of the conventional theatrical assumption that female religion means an inhumanly ferocious chastity. But for the most part Shakespear differentiates his heroes from his villains much more by what they do than by what they are. Don Juan in Much Ado is a true villain: a man with a malicious will; but he is too dull a duffer to be of any use in a leading part; and when we come to the great villains like Macbeth, we find, as Mr Harris points out, that they are precisely identical with the heroes: Macbeth is only Hamlet incongruously committing murders and engaging in hand-to-hand combats. And Hamlet, who does not dream of apologizing for the three murders he commits, is always apologizing because he has not yet committed a fourth, and finds, to his great bewilderment, that he does not want to commit it. "It cannot be," he says, "but I am pigeon-livered, and lack gall to make oppression bitter; else, ere this, I should have fatted all the region kites with this slave's offal." Really one is tempted to suspect that when Shylock asks "Hates any man the thing he would not kill?" he is expressing the natural and proper sentiments of the human race as Shakespear understood them, and not the vindictiveness of a stage Jew.

Gaiety of Genius

In view of these facts, it is dangerous to cite Shakespear's pessimism as evidence of the despair of a heart broken by the Dark Lady. There is an irrepressible gaiety of genius which enables it to bear the whole weight of the world's misery without blenching. There is a laugh always ready to avenge its tears of discouragement. In the lines which Mr Harris quotes only to declare that he can make nothing of them, and to condemn them as out of character, Richard III, immediately after pitying himself because

> There is no creature loves me
> And if I die no soul will pity me,

adds, with a grin,

> Nay, wherefore should they, since that I myself
> Find in myself no pity for myself?

Let me again remind Mr Harris of Oscar Wilde. We all dreaded to read De Profundis: our instinct was to stop our ears, or run away from the wail of a broken, though by no means contrite, heart. But we were throwing away our pity. De Profundis was de profundis indeed: Wilde was too good a dramatist to throw away so powerful an effect; but none the less it was de profundis in excelsis. There was more laughter between the lines of that book than in a thousand farces by men of no genius. Wilde, like Richard and Shakespear, found in himself no pity for himself. There is nothing that marks the born dramatist more unmistakeably than this discovery of comedy in his own misfortunes almost in proportion to the pathos with which the ordinary man announces their tragedy. I cannot for the life of me see the broken heart in Shakespear's latest works. "Hark, hark! the lark at heaven's gate sings" is not the lyric of a broken man; nor is Cloten's comment that if Imogen does not appreciate it, "it is a vice in her ears which horse hairs, and cats' guts, and the voice of unpaved eunuch to boot, can never amend," the sally of a saddened one. Is it not clear that to the last there was in Shakespear an incorrigible divine levity, an inexhaustible joy that derided sorrow? Think of the poor Dark Lady having to stand up to this unbearable power of extracting a grim fun from everything. Mr Harris writes as if Shakespear did all the suffering and the Dark Lady all the cruelty. But why does he not put himself in the Dark Lady's place for a moment as he has put himself so successfully in Shakespear's? Imagine her reading the hundred and thirtieth sonnet!

> My mistress' eyes are nothing like the sun;
> Coral is far more red than her lips' red;
> If snow be white, why then her breasts are dun;
> If hairs be wire, black wires grow on her head;
> I have seen roses damasked, red and white,
> But no such roses see I in her cheeks;
> And in some perfumes is there more delight
> Than in the breath that from my mistress reeks.
> I love to hear her speak; yet well I know
> That music hath a far more pleasing sound.
> I grant I never saw a goddess go:
> My mistress, when she walks, treads on the ground.
>   And yet, by heaven, I think my love as rare
>   As any she belied with false compare.

Take this as a sample of the sort of compliment from which she was never for a moment safe with Shakespear. Bear in mind that she was not a comedian; that the Elizabethan fashion of treating brunettes as ugly women must have made her rather sore on the subject of her complexion; that no human being, male or female, can conceivably enjoy being chaffed on that point in the fourth couplet about the perfumes; that Shakespear's revulsions, as the sonnet immediately preceding shews, were as violent as his ardors, and were expressed with the realistic power and horror that makes Hamlet say that the heavens got sick when they saw the queen's conduct; and then ask Mr Harris whether any woman could have stood it for long, or have thought the "sugred" compliment worth the cruel wounds, the cleaving of the heart in twain, that seemed to Shakespear as natural and amusing a reaction as the burlesquing of his heroics by Pistol, his sermons by Falstaff, and his poems by Cloten and Touchstone.

Jupiter and Semele

This does not mean that Shakespear was cruel: evidently he was not; but it was not cruelty that made Jupiter reduce Semele to ashes: it was the fact that he could not help being a god nor she help being a mortal. The one thing Shakespear's passion for the Dark Lady was not, was what Mr Harris in one passage calls it: idolatrous. If it had been, she might have been able to stand it. The man who dotes "yet doubts; suspects, yet strongly loves," is tolerable even by a spoilt and tyrannical mistress; but what woman could possibly endure a man who dotes without doubting; who *knows* and who is hugely amused at the absurdity of his infatuation for a woman of whose mortal imperfections not one escapes him: a man always exchanging grins with Yorick's skull, and inviting "my lady" to laugh at the sepulchral humor of the fact that though she paint an inch thick (which the Dark Lady may have done), to Yorick's favor she must come at last. To the Dark Lady he must sometimes have seemed cruel beyond description: an intellectual Caliban. True, a Caliban who could say

> Be not afeard: the isle is full of noises,
> Sounds and sweet airs that give delight and hurt not.
> Sometimes a thousand twangling instruments
> Will hum about mine ears; and sometimes voices,
> That, if I then had waked after long sleep,
> Will make me sleep again; and then, in dreaming,
> The clouds, methought, would open and shew riches
> Ready to drop on me: that when I wak'd
> I cried to dream again.

which is very lovely; but the Dark Lady may have had that vice in her ears which Cloten dreaded: she may not have seen the beauty of it, whereas there can be no doubt at all that of "My mistress' eyes are nothing like the sun," &c., not a word was lost on her.

And is it to be supposed that Shakespear was too stupid or too modest not to see at last that it was a case of Jupiter and Semele? Shakespear was most certainly not modest in that sense. The timid cough of the minor poet was never heard from him.

> Not marble, nor the gilded monuments
> Of princes, shall outlive this powerful rhyme

is only one out of a dozen passages in which he (possibly with a keen sense of the fun of scandalizing the modest coughers) proclaimed his place and his power in "the wide world dreaming of things to come." The Dark Lady most likely thought this side of him insufferably conceited; for there is no reason to suppose that she liked his plays any better than Minna Wagner liked Richard's music dramas: as likely as not, she thought The Spanish Tragedy worth six Hamlets. He was not stupid either: if his class limitations and a profession that cut him off from actual participation in great affairs of State had not confined his opportunities of intellectual and political training to private conversation and to the Mermaid Tavern, he would probably have become one of the ablest men of his time instead of being merely its ablest playwright. One might surmise that Shakespear found out that the Dark Lady's brains could no more keep pace with his than Anne Hathaway's, if there were any evidence that their friendship ceased when he stopped writing sonnets to her. As a matter of fact the consolidation of a passion into an enduring intimacy generally puts an end to sonnets.

That the Dark Lady broke Shakespear's heart, as Mr Harris will have it she did, is an extremely unShakespearean hypothesis. "Men have died from time to time, and worms have eaten them; but not for love," says Rosalind. Richard of Gloster, into whom Shakespear put all his own impish superiority to vulgar sentiment, exclaims

> And this word "love," which greybeards call divine,
> Be resident in men like one another
> And not in me: I am myself alone.

Hamlet has not a tear for Ophelia: her death moves him to

fierce disgust for the sentimentality of Laertes by her grave; and when he discusses the scene with Horatio immediately after, he utterly forgets her, though he is sorry he forgot himself, and jumps at the proposal of a fencing match to finish the day with. As against this view Mr Harris pleads Romeo, Orsino, and even Antonio; and he does it so penetratingly that he convinces you that Shakespear did betray himself again and again in these characters; but self-betrayal is one thing; and self-portrayal, as in Hamlet and Mercutio, is another. Shakespear never "saw himself," as actors say, in Romeo or Orsino or Antonio. In Mr Harris's own play Shakespear is presented with the most pathetic tenderness. He is tragic, bitter, pitiable, wretched, and broken among a robust crowd of Jonsons and Elizabeths; but to me he is not Shakespear because I miss the Shakespearean irony and the Shakespearean gaiety. Take these away and Shakespear is no longer Shakespear: all the bite, the impetus, the strength, the grim delight in his own power of looking terrible facts in the face with a chuckle, is gone; and you have nothing left but that most depressing of all things: a victim. Now who can think of Shakespear as a man with a grievance? Even in that most thoroughgoing and inspired of all Shakespear's loves: his love of music (which Mr Harris has been the first to appreciate at anything like its value), there is a dash of mockery. "Spit in the hole, man; and tune again." "Divine air! Now is his soul ravished. Is it not strange that sheep's guts should hale the souls out of men's bodies?" "An he had been a dog that should have howled thus, they would have hanged him." There is just as much Shakespear here as in the inevitable quotation about the sweet south and the bank of violets.

I lay stress on this irony of Shakespear's, this impish rejoicing in pessimism, this exultation in what breaks the hearts of common men, not only because it is diagnostic of that immense energy of life which we call genius, but because its omission is the one glaring defect in Mr Harris's otherwise extraordinarily penetrating book. Fortunately, it is an omission that does not disable the book as (in my judgment) it disabled the hero of the play, because Mr Harris left himself out of his play, whereas he pervades his book, mordant, deep-voiced, and with an unconquerable style which is the man.

THE IDOL OF THE BARDOLATERS

There is even an advantage in having a book on Shakespear with the Shakespearean irony left out of account. I do not say that the missing chapter should not be added in the next edition: the hiatus is too great: it leaves the reader too uneasy before this touching picture of a writhing worm substituted for the invulnerable giant. But it is none the less probable that in no other way could Mr Harris have got at his man as he has. For, after all, what is the secret of the hopeless failure of the academic Bardolaters to give us a credible or even interesting Shakespear, and the easy triumph of Mr Harris in giving us both? Simply that Mr Harris has assumed that he was dealing with a man, whilst the others have assumed that they were writing about a god, and have therefore rejected every consideration of fact, tradition, or interpretation, that pointed to any human imperfection in their hero. They thus leave themselves with so little material that they are forced to begin by saying that we know very little about Shakespear. As a matter of fact, with the plays and sonnets in our hands, we know much more about Shakespear than we know about Dickens or Thackeray: the only difficulty is that we deliberately suppress it because it proves that Shakespear was not only very unlike the conception of a god current in Clapham, but was not, according to the same reckoning, even a respectable man. The academic view starts with a Shakespear who was not scurrilous; therefore the verses about "lousy Lucy" cannot have been written by him, and the cognate passages in the plays are either strokes of character-drawing or gags interpolated by the actors. This ideal Shakespear was too well behaved to get drunk; therefore the tradition that his death was hastened by a drinking bout with Jonson and Drayton must be rejected, and the remorse of Cassio treated as a thing observed, not experienced: nay, the disgust of Hamlet at the drinking customs of Denmark is taken to establish Shakespear as the superior of Alexander in self-control, and the greatest of teetotalers.

Now this system of inventing your great man to start with, and then rejecting all the materials that do not fit him, with the ridiculous result that you have to declare that there are no materials at all (with your waste-paper basket full of them), ends in leaving Shakespear with a much worse character than he deserves. For though it does not greatly matter whether he wrote the lousy Lucy lines or not, and does not really matter at all whether he got drunk when he made a night of it with Jonson and Drayton, the sonnets raise an unpleasant question which does matter a good deal; and the refusal of the academic Bardolaters to discuss or even mention this question has had the effect of producing a silent verdict against Shakespear. Mr Harris tackles the question openly, and has no difficulty whatever in convincing us that Shakespear was a man of normal constitution sexually, and was not the victim of that most cruel and pitiable of all the freaks of nature: the freak which transposes the normal aim of the affections. Silence on this point means condemnation; and the condemnation has been general throughout the present generation, though it only needed Mr Harris's fearless handling of the matter to sweep away what is nothing but a morbid and very disagreeable modern fashion. There is always some stock accusation brought against eminent persons. When I was a boy every well-known man was accused of beating his wife. Later on, for some unexplained reason, he was accused of psychopathic derangement. And this fashion is retrospective. The cases of Shakespear and Michel Angelo are cited as proving that every genius of the first magnitude was a sufferer; and both here and in Germany there are circles in which such derangement is grotesquely reverenced as part of the stigmata of heroic powers. All of which is gross nonsense. Unfortunately, in Shakespear's case, prudery, which cannot prevent the accusation from being whispered, does prevent the refutation from being shouted. Mr Harris, the deep-voiced, refuses to be silenced. He dismisses with proper contempt the stupidity which places an outrageous construction on Shakespear's apologies in the sonnets for neglecting that "perfect ceremony" of love which consists in returning calls and making protestations and giving presents and paying the trumpery attentions which men of genius always refuse to bother about, and to which touchy people who have no genius attach so much importance. No reader who had not been tampered with by the psychopathic monomaniacs could ever put any construction but the obvious and innocent one on these passages. But the general vocabulary of the sonnets to Pembroke (or whoever "Mr W. H." really was) is so overcharged according to modern ideas that a reply on the general case is necessary.

Shakespear's alleged Sycophancy and Perversion

That reply, which Mr Harris does not hesitate to give, is twofold: first, that Shakespear was, in his attitude towards earls, a sycophant; and, second, that the normality of Shakespear's sexual constitution is only too well attested by the excessive susceptibility to the normal impulse shewn in the whole mass of his writings. This latter is the really conclusive reply. In the case of Michel Angelo, for instance, one must admit that if his works are set beside those of Titian or Paul Veronese, it is impossible not to be struck by the absence in the Florentine of that susceptibility to feminine charm which pervades the pictures of the Venetians. But, as Mr Harris points out (though he does not use this particular illustration) Paul Veronese is an anchorite compared to Shakespear. The language of the sonnets addressed to Pembroke, extravagant as it now seems, is the language of compliment and fashion, transfigured no doubt by Shakespear's verbal magic, and hyperbolical, as Shakespear always seems to people who cannot conceive so vividly as he, still unmistakeable for anything else than the expression of a friendship delicate enough to be wounded, and a manly loyalty deep enough to be outraged. But the language of the sonnets to the Dark Lady is the language of passion: their cruelty shews it. There is no evidence that Shakespear was capable of being unkind in cold blood. But in his revulsions from love, he was bitter, wounding, even ferocious; sparing neither himself nor the unfortunate woman whose only offence was that she had reduced the great man to the common human denominator.

In seizing on these two points Mr Harris has made so sure a stroke, and places his evidence so featly that there is nothing left for me to do but to plead that the second is sounder than the first, which is, I think, marked by the prevalent mistake as to Shakespear's social position, or, if you prefer it, the confusion between his actual social position as a penniless tradesman's son taking to the theatre for a livelihood, and his own conception of himself as a gentleman of good family. I am prepared to contend that though Shakespear was undoubtedly sentimental in his expressions of devotion to Mr W. H. even to a point which nowadays makes both ridiculous, he was not syncophantic if Mr W. H. was really attractive and promising, and Shakespear deeply attached to him. A sycophant does not tell his patron that his fame will survive, not in the renown of his own actions, but in the sonnets of his sycophant. A sycophant, when his patron cuts him out in a love affair, does not tell his patron exactly what he thinks of him. Above all, a sycophant does not write to his patron precisely as he feels on all occasions; and this rare kind of sincerity is all over the sonnets. Shakespear, we are told, was "a very civil gentleman." This must mean that his desire to please people and be liked by them, and his reluctance to hurt their feelings, led him into amiable flattery even when his feelings were not strongly stirred. If this be taken into account along with the fact that Shakespear conceived and expressed all his emotions with a vehemence that sometimes carried him into ludicrous extravagance, making Richard offer his kingdom for a horse and Othello declare of Cassio that

> Had all his hairs been lives, my great revenge
> Had stomach for them all,

we shall see more civility and hyperbole than sycophancy even in the earlier and more coldblooded sonnets.

Shakespear and Democracy

Now take the general case pled against Shakespear as an enemy of democracy by Tolstoy, the late Ernest Crosbie and others, and endorsed by Mr Harris. Will it really stand fire? Mr Harris emphasizes the passages in which Shakespear spoke of mechanics and even of small master tradesmen as base persons whose clothes were greasy, whose breath was rank, and whose political imbecility and caprice moved Coriolanus to say to the Roman Radical who demanded at least "good words" from him

> He that will give good words to thee will flatter
> Beneath abhorring.

But let us be honest. As political sentiments these lines are an abomination to every democrat. But suppose they are not political sentiments! Suppose they are merely a record of observed fact. John Stuart Mill told our British workmen that they were mostly liars. Caryle told us all that we are mostly fools. Matthew Arnold and Ruskin were more circumstantial and more abusive. Everybody, including the workers themselves, know that they are dirty, drunken, foul-mouthed, ignorant, gluttonous, prejudiced: in short, heirs to the peculiar ills of poverty and slavery, as well as co-heirs with the plutocracy to all the failings of human nature. Even Shelley admitted, 200 years after Shakespear wrote Coriolanus, that universal suffrage was out of the question. Surely the real test, not of Democracy, which was not a live political issue in Shakespear's time, but of impartiality in judging classes, which is what one demands from a great human poet, is not that he should flatter the poor and denounce the rich, but that he should weigh them both in the same balance. Now whoever will read Lear and Measure for Measure will find stamped on his mind such an appalled sense of the danger of dressing man in a little brief authority, such a merciless stripping of the purple from the "poor, bare, forked animal" that calls itself a king and fancies itself a god, that one wonders what was the real nature of the mysterious restraint that kept

"Eliza and our James" from teaching Shakespear to be civil to crowned heads, just as one wonders why Tolstoy was allowed to go free when so many less terrible levellers went to the galleys or Siberia. From the mature Shakespear we get no such scenes of village snobbery as that between the stage country gentleman Alexander Iden and the stage Radical Jack Cade. We get the shepherd in As You Like It, and many honest, brave, human, and loyal servants, beside the inevitable comic ones. Even in the Jingo play, Henry V, we get Bates and Williams drawn with all respect and honor as normal rank and file men. In Julius Caesar, Shakespear went to work with a will when he took his cue from Plutarch in glorifying regicide and transfiguring the republicans. Indeed hero-worshippers have never forgiven him for belittling Caesar and failing to see that side of his assassination which made Goethe denounce it as the most senseless of crimes. Put the play beside the Charles I of Wills, in which Cromwell is written down to a point at which the Jack Cade of Henry VI becomes a hero in comparison; and then believe, if you can, that Shakespear was one of them that "crook the pregnant hinges of the knee where thrift may follow fawning." Think of Rosencrantz, Guildenstern, Osric, the fop who annoyed Hotspur, and a dozen passages concerning such people! If such evidence can prove anything (and Mr Harris relies throughout on such evidence) Shakespear loathed courtiers.

If, on the other hand, Shakespear's characters are mostly members of the leisured classes, the same thing is true of Mr Harris's own plays and mine. Industrial slavery is not compatible with that freedom of adventure, that personal refinement and intellectual culture, that scope of action, which the higher and subtler drama demands. Even Cervantes had finally to drop Don Quixote's troubles with innkeepers demanding to be paid for his food and lodging, and make him as free of economic difficulties as Amadis de Gaul. Hamlet's experiences simply could not have happened to a plumber. A poor man is useful on the stage only as a blind man is: to excite sympathy. The poverty of the apothecary in Romeo and Juliet produces a great effect, and even points the sound moral that a poor man cannot afford to have a conscience; but if all the characters of the play had been as poor as he, it would have been nothing but a melodrama of the sort that the Sicilian players gave us here; and that was not the best that lay in Shakespear's power. When poverty is abolished, and leisure and grace of life become general, the only plays surviving from our epoch which will have any relation to life as it will be lived then will be those in which none of the persons represented are troubled with want of money or wretched drudgery. Our plays of poverty and squalor, now the only ones that are true to the life of the majority of living men, will then be classed with the records of misers and monsters, and read only by historical students of social pathology.

Then consider Shakespear's kings and lords and gentlemen! Would even John Ball or Jeremiah complain that they are flattered? Surely a more mercilessly exposed string of scoundrels never crossed the stage. The very monarch who paralyses a rebel by appealing to the divinity that hedges a king, is a drunken and sensual assassin, and is presently killed contemptuously before our eyes in spite of his hedge of divinity. I could write as convincing a chapter on Shakespear's Dickensian prejudice against the throne and the nobility and gentry in general as Mr Harris or Ernest Crosbie on the other side. I could even go so far as to contend that one of Shakespear's defects is his lack of an intelligent comprehension of feudalism. He had of course no prevision of democratic Collectivism. He was, except in the commonplaces of war and patriotism, a privateer through and through. Nobody in his plays, whether king or citizen, has any civil public business or conception of such a thing, except in the method of appointing constables, to the abuses in which he called attention quite in the vein of the Fabian Society. He was concerned about drunkenness and about the idolatry and hypocrisy of our judicial system; but his implied remedy was personal sobriety and freedom from idolatrous illusion in so far as he had any remedy at all, and did not merely despair of human nature. His first and last word on parliament was "Get thee glass eyes, and, like a scurvy politician, seem to see the thing thou dost not." He had no notion of the feeling with which the land nationalizers of today regard the fact that he was a party to the enclosure of common lands at Wellcome. The explanation is, not a general deficiency in his mind, but the simple fact that in his day what English land needed was individual appropriation and cultivation, and what the English Constitution needed was the incorporation of Whig principles of individual liberty.

Shakespear and the British Public

I have rejected Mr Harris's view that Shakespear died brokenhearted of "the pangs of love despised." I have given my reasons for believing that Shakespear died game, and indeed in a state of levity which would have been considered unbecoming in a bishop. But Mr Harris's evidence does prove that Shakespear had a grievance and a very serious one. He might have been jilted by ten dark ladies and been none the worse for it; but his treatment by the British Public was another matter. The idolatry which exasperated Ben Jonson was by no means a popular movement; and, like all such idolatries, it was excited by the magic of Shakepear's art rather than by his views. He was launched on his career as a successful playwright by the Henry VI trilogy, a work of no originality, depth, or subtlety except the originality, depth, and subtlety of the feelings and fancies of the common people. But Shakespear was not satisfied with this. What is the use of being Shakespear if you are not allowed to express any notions but those of Autolycus? Shakespear did not see the world as Autolycus did: he saw it, if not exactly as Ibsen did (for it was not quite the same world), at least with much of Ibsen's power of penetrating its illusions and idolatries, and with all Swift's horror of its cruelty and uncleanliness.

Now it happens to some men with these powers that they are forced to impose their fullest exercise on the world because they cannot produce popular work. Take Wagner and

Ibsen for instance! Their earlier works are no doubt much cheaper than their later ones; still, they were not popular when they were written. The alternative of doing popular work was never really open to them: had they stooped they would have picked up less than they snatched from above the people's heads. But Handel and Shakespear were not held to their best in this way. They could turn out anything they were asked for, and even heap up the measure. They reviled the British Public, and never forgave it for ignoring their best work and admiring their splendid commonplaces; but they produced the commonplaces all the same, and made them sound magnificent by mere brute faculty for their art. When Shakespear was forced to write popular plays to save his theatre from ruin, he did it mutinously, calling the plays As *You* Like it, and Much Ado About Nothing. All the same, he did it so well that to this day these two genial vulgarities are the main Shakespearean stock-in-trade of our theatres. Later on Burbage's power and popularity as an actor enabled Shakespear to free himself from the tyranny of the box office, and to express himself more freely in plays consisting largely of monologue to be spoken by a great actor from whom the public would stand a good deal. This history of Shakespear's tragedies has thus been the history of a long line of famous actors, from Burbage and Betterton to Forbes Robertson; and the man of whom we are told that "when he would have said that Richard died, and cried A horse! A horse! he Burbage cried" was the father of nine generations of Shakespearean playgoers, all speaking of Garrick's Richard, and Kean's Othello, and Irving's Shylock, and Forbes Robertson's Hamlet without knowing or caring how much these had to do with Shakespear's Richard and Othello and so forth. And the plays which were written without great and predominant parts, such as Troilus and Cressida, All's Well That Ends Well, and Measure for Measure, have dropped on our stage as dead as the second part of Goethe's Faust or Ibsen's Emperor or Galilean.

Here, then, Shakespear had a real grievance; and though it is a sentimental exaggeration to describe him as a broken-hearted man in the face of the passages of reckless jollity and serenely happy poetry in his latest plays, yet the discovery that his most serious work could reach success only when carried on the back of a very fascinating actor who was enormously overcharging his part, and that the serious plays which did not contain parts big enough to hold the overcharge were left on the shelf, amply accounts for the evident fact that Shakespear did not end his life in a glow of enthusiastic satisfaction with mankind and with the theatre, which is all that Mr Harris can allege in support of his broken-heart theory. But even if Shakespear had had no failures, it was not possible for a man of his powers to observe the political and moral conduct of his contemporaries without perceiving that they were incapable of dealing with the problems raised by their own civilization, and that their attempts to carry out the codes of law and to practice the religions offered to them by great prophets and law-givers were and still are so foolish that we now call for The Superman, virtually a new species, to rescue the world from mismanagement. This is the real sorrow of great men; and in the face of it the notion that when a great man speaks bitterly or looks melancholy he must be troubled by a disappointment in love seems to me sentimental trifling.

If I have carried the reader with me thus far, he will find that trivial as this little play of mine is, its sketch of Shakespear is more complete than its levity suggests. Alas! its appeal for a National Theatre as a monument to Shakespear failed to touch the very stupid people who cannot see that a National Theatre is worth having for the sake of the National Soul. I had unfortunately represented Shakespear as treasuring and using (as I do myself) the jewels of unconsciously musical speech which common people utter and throw away every day; and this was taken as a disparagement of Shakespear's "originality." Why was I born with such contemporaries? Why is Shakespear made ridiculous by such a posterity?

THE DARK LADY OF THE SONNETS

Fin de siècle 15–1600. *Midsummer night on the terrace of the Palace at Whitehall, overlooking the Thames. The Palace clock chimes four quarters and strikes eleven.*

A Beefeater on guard. A Cloaked Man approaches.

THE BEEFEATER. Stand. Who goes there? Give the word.

THE MAN. Marry! I cannot. I have clean forgotten it.

THE BEEFEATER. Then cannot you pass here. What is your business? Who are you? Are you a true man?

THE MAN. Far from it, Master Warder. I am not the same man two days together: sometimes Adams, sometimes Benvolio, and anon the Ghost.

THE BEEFEATER [*recoiling*] A ghost! Angels and ministers of grace defend us!

THE MAN. Well said, Master Warder. With your leave I will set that down in writing; for I have a very poor and unhappy brain for remembrance. [*He takes out his tablets and writes*]. Methinks this is a good scene, with you on your lonely watch, and I approaching like a ghost in the moonlight. Stare not so amazedly at me; but mark what I say. I keep tryst here tonight with a dark lady. She promised to bribe the warder. I gave her the wherewithal: four tickets for the Globe Theatre.

THE BEEFEATER. Plague on her! She gave me two only.

THE MAN [*detaching a tablet*] My friend: present this tablet, and you will be welcomed at any time when the plays of Will Shakespear are in hand. Bring your wife. Bring your friends. Bring the whole garrison. There is ever plenty of room.

THE BEEFEATER. I care not for these new-fangled plays. No man can understand a word of them. They are all talk. Will you not give me a pass for The Spanish Tragedy?

THE MAN. To see The Spanish Tragedy one pays, my friend. Here are the means. [*He gives him a piece of gold*].

THE BEEFEATER [*overwhelmed*] Gold! Oh, sir, you are a better paymaster than your dark lady.

THE MAN. Women are thrifty, my friend.

THE BEEFEATER. Tis so, sir. And you have to consider that the most open handed of us must een cheapen that which we buy every day. This lady has to make a present to a warder nigh every night of her life.

THE MAN [*turning pale*] I'll not believe it.

THE BEEFEATER. Now you, sir, I dare be sworn, do not have an adventure like this twice in the year.

THE MAN. Villain: wouldst tell me that my dark lady hath ever done thus before? that she maketh occasions to meet other men?

THE BEEFEATER. Now the Lord bless your innocence, sir, do you think you are the only pretty man in the world? A merry lady, sir: a warm bit of stuff. Go to: I'll not see her pass a deceit on a gentleman that hath given me the first piece of gold I ever handled.

THE MAN. Master Warder: is it not a strange thing that we, knowing that all women are false, should be amazed to find our own particular drab no better than the rest?

THE BEEFEATER. Not all, sir. Decent bodies, many of them.

THE MAN [*intolerantly*] No. All false. All. If thou deny it, thou liest.

THE BEEFEATER. You judge too much by the Court, sir. There, indeed, you may say of frailty that its name is woman.

THE MAN [*pulling out his tablets again*] Prithee say that again: that about frailty: the strain of music.

THE BEEFEATER. What strain of music, sir? I'm no musician, God knows.

THE MAN. There is music in your soul: many of your degree have it very notably. [*Writing*] "Frailty: thy name is woman!" [*Repeating it affectionately*] "Thy name is woman."

THE BEEFEATER. Well, sir, it is but four words. Are you a snapper-up of such unconsidered trifles?

THE MAN [*eagerly*] Snapper-up of—[*he gasps*] Oh! Immortal phrase! [*He writes it down*]. This man is a greater than I.

THE BEEFEATER. You have my lord Pembroke's trick, sir.

THE MAN. Like enough: he is my near friend. But what call you his trick?

THE BEEFEATER. Making sonnets by moonlight. And to the same lady too.

THE MAN. No!

THE BEEFEATER. Last night he stood here on your errand, and in your shoes.

THE MAN. Thou, too, Brutus! And I called him friend!

THE BEEFEATER. Tis ever so, sir.

THE MAN. Tis ever so. Twas ever so. [*He turns away, overcome*]. Two Gentlemen of Verona! Judas! Judas!!

THE BEEFEATER. Is he so bad as that, sir?

THE MAN [*recovering his charity and self-possession*] Bad? O no. Human, Master Warder, human. We call one another names when we are offended, as children do. That is all.

THE BEEFEATER. Ay, sir: words, words, words. Mere wind, sir. We fill our bellies with the east wind, sir, as the Scripture hath it. You cannot feed capons so.

THE MAN. A good cadence. By your leave. [*He makes a note of it*].

THE BEEFEATER. What manner of thing is a cadence, sir? I have not heard of it.

THE MAN. A thing to rule the world with, friend.

THE BEEFEATER. You speak strangely, sir: no offence. But, an't like you, you are a very civil gentleman; and a poor man feels drawn to you, you being, as twere, willing to share your thought with him.

THE MAN. Tis my trade. But alas! the world for the most part will none of my thoughts.

Lamplight streams from the palace door as it opens from within.

THE BEEFEATER. Here comes your lady, sir. I'll to t'other

end of my ward. You may een take your time about your business: I shall not return too suddenly unless my sergeant comes prowling round. Tis a fell sergeant, sir: strict in his arrest. Good een, sir; and good luck! [*He goes*].

THE MAN. "Strict in his arrest"! "Fell sergeant"! [*As if tasting a ripe plum*] O-o-o-h! [*He makes a note of them*].

A Cloaked Lady gropes her way from the palace and wanders along the terrace, walking in her sleep.

THE LADY [*rubbing her hands as if washing them*] Out, damned spot. You will mar all with these cosmetics. God made you one face; and you make yourself another. Think of your grave, woman, not ever of being beautified. All the perfumes of Arabia will not whiten this Tudor hand.

THE MAN. "All the perfumes of Arabia"! "Beautified"! "Beautified"! a poem in a single word. Can this be my Mary? [*To the Lady*] Why do you speak in a strange voice, and utter poetry for the first time? Are you ailing? You walk like the dead. Mary! Mary!

THE LADY [*echoing him*] Mary! Mary! Who would have thought that woman to have had so much blood in her! Is it my fault that my counsellors put deeds of blood on me? Fie! If you were women you would have more wit than to stain the floor so foully. Hold not up her head so: the hair is false. I tell you yet again, Mary's buried: she cannot come out of her grave. I fear her not: these cats that dare jump into thrones though they be fit only for men's laps must be put away. Whats done cannot be undone. Out, I say. Fie! a queen, and freckled!

THE MAN [*shaking her arm*] Mary, I say: art asleep?

The Lady wakes; starts; and nearly faints. He catches her on his arm.

THE LADY. Where am I? What art thou?

THE MAN. I cry your mercy. I have mistook your person all this while. Methought you were my Mary: my mistress.

THE LADY [*outraged*] Profane fellow: how do you dare?

THE MAN. Be not wroth with me, lady. My mistress is a marvellous proper woman. But she does not speak so well as you. "All the perfumes of Arabia"! That was well said: spoken with good accent and excellent discretion.

THE LADY. Have I been in speech with you here?

THE MAN. Why, yes, fair lady. Have you forgot it?

THE LADY. I have walked in my sleep.

THE MAN. Walk ever in your sleep, fair one; for then your words drop like honey.

THE LADY [*with cold majesty*] Know you to whom you speak, sir, that you dare express yourself so saucily?

THE MAN [*unabashed*] Not I, not care neither. You are some lady of the Court, belike. To me there are but two sorts of women: those with excellent voices, sweet and low, and cackling hens that cannot make me dream. Your voice has all manner of loveliness in it. Grudge me not a short hour of its music.

THE LADY. Sir: you are overbold. Season your admiration for a while with—

THE MAN [*holding up his hand to stop her*] "Season your admiration for a while—"

THE LADY. Fellow: do you dare mimic me to my face?

THE MAN. Tis music. Can you not hear? When a good musician sings a song, do you not sing it and sing it again til you have caught and fixed its perfect melody? "Season your admiration for a while": God! the history of man's heart is in that one word admiration. Admiration! [*Taking up his tablets*] What was it? "Suspend your admiration for a space—"

THE LADY. A very vile jingle of esses. I said "Season your—

THE MAN [*hastily*] Season: ay, season, season, season. Plague on my memory, my wretched memory! I must een write it down. [*He begins to write, but stops, his memory failing him*]. Yet tell me which was the vile jingle? You said very justly: mine own ear caught it even as my false tongue said it.

THE LADY. You said "for a space." I said "for a while."

THE MAN. "For a while" [*he corrects it*]. Good! [*Ardently*]

And now be mine neither for a space nor a while, but for ever.

THE LADY. Odds my life! Are you by chance making love to me, knave?

THE MAN. Nay: tis you who have made the love: I but pour it out at your feet. I cannot but love a lass that sets such store by an apt word. Therefore vouchsafe, divine perfection of a woman—no: I have said that before somewhere; and the wordy garment of my love for you must be fire-new—

THE LADY. You talk too much, sir. Let me warn you: I am more accustomed to be listened to than preached at.

THE MAN. The most are like that that do talk well. But though you spake with the tongues of angels, as indeed you do, yet know that I am king of words—

THE LADY. A king, ha!

THE MAN. No less. We are poor things, we men and women—

THE LADY. Dare you call me woman?

THE MAN. What nobler name can I tender you? How else can I love you? Yet you may well shrink from the name: have I not said we are but poor things? Yet there is a power that can redeem us.

THE LADY. Gramercy for your sermon, sir. I hope I know my duty.

THE MAN. This is no sermon, but the living truth. The power I speak of is the power of immortal poesy. For know that vile as this world is, and worms as we are, you have but to invest all this vileness with a magical garment of words to transfigure us and uplift our souls til earth flowers into a million heavens.

THE LADY. You spoil your heaven with your million. You are extravagant. Observe some measure in your speech.

THE MAN. You speak now as Ben does.

THE LADY. And who, pray, is Ben?

THE MAN. A learned bricklayer who thinks that the sky is at the top of his ladder, and so takes it on him to rebuke me for flying. I tell you there is no word yet coined and no melody yet sung that is extravagant and majestical enough for the glory that lovely words can reveal. It is heresy to deny it: have you not been taught that in the beginning was the Word? that the Word was with God? nay, that the Word was God?

THE LADY. Beware, fellow, how you presume to speak of holy things. The Queen is the head of the Church.

THE MAN. You are the head of my Church when you speak as you did at first. "All the perfumes of Arabia"! Can the Queen speak thus? They say she playeth well upon the virginals. Let her play so to me; and I'll kiss her hands. But until then, you are my Queen; and I'll kiss those lips that have dropt music on my heart. [*He puts his arms about her*].

THE LADY. Unmeasured impudence! On your life, take your hands from me.

The Dark Lady comes stooping along the terrace behind them like a running thrush. When she sees how they are employed, she rises angrily to her full height, and listens jealously.

THE MAN [*unaware of the Dark Lady*] Then cease to make my hands tremble with the streams of life you poured through them. You hold me as the lodestar holds the iron: I cannot but cling to you. We are lost, you and I: nothing can separate us now.

THE DARK LADY. We shall see that, false lying hound, you and your filthy trull. [*With two vigorous cuffs, she knocks the pair asunder, sending the man, who is unlucky enough to receive a right-handed blow, sprawling on the flags*]. Take that, both of you!

THE CLOAKED LADY [*in towering wrath, throwing off her cloak and turning in outraged majesty on her assailant*] High treason!

THE DARK LADY [*recognizing her and falling on her knees in abject terror*] Will: I am lost: I have struck the Queen.

THE MAN [*sitting up as majestically as his ignominious posture allows*] Woman: you have struck WILLIAM SHAKESPEAR!!!!!!

QUEEN ELIZABETH [*stupent*] Marry, come up!!! Struck William Shakespear quotha! And who in the name of all the sluts and jades and light-o'-loves and fly-by-nights that infest this palace of mine, may William Shakespear be?

THE DARK LADY. Madam: he is but a player. Oh, I could have my hand cut off—

QUEEN ELIZABETH. Belike you will, mistress. Have you bethought you that I am like to have your head cut off as well?

THE DARK LADY. Will: save me. Oh, save me.

ELIZABETH. Save you! A likely savior, on my royal word! I had thought this fellow at least an esquire; for I had hoped that even the vilest of my ladies would not have dishonored my Court by wantoning with a baseborn servant.

SHAKESPEAR [*indignantly scrambling to his feet*] Baseborn! I, a Shakespear of Stratford! I, whose mother was an Arden! baseborn! You forget yourself, madam.

ELIZABETH [*furious*] S'blood! do I so? I will teach you—

THE DARK LADY [*rising from her knees and throwing herself between them*] Will: in God's name anger her no further. It is death. Madam: do not listen to him.

SHAKESPEAR. Not were it een to save your life, Mary, not to mention mine own, will I flatter a monarch who forgets what is due to my family. I deny not that my father was brought down to be a poor bankrupt; but twas his gentle blood that was ever too generous for trade. Never did he disown his debts. Tis true he paid them not; but it is an attested truth that he gave bills for them; and twas those bills, in the hands of base hucksters, that were his undoing.

ELIZABETH [*grimly*] The son of your father shall learn his place in the presence of the daughter of Harry the Eighth.

SHAKESPEAR [*swelling with intolerant importance*] Name not that inordinate man in the same breath with Stratford's worthiest alderman. John Shakespear wedded but once: Harry Tudor was married six times. You should blush to utter his name.

THE DARK LADY } *crying out together* { Will: for pity's sake—
ELIZABETH } { Insolent dog—

SHAKESPEAR [*cutting them short*] How know you that King Harry was indeed your father?

ELIZABETH } Zounds! Now by— [*she stops to grind her teeth with rage*].

THE DARK LADY } She will have me whipped through the streets. Oh God! Oh God!

SHAKESPEAR. Learn to know yourself better, madam. I am an honest gentleman of unquestioned parentage, and have already sent in my demand for the coat-of-arms that is lawfully mine. Can you say as much for yourself?

ELIZABETH [*almost beside herself*] Another word; and I begin with mine own hands the work the hangman shall finish.

SHAKESPEAR. You are no true Tudor: this baggage here has as good a right to your royal seat as you. What maintains you on the throne of England? Is it your renownéd wit? your wisdom that sets at nought the craftiest statesmen of the Christian world? No. Tis the mere chance that might have happened to any milkmaid, the caprice of Nature that made you the most wondrous piece of beauty the age hath seen. [*Elizabeth's raised fists, on the point of striking him, fall to her side*]. That is what hath brought all men to your feet, and founded your throne on the impregnable rock of your proud heart, a stony island in a sea of desire. There, madam, is some wholesome blunt honest speaking for you. Now do your worst.

ELIZABETH [*with dignity*] Master Shakespear: it is well for you that I am a merciful prince. I make allowance for your rustic ignorance. But remember that there are things which be true, and are yet not seemly to be said (I will not say to a queen; for you will have it that I am none) but to a virgin.

SHAKESPEAR [*bluntly*] It is no fault of mine that you are a virgin, madam, albeit tis my misfortune.

THE DARK LADY [*terrified again*] In mercy, madam, hold no further discourse with him. He hath ever some lewd jest on his tongue. You hear how he useth me! calling me baggage and the like to your Majesty's face.

ELIZABETH. As for you, mistress, I have yet to demand

what your business is at this hour in this place, and how you come to be so concerned with a player that you strike blindly at your sovereign in your jealousy of him.

THE DARK LADY. Madam: as I live and hope for salvation—

SHAKESPEAR [*sardonically*] Ha!

THE DARK LADY [*angrily*] —ay, I'm as like to be saved as thou that believest naught save some black magic of words and verses—I say, madam, as I am a living woman I came here to break with him for ever. Oh, madam, if you would know what misery is, listen to this man that is more than man and less at the same time. He will tie you down to anatomize your very soul: he will wring tears of blood from your humiliation; and then he will heal the wound with flatteries that no woman can resist.

SHAKESPEAR. Flatteries! [*Kneeling*] Oh, madam, I put my case at your royal feet. I confess to much. I have a rude tongue: I am unmannerly: I blaspheme against the holiness of anointed royalty; but oh, my royal mistress, AM I a flatterer?

ELIZABETH. I absolve you as to that. You are far too plain a dealer to please me. [*He rises gratefully*].

THE DARK LADY. Madam: he is flattering you even as he speaks.

ELIZABETH [*a terrible flash in her eye*] Ha! Is it so?

SHAKESPEAR. Madam: she is jealous; and, heaven help me! not without reason. Oh, you say you are a merciful prince; but that was cruel of you, that hiding of your royal dignity when you found me here. For how can I ever be content with this black-haired, black-eyed, black-avised devil again now that I have looked upon real beauty and real majesty?

THE DARK LADY [*wounded and desperate*] He hath swore to me ten times over that the day shall come in England when black women, for all their foulness, shall be more thought on than fair ones. [*To Shakespear, scolding at him*] Deny it if thou canst. Oh, he is compact of lies and scorns. I am tired of being tossed up to heaven and dragged down to hell at every whim that takes him. I am ashamed to my very soul that I have abased myself to love one that my father would not have deemed fit to hold my stirrup—one that will talk to all the world about me—that will put my love and my shame into his plays and make me blush for myself there—that will write sonnets about me that no man of gentle strain would put his hand to. I am all disordered: I know not what I am saying to your Majesty: I am of all ladies most deject and wretched—

SHAKESPEAR. Ha! At last sorrow hath struck a note of music out of thee. "Of all ladies most deject and wretched." [*He makes a note of it*].

THE DARK LADY. Madam: I implore you give me leave to go. I am distracted with grief and shame. I—

ELIZABETH. Go. [*The Dark Lady tries to kiss her hand*]. No more. Go. [*The Dark Lady goes, convulsed*]. You have been cruel to that poor fond wretch, Master Shakespear.

SHAKESPEAR. I am not cruel, madam; but you know the fable of Jupiter and Semele. I could not help my lightnings scorching her.

ELIZABETH. You have an overweening conceit of yourself, sir, that displeases your Queen.

SHAKESPEAR. Oh, madam, can I go about with the modest cough of a minor poet, belittling my inspiration and making the mightiest wonder of your reign a thing of nought? I have said that "not marble nor the gilded monuments of princes shall outlive" the words with which I make the world glorious or foolish at my will. Besides, I would have you think me great enough to grant me a boon.

ELIZABETH. I hope it is a boon that may be asked of a virgin Queen without offence, sir. I mistrust your forwardness; and I bid you remember that I do not suffer persons of your degree (if I may say so without offence to your father the alderman) to presume too far.

SHAKESPEAR. Oh, madam, I shall not forget myself again; though by my life, could I make you a serving wench, neither a queen nor a virgin should you be for so much longer as a flash of lightning might take to cross the river to the Bankside. But since you are a queen and will none of me, nor of Philip of Spain, nor of any other mortal man, I must een contain myself as best I may, and ask you only for a boon of State.

ELIZABETH. A boon of State already! You are becoming a courtier like the rest of them. You lack advancement.

SHAKESPEAR. "Lack advancement." By your Majesty's leave: a queenly phrase. [*He is about to write it down*].

ELIZABETH [*striking the tablets from his hand*] Your tables begin to anger me, sir. I am not here to write your plays for you.

SHAKESPEAR. You are here to inspire them, madam. For this, among the rest, were you ordained. But the boon I crave is that you do endow a great playhouse, or, if I may make bold to coin a scholarly name for it, a National Theatre, for the better instruction and gracing of your Majesty's subjects.

ELIZABETH. Why, sir, are there not theatres enow on the Bankside and in Blackfriars?

SHAKESPEAR. Madam: these are the adventures of needy and desperate men that must, to save themselves from perishing of want, give the sillier sort of people what they best like; and what they best like, God knows, is not their own betterment and instruction, as we well see by the example of the churches, which must needs compel men to frequent them, though they be open to all without charge. Only when there is a matter of a murder, or a plot, or a pretty youth in petticoats, or some naughty tale of wantonness, will your subjects pay the great cost of good players and their finery, with a little profit to boot. To prove this I will tell you that I have written two noble and excellent plays setting forth the advancement of women of high nature and fruitful industry even as your Majesty is: the one a skilful physician, the other a sister devoted to good works. I have also stole from a book of idle wanton tales two of the most damnable foolishnesses in the world, in the one of which a woman goeth in man's attire and maketh impudent love to her swain, who pleaseth the groundlings by overthrowing a wrestler; whilst, in the other, one of the same kidney sheweth her wit by saying endless naughtinesses to a gentleman as lewd as herself. I have writ these to save my friends from penury, yet shewing my scorn for such follies and for them that praise them by calling the one As You Like It, meaning that it is not as *I* like it, and the other Much Ado About Nothing, as it truly is. And now these two filthy pieces drive their nobler fellows from the stage, where indeed I cannot have my lady physician presented at all, she being too honest a woman for the taste of the town. Wherefore I humbly beg your Majesty to give order that a theatre be endowed out of the public revenue for the playing of those pieces of mine which no merchant will touch, seeing that his gain is so much greater with the worse than with the better. Thereby you shall also encourage other men to undertake the writing of plays who do now despise it and leave it wholly to those whose counsels will work little good to your realm. For this writing of plays is a great matter, forming as it does the minds and affections of men in such sort that whatsoever they see done in show on the stage, they will presently be doing in earnest in the world, which is but a larger stage. Of late, as you know, the Church taught the people by means of plays; but the people flocked only to such as were full of superstitious miracles and bloody martyrdoms; and so the Church, which also was just then brought into straits by the policy of your royal father, did abandon and discountenance the art of playing; and thus it fell into the hands of poor players and greedy merchants that had their pockets to look to and not the greatness of this your kingdom. Therefore now must your Majesty take up that good work that your Church hath abandoned, and restore the art of playing to its former use and dignity.

ELIZABETH. Master Shakespear: I will speak of this matter to the Lord Treasurer.

SHAKESPEAR. Then am I undone, madam; for there was never yet a Lord Treasurer that could find a penny for anything over and above the necessary expenses of your government, save for a war or a salary for his own nephew.

ELIZABETH. Master Shakespear: you speak sooth; yet cannot I in any wise mend it. I dare not offend my unruly Puritans by making so lewd a place as the playhouse a public charge; and there be a thousand things to be done in this London of mine before your poetry can have its penny from the general purse. I tell thee, Master Will, it will be three hundred years and more before my subjects learn that man cannot live by bread alone, but by every word that cometh from the mouth of those whom God inspires. By that time you and I will be dust beneath the feet of the horses, if indeed there be any horses then, and men be still riding instead of flying. Now it may be that by then your works will be dust also.

SHAKESPEAR. They will stand, madam: fear not for that.

ELIZABETH. It may prove so. But of this I am certain (for I know my countrymen) that until every other country in the Christian world, even to barbarian Muscovy and the hamlets of the boorish Germans, have its playhouse at the public charge, England will never adventure. And she will adventure then only because it is her desire to be ever in the fashion, and do humbly and dutifully whatso she seeth everybody else doing. In the meantime you must content yourself as best you can by the playing of those two pieces which you give out as the most damnable ever writ, but which your countrymen, I warn you, will swear are the best you have ever done. But this I will say, that if I could speak across the ages to our descendants, I should heartily recommend them to fulfil your wish; for the Scottish minstrel hath well said that he that maketh the songs of a nation is mightier than he that maketh its laws; and the same may well be true of plays and interludes. [*The clock chimes the first quarter. The warder returns on his round*]. And now, sir, we are upon the hour when it better beseems a virgin queen to be abed than to converse alone with the naughtiest of her subjects. Ho there! Who keeps ward on the queen's lodgings tonight?

THE WARDER. I do, an't please your majesty.

ELIZABETH. See that you keep it better in future. You have let pass a most dangerous gallant even to the very door of our royal chamber. Lead him forth; and bring me word when he is safely locked out; for I shall scarce dare disrobe until the palace gates are between us.

SHAKESPEAR [*kissing her hand*] My body goes through the gate into the darkness, madam; but my thoughts follow you.

ELIZABETH. How! to my bed!

SHAKESPEAR. No, madam, to your prayers, in which I beg you to remember my theatre.

ELIZABETH. That is my prayer to posterity. Forget not your own to God; and so goodnight, Master Will.

SHAKESPEAR. Goodnight, great Elizabeth. God save the Queen!

ELIZABETH. Amen.

Exeunt severally: she to her chamber: he, in custody of the warder, to the gate nearest Blackfriars.

AYOT ST LAWRENCE,
20*th June* 1910.

OVERRULED

Overruled was first produced at the Duke of York's Theatre, London, on 14 October 1912, with the following cast:

GREGORY LUNN	*Claude King*
SIBTHORPE JUNO	*Adolphus Vane Tempest*
MRS. JUNO	*Miriam Lewes*
MRS. LUNN	*Geraldine Olliffe*

PREFACE TO OVERRULED

The Alleviations of Monogamy

This piece is not an argument for or against polygamy. It is a clinical study of how the thing actually occurs among quite ordinary people, innocent of all unconventional views concerning it. The enormous majority of cases in real life are those of people in that position. Those who deliberately and conscientiously profess what are oddly called advanced views by those others who believe them to be retrograde, are often, and indeed mostly, the last people in the world to engage in unconventional adventures of any kind, not only because they have neither time nor disposition for them, but because the friction set up between the individual and the community by the expression of unusual views of any sort is quite enough hindrance to the heretic without being complicated by personal scandals. Thus the theoretic libertine is usually a person of blameless family life, whilst the practical libertine is mercilessly severe on all other libertines, and excessively conventional in professions of social principle.

What is more, these professions are not hypocritical: they are for the most part quite sincere. The common libertine, like the drunkard, succumbs to a temptation which he does not defend, and against which he warns others with an earnestness proportionate to the intensity of his own remorse. He (or she) may be a liar and a humbug, pretending to be better than the detected libertines, and clamoring for their condign punishment; but this is mere self-defence. No reasonable person expects the burglar to confess his pursuits, or to refrain from joining in the cry of Stop Thief when the police get on the track of another burglar. If society chooses to penalize candor, it has itself to thank if its attack is countered by falsehood. The clamorous virtue of the libertine is therefore no more hypocritical than the plea of Not Guilty which is allowed to every criminal. But one result is that the theorists who write most sincerely and favorably about polygamy know least about it; and the practitioners who know most about it keep their knowledge very jealously to themselves. Which is hardly fair to the practice.

Inaccessibility of the Facts

Also, it is impossible to estimate its prevalence. A practice to which nobody confesses may be both universal and unsuspected, just as a virtue which everybody is expected, under heavy penalties, to claim, may have no existence. It is often assumed—indeed it is the official assumption of the Churches and the divorce courts—that a gentleman and a lady cannot be alone together innocently. And that is manifest blazing nonsense, though many women have been stoned to death in the east, and divorced in the west, on the strength of it. On the other hand, the innocent and conventional people who regard gallant adventures as crimes of so horrible a nature that only the most depraved and desperate characters engage in them or would listen to advances in that direction without raising an alarm with the noisiest indignation, are clearly examples of the fact that most sections of society do not know how the other sections live. Industry is the most effective check on gallantry. Women may, as Napoleon said, be the occupation of the idle man just as men are the preoccupation of the idle woman; but the mass of mankind is too busy and too poor for the long and expensive sieges which the professed libertine lays to virtue. Still, wherever there is idleness or even a reasonable supply of elegant leisure there is a good deal of coquetry and philandering. It is so much pleasanter to dance on the edge of a precipice than to go over it that leisured society is full of people who spend a great part of their lives in flirtation, and conceal nothing but the humiliating secret that they have never gone any further. For there is no pleasing people in the matter of reputation in this department: every insult is a flattery: every testimonial is a disparagement: Joseph is despised and promoted, Potiphar's wife admired and condemned: in short, you are never on solid ground until you get away from the subject altogether. There is a continual and irreconcilable conflict between the natural and conventional sides of the case, between spontaneous human relations between independent men and women on the one hand and the property relation between husband and wife on the other, not to mention the confusion under the common name of love of a generous natural attraction and interest with the murderous jealousy that fastens on and clings to its mate (especially a hated mate) as a tiger fastens on a carcase. And the confusion is natural; for these extremes are extremes of the same passion; and most cases lie somewhere on the scale between them, and are so complicated by ordinary likes and dislikes, by incidental wounds to vanity or gratifications of it, and by class feeling, that A will be jealous of B and not of C, and will tolerate infidelities on the part of D whilst being furiously angry when they are committed by E.

The Convention of Jealousy

That jealousy is independent of sex is shewn by its intensity in children, and by the fact that very jealous people are jealous of everybody without regard to relationship or sex, and cannot bear to hear the person they "love" speak favorably of anyone under any circumstances (many women, for instance, are much more jealous of their husbands' mothers and sisters than of unrelated women whom they suspect him of fancying); but it is seldom possible to disentangle the two passions in practice. Besides, jealousy is an inculcated passion, forced by society on people in whom it would not occur spontaneously. In Brieux's Bourgeois aux Champs, the benevolent hero finds himself detested by the neighboring peasants and farmers, not because he preserves game, and sets mantraps for poachers, and defends his legal rights over his land to the extremest point of unsocial savagery, but because, being an amiable and public-spirited person, he refuses to do all this, and thereby offends and disparages the sense of property in his neighbors. The same thing is true of matrimonial jealousy: the man who does not at least pretend to feel it, and behave as badly as if he really felt it, is despised and insulted; and many a man has shot or stabbed a friend or been shot or stabbed by him in a duel, or disgraced himself and ruined his own wife in a divorce scandal, against his conscience, against his instinct, and to the destruction of his home, solely because Society conspired to drive him to keep its own lower morality in countenance in this miserable and undignified manner.

Morality is confused in such matters. In an elegant plutocracy, a jealous husband is regarded as a boor. Among the tradesmen who supply that plutocracy with its meals, a husband who is not jealous, and refrains from assailing his rival with his fists, is regarded as a ridiculous, contemptible, and cowardly cuckold. And the laboring class is divided into the respectable section which takes the tradesman's view, and the disreputable section which enjoys the license of the plutocracy without its money: creeping below the law as its exemplars prance above it; cutting down all expenses of respectability and even decency; and frankly accepting squalor and disrepute as the price of anarchic self-indulgence. The conflict between Malvolio and Sir Toby, between the marquis and the bourgeois, the cavalier and the puritan, the ascetic and the voluptuary, goes on continually, and goes on not only between class and class and individual and individual, but in the selfsame breast in a series of reactions and revulsions in which the irresistible becomes the unbearable, and the unbearable the irresistible, until none of us can say what our characters really are in this respect.

The Missing Data of a Scientific Natural History of Marriage

Of one thing I am persuaded: we shall never attain to a reasonably healthy public opinion on sex questions until we offer, as the data for that opinion, our actual conduct and our real thoughts instead of a moral fiction which we agree to call virtuous conduct, and which we then—and here comes in the mischief—pretend is our conduct and our thoughts. If the result were that we all believed one another to be better than we really are, there would be something to be said for it; but the actual result appears to be a monstrous exaggeration of the power and continuity of sexual passion. The whole world shares the fate of Lucrezia Borgia, who, though she seems on investigation to have been quite a suitable wife for a modern British Bishop, has been invested by the popular historical imagination with all the extravagances of a Messalina or a Cenci. Writers of belles lettres who are rash enough to admit that their whole life is not one constant preoccupation with adored members of the opposite sex, and who even countenance La Rochefoucauld's remark that very few people would ever imagine themselves in love if they had never read anything about it, are gravely declared to be abnormal or physically defective by critics of crushing unadventurousness and domestication. French authors of saintly temperament are forced to include in their retinue countesses of ardent complexion with whom they are supposed to live in sin. Sentimental controversies on the subject are endless; but they are useless, because nobody tells the truth. Rousseau did it by an extraordinary effort, aided by a superhuman faculty for human natural history; but the result was curiously disconcerting because, though the facts were so conventionally shocking that people felt that they ought to matter a great deal, they actually mattered very little. And even at that everybody pretends not to believe him.

Artificial Retribution

The worst of this is that busybodies with perhaps rather more than a normal taste for mischief are continually trying to make negligible things matter as much in fact as they do in convention by deliberately inflicting injuries—sometimes atrocious injuries—on the parties concerned. Few people have any knowledge of the savage punishments that are legally inflicted for aberrations and absurdities to which no sanely instructed community would call any attention. We create an artificial morality, and consequently an artificial conscience, by manufacturing disastrous consequences for events which, left to themselves, would do very little harm (sometimes not any) and be forgotten in a few days.

But the artificial morality is not therefore to be condemned offhand. In many cases it may save mischief instead of making it: for example, though the hanging of a murderer is the duplication of a murder, yet it may be less murderous than leaving the matter to be settled by blood feud or vendetta. As long as human nature insists on revenge, the official organization and satisfaction of revenge by the State may be also its minimization. The mischief begins when the official revenge persists after the passion it satisfies has died out of the race. Stoning a woman to death in the east because she has ventured to marry again after being deserted by her husband may be more merciful than allowing her to be mobbed to death; but the official stoning or burning of an adulteress in the west would be an atrocity, because few of us hate an adulteress to the extent of desiring such a penalty, or of being prepared to take the law into our own hands if it were withheld. Now what applies to this extreme case applies also in due degree to the other cases. Offences in which sex is concerned are often needlessly magnified by penalties, ranging from various forms of social ostracism to long sentences of penal servitude, which would be seen to be monstrously disproportionate to the real feeling against them if the removal of both the penalties and the taboo on their discussion made it possible for us to ascertain their real prevalence and estimation. Fortunately there is one outlet for the truth. We are permitted to discuss in jest what we may not discuss in earnest. A serious comedy about sex is taboo: a farcical comedy is privileged.

The Favorite Subject of Farcical Comedy

The little piece which follows this preface accordingly takes the form of a farcical comedy, because it is a contribution to the very extensive dramatic literature which takes as its special department the gallantries of married people. The stage has been preoccupied by such affairs for centuries, not only in the jesting vein of Restoration Comedy and Palais Royal farce, but in the more tragically turned adulteries of the Parisian school which dominated the stage until Ibsen put them out of countenance and relegated them to their proper place as articles of commerce. Their continued vogue in that department maintains the tradition that adultery is the dramatic subject *par excellence,* and indeed that a play that is not about adultery is not a play at all. I was considered a heresiarch of the most extravagant kind when I expressed my opinion, at the outset of my career as a playwright, that adultery is the dullest of themes on the stage, and that from Francesca and Paolo down to the latest guilty couple of the school of Dumas *fils,* the romantic adulterers have all been intolerable bores.

The Pseudo Sex Play

Later on, I had occasion to point out to the defenders of sex as the proper theme of drama, that though they were right in ranking sex as an intensely interesting subject, they were wrong in assuming that sex is an indispensable motive in popular plays. The plays of Molière are, like the novels of the Victorian epoch or Don Quixote, as nearly sexless as anything not absolutely inhuman can be; and some of Shakespear's plays are sexually on a par with the census: they contain women as well as men, and that is all. This had to be admitted; but it was still assumed that the plays of the nineteenth century Paris school are, in contrast with the sexless masterpieces, saturated with sex; and this I strenuously denied. A play about the convention that a man should fight a duel or come to fisticuffs with his wife's lover if she has one, or the convention that he should strangle her like Othello, or turn her out of the house and never see her or allow her to see her children again, or the convention that she should never be spoken to again by any decent person and should finally drown herself, or the convention that persons involved in scenes of recrimination or confession by these conventions should call each other certain abusive names and describe their conduct as guilty and frail and so on: all these may provide material for very effective plays; but such plays are not dramatic studies of sex: one might as well say that Romeo and Juliet is a dramatic study of pharmacy because the catastrophe is brought about through an apothecary. Duels are not sex; divorce cases are not sex; the Trade Unionism of married women is not sex. Only the most insignificant fraction of the gallantries of married people produce any of the conventional results; and plays occupied wholly with the conventional results are therefore utterly unsatisfying as sex plays, however interesting they may be as plays of intrigue and plot puzzles.

The world is finding this out rapidly. The Sunday papers, which in the days when they appealed almost exclusively to the lower middle class were crammed with police intelligence, and more especially with divorce and murder cases, now lay no stress on them; and police papers which confined themselves entirely to such matters, and were once eagerly read, have perished through the essential dulness of their topics. And yet the interest in sex is stronger than ever: in fact, the literature that has driven out the journalism of the divorce courts is a literature occupied with sex to an extent and with an intimacy and frankness that would have seemed utterly impossible to Thackeray or Dickens if they had been told that the change would complete itself within fifty years of their own time.

Art and Morality

It is ridiculous to say, as inconsiderate amateurs of the arts do, that art has nothing to do with morality. What is true is that the artist's business is not that of the policeman; and that such factitious consequences and put-up jobs as divorces and executions and the detective operations that lead up to them are no essential part of life, though, like poisons and buttered slides and red-hot pokers, they provide material for plenty of thrilling or amusing stories suited to people who are incapable of any interest in psychology. But the fine artist must keep the policeman out of his studies of sex and studies of crime. It is by clinging nervously to the policeman that most of the pseudo sex plays convince me that the writers have either never had any serious personal experience of their ostensible subject, or else have never conceived it possible that the stage dare present the phenomena of sex as they appear in nature.

The Limits of Stage Presentation

But the stage presents much more shocking phenomena than those of sex. There is, of course, a sense in which you cannot present sex on the stage, just as you cannot present murder. Macbeth must no more really kill Duncan than he must himself be really slain by Macduff. But the feelings of a murderer can be expressed in a certain artistic convention; and a carefully prearranged sword exercise can be gone through with sufficient pretence of earnestness to be accepted by the willing imaginations of the younger spectators as a desperate combat.

The tragedy of love has been presented on the stage in the same way. In Tristan and Isolde, the curtain does not, as in Romeo and Juliet, rise with the lark: the whole night of love is played before the spectators. The lovers do not discuss marriage in an elegantly sentimental way: they utter the visions and feelings that come to lovers at the supreme moments of their love, totally forgetting that there are such things in the world as husbands and lawyers and duelling codes and theories of sin and notions of propriety and all the other irrelevancies which provide hackneyed and bloodless material for our so-called plays of passion.

Pruderies of the French Stage

To all stage presentations there are limits. If Macduff were to stab Macbeth, the spectacle would be intolerable; and even the pretence which we allow on our stage is ridiculously destructive to the illusion of the scene. Yet pugilists and gladiators will actually fight and kill in public without shame, even as a spectacle for money. But no sober couple of lovers of any delicacy could endure to be watched. We in England, accustomed to consider the French stage much more licentious than the British, are always surprised and puzzled when we learn, as we may do any day if we come within reach of such information, that French actors are often scandalized by what they consider the indecency of the English stage, and that French actresses who desire a greater license in appealing to the sexual instincts than the French stage allows them, learn English and establish themselves on the English stage. The German and Russian stages are in the same relation to the French and, perhaps more or less, all the Latin stages. The reason is that, partly from a want of respect for the theatre, partly from a sort of respect for art in general which moves them to accord moral privileges to artists, partly from the very objectionable tradition that the realm of art is Alsatia and the contemplation of works of art a holiday from the burden of virtue, partly because French prudery does not attach itself to the same points of behavior as British prudery, and has a different code of the mentionable and the unmentionable, and for many other reasons, the French tolerate plays which are never performed in England until they have been spoiled by a process of bowdlerization; yet French taste is more fastidious than ours as to the exhibition and treatment on the stage of the physical incidents of sex. On the French stage a kiss is as obvious a convention as the thrust under the arm by which Macduff runs Macbeth through. It is even a purposely unconvincing convention: the actors rather insisting that it shall be impossible for any spectator to mistake a stage kiss for a real one. In England, on the contrary, realism is carried to the point at which nobody except the two performers can perceive that the caress is not genuine. And here the English stage is certainly in the right; for whatever question there arises as to what incidents are proper for representation on the stage or not, my experience as a playgoer leaves me in no doubt that once it is decided to represent an incident, it will be offensive, no matter whether it be a prayer or a kiss, unless it is presented with a convincing appearance of sincerity.

Our Disillusive Scenery

For example, the main objection to the use of illusive scenery (in most modern plays scenery is not illusive: everything visible is as real as in your drawing room at home) is that it is unconvincing; whilst the imaginary scenery with which the audience transfigures a platform or tribune like the Elizabethan stage or the Greek stage used by Sophocles, is quite convincing. In fact, the more scenery you have the less illusion you produce. The wise playwright, when he cannot get absolute reality of presentation, goes to the other extreme, and aims at atmosphere and suggestion of mood rather than at direct simulative illusion. The theatre, as I first knew it, was a place of wings and flats which destroyed both atmosphere and illusion. This was tolerated, and even intensely enjoyed, but not in the least because nothing better was possible; for all the devices employed in the productions of Mr Granville Barker or Max Reinhardt or the Moscow Art Theatre were equally available for Colley Cibber and Garrick, except the intensity of our artificial light. When Garrick played Richard III in slashed trunk hose and plumes, it was not because he believed that the Plantagenets dressed like that, or because the costumiers could not have made him a XV century dress as easily as a nondescript combination of the state robes of George III with such scraps of older fashions as seemed to playgoers for some reason to be romantic. The charm of the theatre in those days was its makebelieve. It has that charm still, not only for the amateurs, who are happiest when they are most unnatural and impossible and absurd, but for audiences as well. I have seen performances of my own plays which were to me far wilder burlesques than Sheridan's Critic or Buckingham's Rehearsal; yet they have produced sincere laughter and tears such as the most finished metropolitan productions have failed to elicit. Fielding was entirely right when he represented Partridge as enjoying intensely the performance of the king in Hamlet because anybody could see that the king was an actor, and resenting Garrick's Hamlet because it might have been a real man. Yet we have only to look at the portraits of Garrick to see that his performances would nowadays seem almost as extravagantly stagey as his costumes. In our day Calvé's intensely real Carmen never pleased the mob as much as the obvious fancy ball masquerading of suburban young ladies in the same character.

Holding the Mirror up to Nature

Theatrical art begins as the holding up to Nature of a distorting mirror. In this phase it pleases people who are childish enough to believe that they can see what they look like and what they are when they look at a true mirror. Naturally they think that a true mirror can teach them nothing. Only by giving them back some monstrous image can the mirror amuse them or terrify them. It is not until they grow up to the point at which they learn that they know very little about themselves, and that they do not see themselves in a true mirror as other people see them, that they become consumed with curiosity as to what they really are like, and begin to demand that the stage shall be a mirror of such accuracy and intensity of illumination that they shall be able to get glimpses of their real selves in it, and also learn a little how they appear to other people.

For audiences of this highly developed class, sex can no longer be ignored or conventionalized or distorted by the playwright who makes the mirror. The old sentimental extravagances and the old grossnesses are of no further use to him. Don Giovanni and Zerlina are not gross: Tristan and Isolde are not extravagant or sentimental. They say and do nothing that you cannot bear to hear and see; and yet they give you, the one pair briefly and slightly, and the other fully and deeply, what passes in the minds of lovers. The love depicted may be that of a philosophic adventurer tempting an ignorant country girl, or of a tragically serious poet entangled with a woman of noble capacity in a passion which has become for them the reality of the whole universe. No matter: the thing is dramatized and dramatized directly, not talked about as something that happened before the curtain rose, or that will happen after it falls.

Farcical Comedy Shirking its Subject

Now if all this can be done in the key of tragedy and philosophic comedy, it can, I have always contended, be done in the key of farcical comedy; and Overruled is a trifling experiment in that manner. Conventional farcical comedies are always finally tedious because the heart of them, the inevitable conjugal infidelity, is always evaded. Even its consequences are evaded. Mr Granville Barker has pointed out rightly that if the third acts of our farcical comedies dared to describe the consequences that would follow from the first and second in real life, they would end as squalid tragedies; and in my opinion they would be greatly improved thereby even as entertainments; for I have never seen a three-act farcical comedy without being bored and tired by the third act, and observing that the rest of the audience were in the same condition, though they were not vigilantly introspective enough to find that out, and were apt to blame one another, especially the husbands and wives, for their crossness. But it is happily by no means true that conjugal infidelities always produce tragic consequences, or that they need produce even the unhappiness which they often do produce. Besides, the more momentous the consequences, the more interesting become the impulses and imaginations and reasonings, if any, of the people who disregard them. If I had an opportunity of conversing with the ghost of an executed murderer, I have no doubt he would begin to tell me eagerly about his trial, with the names of the distinguished ladies and gentlemen who honored him with their presence on that occasion, and then about his execution. All of which would bore me exceedingly. I should say, "My dear sir: such manufactured ceremonies do not interest me in the least. I know how a man is tried, and how he is hanged. I should have had you killed in a much less disgusting, hypocritical, and unfriendly manner if the matter had been in my hands. What I want to know about is the murder. How did you feel when you committed it? Why did you do it? What did you say to yourself about it? If, like most murderers, you had not been hanged, would you have committed other murders? Did you really dislike the victim, or did you want his money, or did you murder a person whom you did not dislike, and from whose death you had nothing to gain, merely for the sake of murdering? If so, can you describe the charm to me? Does it come upon you periodically; or is it chronic? Has curiosity anything to do with it?" I would ply him with all manner of questions to find out what murder is really like; and I should not be satisfied until I had realized that I, too, might commit a murder, or else that there is some specific quality present in a murderer and lacking in me. And, if so, what that quality is.

In just the same way, I want the unfaithful husband or the unfaithful wife in a farcical comedy not to bother me with their divorce cases or the stratagems they employ to avoid a divorce case, but to tell me how and why married couples are unfaithful. I don't want to hear the lies they tell one another to conceal what they have done, but the truths they tell one another when they have to face what they have done without concealment or excuse. No doubt prudent and considerate people conceal such adventures, when they can, from those who are most likely to be wounded by them; but it is not to be presumed that, when found out, they necessarily disgrace themselves by irritating lies and transparent subterfuges.

My playlet, which I offer as a model to all future writers of farcical comedy, may now, I hope, be read without shock. I may just add that Mr Sibthorpe Juno's view that morality demands, not that we should behave morally (an impossibility to our sinful nature) but that we shall not attempt to defend our immoralities, is a standard view in England, and was advanced in all seriousness by an earnest and distinguished British moralist shortly after the first performance of Overruled. My objection to that aspect of the doctrine of original sin is that no necessary and inevitable operation of human nature can reasonably be regarded as sinful at all, and that a morality which assumes the contrary is an absurd morality, and can be kept in countenance only by hypocrisy. When people were ashamed of sanitary problems, and refused to face them, leaving them to solve themselves clandestinely in dirt and secrecy, the solution arrived at was the Black Death. A similar policy as to sex problems has solved itself by an even worse plague than the Black Death; and the remedy for that is not salvarsan, but sound moral hygiene, the first foundation of which is the discontinuance of our habit of telling not only the comparatively harmless lies that we know we ought not to tell, but the ruinous lies that we foolishly think we ought to tell.

OVERRULED

A lady and gentleman are sitting together on a chesterfield in a retired corner of the lounge of a seaside hotel. It is a summer night: the French window behind them stands open. The terrace without overlooks a moonlit harbor. The lounge is dark. The chesterfield, upholstered in silver grey, and the two figures on it in evening dress, catch the light from an arc lamp somewhere; but the walls, covered with a dark green paper, are in gloom. There are two stray chairs, one on each side. On the gentleman's right, behind him up near the window, is an unused fireplace. Opposite it on the lady's left is a door. The gentleman is on the lady's right.

The lady is very attractive, with a musical voice and soft appealing manners. She is young: that is, one feels sure that she is under thirty-five and over twenty-four. The gentleman does not look much older. He is rather handsome, and has ventured as far in the direction of poetic dandyism in the arrangement of his hair as any man who is not a professional artist can afford to in England. He is obviously very much in love with the lady, and is, in fact, yielding to an irresistible impulse to throw his arms round her.

THE LADY. Dont—oh dont be horrid. Please, Mr Lunn! [*She rises from the lounge and retreats behind it*]. Promise me you wont be horrid.

GREGORY LUNN. I'm not being horrid, Mrs Juno. I'm not going to be horrid. I love you: thats all. I'm extraordinarily happy.

MRS JUNO. You will really be good?

GREGORY. I'll be whatever you wish me to be. I tell you I love you. I love loving you. I dont want to be tired and sorry, as I should be if I were to be horrid. I dont want you to be tired and sorry. Do come and sit down again.

MRS JUNO [*coming back to her seat*] Youre sure you dont want anything you oughtnt to?

GREGORY. Quite sure. I only want you. [*She recoils*]. Dont be alarmed: I like wanting you. As long as I have a want, I have a reason for living. Satisfaction is death.

MRS JUNO. Yes; but the impulse to commit suicide is sometimes irresistible.

GREGORY. Not with you.

MRS JUNO. What!

GREGORY. Oh, it sounds uncomplimentary; but it isnt really. Do you know why half the couples who find themselves situated as we are now behave horridly?

MRS JUNO. Because they cant help it if they let things go too far.

GREGORY. Not a bit of it. It's because they have nothing else to do, and no other way of entertaining each other. You dont know what it is to be alone with a woman who has little beauty and less conversation. What is a man to do? She cant talk interestingly; and if he talks that way himself she doesnt understand him. He cant look at her: if he does, he only finds out that she isnt beautiful. Before the end of five minutes they are both hideously bored. Theres only one thing that can save the situation; and thats what you call being horrid. With a beautiful, witty, kind woman, theres no time for such follies. It's so delightful to look at her, to listen to her voice, to hear all she has to say, that nothing else happens. That is why the woman who is supposed to have a thousand lovers seldom has one; whilst the stupid, graceless animals of women have dozens.

MRS JUNO. I wonder! It's quite true that when one feels in danger one talks like mad to stave it off, even when one doesnt quite want to stave it off.

GREGORY. One never does quite want to stave it off. Danger is delicious. But death isnt. We court the danger; but the real delight is in escaping, after all.

MRS JUNO. I dont think we'll talk about it any more. Danger is all very well when you do escape; but sometimes one doesnt. I tell you frankly I dont feel as safe as you do —if you really do.

GREGORY. But surely you can do as you please without injuring anyone, Mrs Juno. That is the whole secret of your extraordinary charm for me.

MRS JUNO. I dont understand.

GREGORY. Well, I hardly know how to begin to explain. But the root of the matter is that I am what people call a good man.

MRS JUNO. I thought so until you began making love to me.

GREGORY. But you knew I loved you all along.

MRS JUNO. Yes, of course; but I depended on you not to tell me so; because I thought you were good. Your blurting it out spoilt it. And it was wicked besides.

GREGORY. Not at all. You see, it's a great many years since Ive been able to allow myself to fall in love. I know lots of charming women; but the worst of it is, theyre all married. Women dont become charming, to my taste, until theyre fully developed; and by that time, if theyre really nice, theyre snapped up and married. And then, because I am a good man, I have to place a limit to my regard for them. I may be fortunate enough to gain friendship and even very warm affection from them; but my loyalty to their husbands and their hearths and their happiness obliges me to draw a line and not overstep it. Of course I value such affectionate regard very highly indeed. I am surrounded with women who are most dear to me. But every one of them has a post sticking up, if I may put it that way, with the inscription: Trespassers Will Be Prosecuted. How we all loathe that notice! In every lovely garden, in every dell full of primroses, on every fair hillside, we meet that confounded board; and there is always a game-keeper round the corner. But what is that to the horror of meeting it on every beautiful woman, and knowing that there is a husband round the corner? I have had this accursed board standing between me and every dear and desirable woman until I thought I had lost the power of letting myself fall really and wholeheartedly in love.

MRS JUNO. Wasnt there a widow?

GREGORY. No. Widows are extraordinarily scarce in modern society. Husbands live longer than they used to; and even when they do die, their widows have a string of names down for their next.

MRS JUNO. Well, what about the young girls?

GREGORY. Oh, who cares for young girls? Theyre unsympathetic. Theyre beginners. They dont attract me. I'm afraid of them.

MRS JUNO. Thats the correct thing to say to a woman of my age. But it doesnt explain why you seem to have put your scruples in your pocket when you met me.

GREGORY. Surely thats quite clear. I—

MRS JUNO. No: please dont explain. I dont want to know. I take your word for it. Besides, it doesnt matter now. Our voyage is over; and tomorrow I start for the north to my poor father's place.

GREGORY [*surprised*] Your poor father! I thought he was alive.

MRS JUNO. So he is. What made you think he wasnt?

GREGORY. You said your poor father.

MRS JUNO. Oh, thats a trick of mine. Rather a silly trick, I suppose; but theres something pathetic to me about men: I find myself calling them poor So-and-So when theres nothing whatever the matter with them.

GREGORY [*who has listened in growing alarm*] But—I—is? —wa—? Oh Lord!

MRS JUNO. Whats the matter?

GREGORY. Nothing.

MRS JUNO. Nothing! [*Rising anxiously*] Nonsense: youre ill.

GREGORY. No. It was something about your late husband—

MRS JUNO. My late husband! What do you mean? [*Clutching him, horror-stricken*] Dont tell me he's dead.

GREGORY [*rising, equally appalled*] Dont tell me he's alive.

MRS JUNO. Oh, dont frighten me like this. Of course he's alive—unless youve heard anything.

GREGORY. The first day we met—on the boat—you spoke to me of your poor dear husband.

MRS JUNO [*releasing him, quite reassured*] Is that all?

GREGORY. Well, afterwards you called him poor Tops. Always poor Tops, or poor dear Tops. What could I think?

MRS JUNO [*sitting down again*] I wish you hadnt given me such a shock about him; for I havent been treating him at all well. Neither have you.

GREGORY [*relapsing into his seat, overwhelmed*] And you mean to tell me youre not a widow!

MRS JUNO. Gracious, no! I'm not in black.

GREGORY. Then I have been behaving like a blackguard! I have broken my promise to my mother. I shall never have an easy conscience again.

MRS JUNO. I'm sorry. I thought you knew.

GREGORY. You thought I was a libertine?

MRS JUNO. No: of course I shouldnt have spoken to you if I had thought that. I thought you liked me, but that you knew, and would be good.

GREGORY [*stretching his hand towards her breast*] I thought the burden of being good had fallen from my soul at last. I saw nothing there but a bosom to rest on: the bosom of a lovely woman of whom I could dream without guilt. What do I see now?

MRS JUNO. Just what you saw before.

GREGORY [*despairingly*] No, no.

MRS JUNO. What else?

GREGORY. Trespassers Will Be Prosecuted: Trespassers Will Be Prosecuted.

MRS JUNO. They wont if they hold their tongues. Dont be such a coward. My husband wont eat you.

GREGORY. I'm not afraid of your husband. I'm afraid of my conscience.

MRS JUNO [*losing patience*] Well! I dont consider myself at all a badly behaved woman; for nothing has passed between us that was not perfectly nice and friendly; but really! to hear a grown-up man talking about promises to his mother!—

GREGORY [*interrupting her*] Yes, yes: I know all about that. It's not romantic: it's not Don Juan: it's not advanced; but we feel it all the same. It's far deeper in our blood and bones than all the romantic stuff. My father got into a scandal once: that was why my mother made me promise never to make love to a married woman. And now Ive done it I cant feel honest. Dont pretend to despise me or laugh at me. You feel it too. You said just now that your own conscience was uneasy when you thought of your husband. What must it be when you think of my wife?

MRS JUNO [*rising aghast*] Your wife!!! You dont dare sit there and tell me coolly that youre a married man!

GREGORY. I never led you to believe I was unmarried.

MRS JUNO. Oh! You never gave me the faintest hint that you had a wife.

GREGORY. I did indeed. I discussed things with you that only married people really understand.

MRS JUNO. Oh!!

GREGORY. I thought it the most delicate way of letting you know.

MRS JUNO. Well, you are a daisy, I must say. I suppose thats vulgar; but really! really!! You and your goodness! However, now weve found one another out theres only one thing to be done. Will you please go?

GREGORY [*rising slowly*] I ought to go.

MRS JUNO. Well, go.

GREGORY. Yes. Er—[*he tries to go*] I—I somehow cant. [*He sits down again helplessly*]. My conscience is active: my will is paralyzed. This is really dreadful. Would you mind ringing the bell and asking them to throw me out? You ought to, you know.

MRS JUNO. What! make a scandal in the face of the whole hotel! Certainly not. Dont be a fool.

GREGORY. Yes; but I cant go.

MRS JUNO. Then I can. Goodbye.

GREGORY [*clinging to her hand*] Can you really?

MRS JUNO. Of course I—[*she wavers*] Oh dear! [*They contemplate one another helplessly*]. I cant. [*She sinks on the lounge, hand in hand with him*].

GREGORY. For heaven's sake pull yourself together. It's a question of self-control.

MRS JUNO [*dragging her hand away and retreating to the end of the chesterfield*] No: it's a question of distance. Self-control is all very well two or three yards off, or on a ship, with everybody looking on. Dont come any nearer.

GREGORY. This is a ghastly business. I want to go away; and I cant.

MRS JUNO. I think you ought to go [*he makes an effort; and she adds quickly*] but if you try to I shall grab you round the neck and disgrace myself. I implore you to sit still and be nice.

GREGORY. I implore you to run away. I believe I can trust myself to let you go for your own sake. But it will break my heart.

MRS JUNO. I dont want to break you heart. I cant bear to think of your sitting here alone. I cant bear to think of sitting alone myself somewhere else. It's so senseless—so ridiculous—when we might be so happy. I dont want to be wicked, or coarse. But I like you very much; and I do want to be affectionate and human.

GREGORY. I ought to draw a line.

MRS JUNO. So you shall, dear. Tell me: do you really like me? I dont mean love me: you might love the housemaid—

GREGORY [*vehemently*] No!

MRS JUNO. Oh yes you might; and what does that matter, anyhow? Are you really fond of me? Are we friends—comrades? Would you be sorry if I died?

GREGORY [*shrinking*] Oh dont.

MRS JUNO. Or was it the usual aimless man's lark: a mere shipboard flirtation?

GREGORY. Oh no, no: nothing half so bad, so vulgar, so wrong. I assure you I only meant to be agreeable. It grew on me before I noticed it.

MRS JUNO. And you were glad to let it grow?

GREGORY. I let it grow because the board was not up.

MRS JUNO. Bother the board! I am just as fond of Sibthorpe as—

GREGORY. Sibthorpe!

MRS JUNO. Sibthorpe is my husband's Christian name. I oughtnt to call him Tops to you now.

GREGORY [*chuckling*] It sounded like something to drink. But I have no right to laugh at him. My Christian name is Gregory, which sounds like a powder.

MRS JUNO [*chilled*] That is so like a man! I offer you my heart's warmest friendliest feeling; and you think of nothing but a silly joke. A quip like that makes you forget me.

GREGORY. Forget you! Oh, if only I could!

MRS JUNO. If you could, would you?

GREGORY [*burying his shamed face in his hands*] No: I'd die first. Oh, I hate myself.

MRS JUNO. I glory in myself. It's so jolly to be reckless. Can a man be reckless, I wonder?

GREGORY [*straightening himself desperately*] No. I'm not reckless. I know what I'm doing: my conscience is awake. Oh, where is the intoxication of love? the delirium? the madness that makes a man think the world well lost for the woman he adores? I dont think anything of the sort: I see that it's not worth it: I know that it's wrong: I have never in my life been cooler, more businesslike.

MRS JUNO [*opening her arms to him*] But you cant resist me.

GREGORY. I must. I ought. [*Throwing himself into her arms*] Oh my darling, my treasure, we shall be sorry for this.

MRS JUNO. We can forgive ourselves. Could we forgive ourselves if we let this moment slip?

GREGORY. I protest to the last. I'm against this. I have been pushed over a precipice. I'm innocent. This wild joy, this exquisite tenderness, this ascent into heaven can thrill me to the uttermost fibre of my heart [*with a gesture of ecstasy she hides her face on his shoulder*]; but it cant subdue my mind or corrupt my conscience, which still shouts to the skies that I'm not a willing party to this outrageous conduct. I repudiate the bliss with which you are filling me.

MRS JUNO. Never mind your conscience. Tell me how happy you are.

GREGORY. No: I recall you to your duty. But oh, I will give you my life with both hands if you can tell me that you feel for me one millionth part of what I feel for you now.

MRS JUNO. Oh yes, yes. Be satisfied with that. Ask for no more. Let me go.

GREGORY. I cant. I have no will. Something stronger than either of us is in command here. Nothing on earth or in heaven can part us now. You know that, dont you?

MRS JUNO. Oh, dont make me say it. Of course I know. Nothing—not life nor death nor shame nor anything can part us.

A MATTER-OF-FACT MALE VOICE IN THE CORRIDOR. All right. This must be it.

The two recover with a violent start; release one another; and spring back to opposite sides of the lounge.

GREGORY. That did it.

MRS JUNO [*in a thrilling whisper*] Sh-sh-sh! That was my husband's voice.

GREGORY. Impossible: it's only our guilty fancy.

A WOMAN'S VOICE. This is the way to the lounge. I know it.

GREGORY. Great Heaven! we're both mad. Thats my wife's voice.

MRS JUNO. Ridiculous! Oh, we're dreaming it all. We— [*The door opens; and Sibthorpe Juno appears in the roseate glow of the corridor* (*which happens to be papered in pink*) *with Mrs Lunn, like Tannhäuser in the hill of Venus. He is a fussily energetic little man, who gives himself an air of gallantry by greasing the points of his moustaches and dressing very carefully. She is a tall, imposing, handsome, languid woman, with flashing dark eyes and long lashes. They make for the chesterfield, not noticing the two palpitating figures blotted against the walls in the gloom on either side. The figures flit away noiselessly through the window and disappear*].

JUNO [*officiously*] Ah: here we are. [*He leads the way to the sofa*]. Sit down: I'm sure youre tired. [*She sits*]. Thats right. [*He sits beside her on her left*]. Hullo! [*he rises*] this sofa's quite warm.

MRS LUNN [*bored*] Is it? I dont notice it. I expect the sun's been on it.

JUNO. I felt it quite distinctly: I'm more thinly clad than you. [*He sits down again, and proceeds, with a sigh of satisfaction*] What a relief to get off the ship and have a private room! Thats the worst of a ship. Youre under observation all the time.

MRS LUNN. But why not?

JUNO. Well, of course theres no reason: at least I suppose not. But, you know, part of the romance of a journey is that a man keeps imagining that something might happen; and he cant do that if there are a lot of people about and it simply cant happen.

MRS LUNN. Mr Juno: romance is all very well on board ship; but when your foot touches the soil of England theres an end of it.

JUNO. No: believe me, thats a foreigner's mistake: we are the most romantic people in the world, we English. Why, my very presence here is a romance.

MRS LUNN [*faintly ironical*] Indeed?

JUNO. Yes. Youve guessed, of course, that I'm a married man.

MRS LUNN. Oh, thats all right. I'm a married woman.

JUNO. Thank Heaven for that! To my English mind, passion is not real passion without guilt. I am a red-blooded man, Mrs Lunn: I cant help it. The tragedy of my life is that I married, when quite young, a woman whom I couldnt help being very fond of. I longed for a guilty passion—for the real thing—the wicked thing; and yet I couldnt care twopence for any other woman when my wife was about. Year after year went by: I felt my youth slipping away without ever having had a romance in my life; for marriage is all very well; but it isnt romance. Theres nothing wrong in it, you see.

MRS LUNN. Poor man! How you must have suffered!

JUNO. No: that was what was so tame about it. I wanted to

suffer. You get so sick of being happily married. It's always the happy marriages that break up. At last my wife and I agreed that we ought to take a holiday.

MRS LUNN. Hadnt you holidays every year?

JUNO. Oh, the seaside and so on! Thats not what we meant. We meant a holiday from one another.

MRS LUNN. How very odd!

JUNO. She said it was an excellent idea; that domestic felicity was making us perfectly idiotic; that she wanted a holiday too. So we agreed to go round the world in opposite directions. I started for Suez on the day she sailed for New York.

MRS LUNN [*suddenly becoming attentive*] Thats precisely what Gregory and I did. Now I wonder did he want a holiday from me! What he said was that he wanted the delight of meeting me after a long absence.

JUNO. Could anything be more romantic than that? Would anyone else than an Englishman have thought of it? I daresay my temperament seems tame to your boiling southern blood—

MRS LUNN. My what!

JUNO. Your southern blood. Dont you remember how you told me, that night in the saloon when I sang "Farewell and adieu to you dear Spanish ladies," that you were by birth a lady of Spain? Your splendid Andalusian beauty speaks for itself.

MRS LUNN. Stuff! I was born in Gibraltar. My father was Captain Jenkins. In the artillery.

JUNO [*ardently*] It is climate and not race that determines the temperament. The fiery sun of Spain blazed on your cradle; and it rocked to the roar of British cannon.

MRS LUNN: What eloquence! It reminds me of my husband when he was in love—before we were married. Are you in love?

JUNO. Yes; and with the same woman.

MRS LUNN. Well, of course, I didnt suppose you were in love with two women.

JUNO. I dont think you quite understand. I meant that I am in love with you.

MRS LUNN [*relapsing into deepest boredom*] Oh, that! Men do fall in love with me. They all seem to think me a creature with volcanic passions: I'm sure I dont know why; for all the volcanic women I know are plain little creatures with sandy hair. I dont consider human volcanoes respectable. And I'm so tired of the subject! Our house is always full of women who are in love with my husband and men who are in love with me. We encourage it because it's pleasant to have company.

JUNO. And is your husband as insensible as yourself?

MRS LUNN. Oh, Gregory's not insensible: very far from it; but I am the only woman in the world for him.

JUNO. But you? Are you really as insensible as you say you are?

MRS LUNN. I never said anything of the kind. I'm not at all insensible by nature; but (I dont know whether youve noticed it) I am what people call rather a fine figure of a woman.

JUNO [*passionately*] Noticed it! Oh, Mrs Lunn! Have I been able to notice anything else since we met?

MRS LUNN. There you go, like all the rest of them! I ask you, how do you expect a woman to keep up what you call her sensibility when this sort of thing has happened to her about three times a week ever since she was seventeen? It used to upset me and terrify me at first. Then I got rather a taste for it. It came to a climax with Gregory: that was why I married him. Then it became a mild lark, hardly worth the trouble. After that I found it valuable once or twice as a spinal tonic when I was run down; but now it's an unmitigated bore. I dont mind your declaration: I daresay it gives you a certain pleasure to make it. I quite understand that you adore me; but (if you dont mind) I'd rather you didnt keep on saying so.

JUNO. Is there then no hope for me?

MRS LUNN. Oh, yes. Gregory has an idea that married women keep lists of the men theyll marry if they become widows. I'll put your name down, if that will satisfy you.

JUNO. Is the list a long one?

MRS LUNN. Do you mean the real list? Not the one I shew to Gregory: there are hundreds of names on that; but the little private list that he'd better not see?

JUNO. Oh, will you really put me on that? Say you will.

MRS LUNN. Well, perhaps I will. [*He kisses her hand*]. Now dont begin abusing the privilege.

JUNO. May I call you by your Christian name?

MRS LUNN. No: it's too long. You cant go about calling a woman Seraphita.

JUNO [*ecstatically*] Seraphita!

MRS LUNN. I used to be called Sally at home; but when I married a man named Lunn, of course that became ridiculous. Thats my one little pet joke. Call me Mrs Lunn for short. And change the subject, or I shall go to sleep.

JUNO. I cant change the subject. For me there is no other subject. Why else have you put me on your list?

MRS LUNN. Because youre a solicitor. Gregory's a solicitor. I'm accustomed to my husband being a solicitor and telling me things he oughtnt to tell anybody.

JUNO [*ruefully*] Is that all? Oh, I cant believe that the voice of love has ever thoroughly awakened you.

MRS LUNN. No: it sends me to sleep. [*Juno appeals against this by an amorous demonstration*]. It's no use, Mr Juno: I'm hopelessly respectable: the Jenkinses always were. Dont you realize that unless most women were like that, the world couldnt go on as it does?

JUNO [*darkly*] You think it goes on respectably; but I can tell you as a solicitor—

MRS LUNN. Stuff! of course all the disreputable people who get into trouble go to you, just as all the sick people go to the doctors; but most people never go to a solicitor.

JUNO [*rising, with a growing sense of injury*] Look here, Mrs Lunn: do you think a man's heart is a potato? or a turnip? or a ball of knitting wool? that you can throw it away like this?

MRS LUNN. I dont throw away balls of knitting wool. A man's heart seems to me much like a sponge, it sops up dirty water as well as clean.

JUNO. I have never been treated like this in my life. Here am I, a married man, with a most attractive wife: a wife I adore, and who adores me, and has never as much as looked at any other man since we were married. I come and throw all this at your feet. I! I, a solicitor! braving the risk of your husband putting me into the divorce court and making me a beggar and an outcast! I do this for your sake. And you go on as if I were making no sacrifice: as if I had told you it's a fine evening, or asked you to have a cup of tea. It's not human. It's not right. Love has its rights as well as respectability. [*He sits down again, aloof and sulky*].

MRS LUNN. Nonsense! Here! heres a flower. [*She gives him one*]. Go and dream over it until you feel hungry. Nothing brings people to their senses like hunger.

JUNO [*contemplating the flower without rapture*] What good's this?

MRS LUNN [*snatching it from him*] Oh! you dont love me a bit.

JUNO. Yes I do. Or at least I did. But I'm an Englishman; and I think you ought to respect the conventions of English life.

MRS LUNN. But I am respecting them; and youre not.

JUNO. Pardon me. I may be doing wrong; but I'm doing it in a proper and customary manner. You may be doing right; but youre doing it in an unusual and questionable manner. I am not prepared to put up with that. I can stand being badly treated: I'm no baby, and can take care of myself with anybody. And of course I can stand being well treated. But the one thing I cant stand is being unexpectedly treated. It's outside my scheme of life. So come now! youve got to behave naturally and straightforwardly with me. You can leave husband and child, home, friends, and country, for my sake, and come with me to some southern isle—or say South America—where we can be all in all to one another. Or you can tell your husband and let him jolly well punch my head if he can. But I'm damned if I'm going to stand any eccentricity. It's not respectable.

GREGORY [*coming in from the terrace and advancing with dignity to his wife's end of the chesterfield*] Will you have the goodness, sir, in addressing this lady, to keep your temper and refrain from using profane language?

MRS LUNN [*rising, delighted*] Gregory! Darling! [*She enfolds him in a copious embrace*].

JUNO [*rising*] You make love to another man to my face!

MRS LUNN. Why, he's my husband.

JUNO. That takes away the last rag of excuse for such conduct. A nice world it would be if married people were to carry on their endearments before everybody!

GREGORY. This is ridiculous. What the devil business is it of yours what passes between my wife and myself? Youre not her husband, are you?

JUNO. Not at present; but I'm on the list. I'm her prospective husband: youre only her actual one. I'm the anticipation: youre the disappointment.

MRS LUNN. Oh, my Gregory is not a disappointment. [*Fondly*] Are you, dear?

GREGORY. You just wait, my pet. I'll settle this chap for you. [*He disengages himself from her embrace, and faces Juno. She sits down placidly*]. You call me a disappointment, do you? Well, I suppose every husband's a disappointment. What about yourself? Dont try to look like an unmarried man. I happen to know the lady you disappointed. I travelled in the same ship with her; and—

JUNO. And you fell in love with her.

GREGORY [*taken aback*] Who told you that?

JUNO. Aha! you confess it. Well, if you want to know, nobody told me. Everybody falls in love with my wife.

GREGORY. And do you fall in love with everybody's wife?

JUNO. Certainly not. Only with yours.

MRS LUNN. But whats the good of saying that, Mr Juno? I'm married to him; and theres an end of it.

JUNO. Not at all. You can get a divorce.

MRS LUNN. What for?

JUNO. For his misconduct with my wife.

GREGORY [*deeply indignant*] How dare you, sir, asperse the character of that sweet lady? a lady whom I have taken under my protection.

JUNO. Protection!

MRS JUNO [*returning hastily*] Really you must be more careful what you say about me, Mr Lunn.

JUNO. My precious! [*He embraces her*]. Pardon this betrayal of feeling; but Ive not seen my wife for several weeks; and she is very dear to me.

GREGORY. I call this cheek. Who is making love to his own wife before people now, pray?

MRS LUNN. Wont you introduce me to your wife, Mr Juno?

MRS JUNO. How do you do? [*They shake hands; and Mrs Juno sits down beside Mrs Lunn, on her left*].

MRS LUNN. I'm so glad to find you do credit to Gregory's taste. I'm naturally rather particular about the women he falls in love with.

JUNO [*sternly*] This is no way to take your husband's unfaithfulness. [*To Lunn*] You ought to teach your wife better. Wheres her feelings? It's scandalous.

GREGORY. What about your own conduct, pray?

JUNO. I dont defend it; and theres an end of the matter.

GREGORY. Well, upon my soul! What difference does your not defending it make?

JUNO. A fundamental difference. To serious people I may appear wicked. I dont defend myself: I am wicked, though not bad at heart. To thoughtless people I may even appear comic. Well, laugh at me: I have given myself away. But Mrs Lunn seems to have no opinion at all about me. She doesnt seem to know whether I'm wicked or comic. She doesnt seem to care. She has no moral sense. I say it's not right. I repeat, I have sinned; and I'm prepared to suffer.

MRS JUNO. Have you really sinned, Tops?

MRS LUNN [*blandly*] I dont remember your sinning. I have a shocking bad memory for trifles; but I think I should remember that—if you mean me.

JUNO [*raging*] Trifles! I have fallen in love with a monster.

GREGORY. Dont you dare call my wife a monster.

MRS JUNO [*rising quickly and coming between them*] Please dont lose your temper, Mr Lunn: I wont have my Tops bullied.

GREGORY. Well, then, let him not brag about sinning with

my wife. [*He turns impulsively to his wife; makes her rise; and takes her proudly on his arm*]. What pretension has he to any such honor?

JUNO. I sinned in intention. [*Mrs Juno abandons him and resumes her seat, chilled*]. I'm as guilty as if I had actually sinned. And I insist on being treated as a sinner, and not walked over as if I'd done nothing, by your wife or any other man.

MRS LUNN. Tush! [*She sits down again contemptuously*].

JUNO [*furious*] I wont be belittled.

MRS LUNN [*to Mrs Juno*] I hope youll come and stay with us now that you and Gregory are such friends, Mrs Juno.

JUNO. This insane magnanimity—

MRS LUNN. Dont you think youve said enough, Mr Juno? This is a matter for two women to settle. Wont you take a stroll on the beach with my Gregory while we talk it over. Gregory is a splendid listener.

JUNO. I dont think any good can come of a conversation between Mr Lunn and myself. We can hardly be expected to improve one another's morals. [*He passes behind the chesterfield to Mrs Lunn's end; seizes a chair; deliberately pushes it between Gregory and Mrs Lunn; and sits down with folded arms, resolved not to budge*].

GREGORY. Oh! Indeed! Oh, all right. If you come to that— [*He crosses to Mrs Juno; plants a chair by her side; and sits down with equal determination*].

JUNO. Now we are both equally guilty.

GREGORY. Pardon me. I'm not guilty.

JUNO. In intention. Dont quibble. You were guilty in intention, as I was.

GREGORY. No. I should rather describe myself as being guilty in fact, but not in intention.

<table>
<tr><td>JUNO
MRS JUNO
MRS LUNN</td><td>rising and
exclaiming
simultaneously</td><td>What!
No, really—
Gregory!</td></tr>
</table>

GREGORY. Yes: I maintain that I am responsible for my intentions only, and not for reflex actions over which I have no control. [*Mrs Juno sits down, ashamed*]. I promised my mother that I would never tell a lie, and that I would never make love to a married woman. I never have told a lie—

MRS LUNN [*remonstrating*] Gregory! [*She sits down again*].

GREGORY. I say never. On many occasions I have resorted to prevarication; but on great occasions I have always told the truth. I regard this as a great occasion; and I wont be intimidated into breaking my promise. I solemnly declare that I did not know until this evening that Mrs Juno was married. She will bear me out when I say that from that moment my intentions were strictly and resolutely honorable; though my conduct, which I could not control and am therefore not responsible for, was disgraceful—or would have been had this gentleman not walked in and begun making love to my wife under my very nose.

JUNO [*flinging himself back into his chair*] Well, I like this!

MRS LUNN. Really, darling, theres no use in the pot calling the kettle black.

GREGORY. When you say darling, may I ask which of us you are addressing?

MRS LUNN. I really dont know. I'm getting hopelessly confused.

JUNO. Why dont you let my wife say something? I dont think she ought to be thrust into the background like this.

MRS LUNN. I'm sorry, I'm sure. Please excuse me, dear.

MRS JUNO [*thoughtfully*] I dont know what to say. I must think over it. I have always been rather severe on this sort of thing; but when it came to the point I didnt behave as I thought I should behave. I didnt intend to be wicked; but somehow or other, Nature, or whatever you choose to call it, didnt take much notice of my intentions. [*Gregory instinctively seeks her hand and presses it*]. And I really did think, Tops, that I was the only woman in the world for you.

JUNO [*cheerfully*] Oh, thats all right, my precious. Mrs Lunn thought she was the only woman in the world for him.

GREGORY [*reflectively*] So she is, in a sort of way.

JUNO [*flaring up*] And so is my wife. Dont you set up to be a better husband than I am; for youre not. Ive owned I'm wrong. You havnt.

MRS LUNN. Are you sorry, Gregory?

GREGORY [*perplexed*] Sorry?

MRS LUNN. Yes, sorry. I think it's time for you to say youre sorry, and to make friends with Mr Juno before we all dine together.

GREGORY. Seraphita; I promised my mother—

MRS JUNO [*involuntarlly*] Oh, bother your mother! [*Recovering herself*] I beg your pardon.

GREGORY. A promise is a promise. I cant tell a deliberate lie. I know I ought to be sorry; but the flat fact is that I'm not sorry. I find that in this business, somehow or other, there is a disastrous separation between my moral principles and my conduct.

JUNO. Theres nothing disastrous about it. It doesnt matter about your conduct if your principles are all right.

GREGORY. Bosh! It doesnt matter about your principles if your conduct is all right.

JUNO. But your conduct isnt all right; and my principles are.

GREGORY. Whats the good of your principles being right if they wont work?

JUNO. They will work, sir, if you exercise self-sacrifice.

GREGORY. Oh yes: if, if, if. You know jolly well that self-sacrifice doesnt work either when you really want a thing. How much have you sacrificed yourself, pray?

MRS LUNN. Oh, a great deal, Gregory. Dont be rude. Mr Juno is a very nice man: he has been most attentive to me on the voyage.

GREGORY. And Mrs Juno's a very nice woman. She oughtnt to be; but she is.

JUNO. Why oughtnt she to be a nice woman, pray?

GREGORY. I mean she oughtnt to be nice to me. And you oughtnt to be nice to my wife. And your wife oughtnt to like me. And my wife oughtnt to like you. And if they do, they oughtnt to go on liking us. And I oughtnt to like your wife; and you oughtnt to like mine; and if we do, we oughtnt to go on liking them. But we do, all of us. We oughtnt; but we do.

JUNO. But, my dear boy, if we admit we are in the wrong

wheres the harm of it? We're not perfect; but as long as we keep the ideal before us—

GREGORY. How?

JUNO. By admitting we're wrong.

MRS LUNN [*springing up, out of patience, and pacing round the lounge intolerantly*] Well, really, I must have my dinner. These two men, with their morality, and their promises to their mothers, and their admissions that they were wrong, and their sinning and suffering, and their going on at one another as if it meant anything, or as if it mattered, are getting on my nerves. [*Stooping over the back of the chesterfield to address Mrs Juno*] If you will be so very good, my dear, as to take my sentimental husband off my hands occasionally, I shall be more than obliged to you: I'm sure you can stand more male sentimentality than I can. [*Sweeping away to the fireplace*] I, on my part, will do my best to amuse your excellent husband when you find him tiresome.

JUNO. I call this polyandry.

MRS LUNN. I wish you wouldnt call innocent things by offensive names, Mr Juno. What do you call your own conduct?

JUNO [*rising*] I tell you I have admitted—

<table>
<tr><td>GREGORY</td><td rowspan="3">together</td><td>Whats the good of keeping on at that?</td></tr>
<tr><td>MRS JUNO</td><td>Oh, not that again, please.</td></tr>
<tr><td>MRS LUNN</td><td>Tops: I'll scream if you say that again.</td></tr>
</table>

JUNO. Oh, well, if you wont listen to me—! [*He sits down again*].

MRS JUNO. What is the position now exactly? [*Mrs Lunn shrugs her shoulders and gives up the conundrum. Gregory looks at Juno. Juno turns away his head huffily*]. I mean, what are we going to do?

MRS LUNN. What would you advise, Mr Juno?

JUNO. I should advise you to divorce your husband.

MRS LUNN. You want me to drag your wife into court and disgrace her?

JUNO. No: I forgot that. Excuse me; but for the moment I thought I was married to you.

GREGORY. I think we had better let bygones be bygones. [*To Mrs Juno, very tenderly*] You will forgive me, wont you? Why should you let a moment's forgetfulness embitter all our future life?

MRS JUNO. But it's Mrs Lunn who has to forgive you.

GREGORY. Oh, dash it, I forgot. This is getting ridiculous.

MRS LUNN. I'm getting hungry.

MRS JUNO. Do you really mind, Mrs Lunn?

MRS LUNN. My dear Mrs Juno, Gregory is one of those terribly uxorious men who ought to have ten wives. If any really nice woman will take him off my hands for a day or two occasionally, I shall be greatly obliged to her.

GREGORY. Seraphita: you cut me to the soul. [*He weeps*].

MRS LUNN. Serve you right! Youd think it quite proper if it cut me to the soul.

MRS JUNO. Am I to take Sibthorpe off your hands too, Mrs Lunn?

JUNO [*rising*] Do you suppose I'll allow this?

MRS JUNO. Youve admitted that youve done wrong, Tops. Whats the use of your allowing or not allowing after that?

JUNO. I do not admit that I have been wrong. I admit that what I did was wrong.

GREGORY. Can you explain the distinction?

JUNO. It's quite plain to anyone but an imbecile. If you tell me Ive done something wrong you insult me. But if you say that something that I did is wrong you simply raise a question of morals. I tell you flatly if you say I did anything wrong you will have to fight me. In fact I think we ought to fight anyhow. I dont particularly want to; but I feel that England expects us to.

GREGORY. I wont fight. If you beat me my wife would share my humiliation. If I beat you, she would sympathize with you and loathe me for my brutality.

MRS LUNN. Not to mention that as we are human beings and not reindeer or barndoor fowl, if two men presumed to fight for us we couldnt decently ever speak to either of them again.

GREGORY. Besides, neither of us could beat the other, as we neither of us know how to fight. We should only blacken each other's eyes and make fools of ourselves.

JUNO. I dont admit that. Every Englishman can use his fists.

GREGORY. Youre an Englishman. Can you use yours?

JUNO. I presume so: I never tried.

MRS JUNO. You never told me you couldnt fight, Tops. I thought you were an accomplished boxer.

JUNO. My precious: I never gave you any ground for such a belief.

MRS JUNO. You always talked as if it were a matter of course. You spoke with the greatest contempt of men who didnt kick other men downstairs.

JUNO. Well, I cant kick Mr Lunn downstairs. We're on the ground floor.

MRS JUNO. You could throw him into the harbor.

GREGORY. Do you want me to be thrown into the harbor?

MRS JUNO. No: I only want to shew Tops that he's making a ghastly fool of himself.

GREGORY [*rising and prowling disgustedly between the chesterfield and the windows*] We're all making fools of ourselves.

JUNO [*following him*] Well, if we're not to fight, I must insist at least on your never speaking to my wife again.

GREGORY. Does my speaking to your wife do you any harm?

JUNO. No. But it's the proper course to take. [*Emphatically*] We must behave with some sort of decency.

MRS LUNN. And are you never going to speak to me again, Mr Juno?

JUNO. I'm prepared to promise never to do so. I think your husband has a right to demand that. Then if I speak to you after, it will not be his fault. It will be a breach of my promise; and I shall not attempt to defend my conduct.

GREGORY [*facing him*] I shall talk to your wife as often as she'll let me.

MRS JUNO. I have no objection to your speaking to me, Mr Lunn.

JUNO. Then I shall take steps.

GREGORY. What steps?

JUNO. Steps. Measures. Proceedings. Such steps as may seem advisable.

MRS LUNN [*to Mrs. Juno*] Can your husband afford a scandal, Mrs Juno?

MRS JUNO. No.

MRS LUNN. Neither can mine.

GREGORY. Mrs Juno: I'm very sorry I let you in for all this. I dont know how it is that we contrive to make feelings like ours, which seem to me to be beautiful and sacred feelings, and which lead to such interesting and exciting adventures, end in vulgar squabbles and degrading scenes.

JUNO. I decline to admit that my conduct has been vulgar or degrading.

GREGORY. I promised—

JUNO. Look here, old chap: I dont say a word against your mother; and I'm sorry she's dead; but really, you know, most women are mothers; and they all die some time or other; yet that doesnt make them infallible authorities on morals, does it?

GREGORY. I was about to say so myself. Let me add that if you do things merely because you think some other fool expects you to do them, and he expects you to do them because he thinks you expect him to expect you to do them, it will end in everybody doing what nobody wants to do, which is in my opinion a silly state of things.

JUNO. Lunn: I love your wife; and thats all about it.

GREGORY. Juno: I love yours. What then?

JUNO. Clearly she must never see you again.

MRS JUNO. Why not?

JUNO. Why not! My love: I'm surprised at you.

MRS JUNO. Am I to speak only to men who dislike me?

JUNO. Yes: I think that is, properly speaking, a married woman's duty.

MRS JUNO. Then I wont do it: thats flat. I like to be liked. I liked to be loved. I want everyone round me to love me. I dont want to meet or speak to anyone who doesnt like me.

JUNO. But, my precious, this is the most horrible immorality.

MRS LUNN. I dont intend to give up meeting you, Mr Juno. You amuse me very much. I dont like being loved: it bores me. But I do like to be amused.

JUNO. I hope we shall meet very often. But I hope also we shall not defend our conduct.

MRS JUNO [*rising*] This is unendurable. Weve all been flirting. Need we go on footling about it?

JUNO [*huffily*] I dont know what you call footling—

MRS JUNO [*cutting him short*] You do. Youre footling. Mr Lunn is footling. Cant we admit that we're human and have done with it?

JUNO. I have admitted it all along. I—

MRS JUNO [*almost screaming*] Then stop footling. [*The dinner gong sounds*].

MRS LUNN [*rising*] Thank heaven! Lets go into dinner. Gregory: take in Mrs Juno.

GREGORY. But surely I ought to take in our guest, and not my own wife.

MRS LUNN. Well, Mrs Juno is not your wife, is she?

GREGORY. Oh, of course: I beg your pardon. I'm hopelessly confused. [*He offers his arm to Mrs Juno, rather apprehensively*].

MRS JUNO. You seem quite afraid of me. [*She takes his arm*].

GREGORY. I am. I simply adore you. [*They go out together; and as they pass through the door he turns and says in a ringing voice to the other couple*] I have said to Mrs Juno that I simply adore her. [*He takes her out defiantly*].

MRS LUNN [*calling after him*] Yes, dear. She's a darling. [*To Juno*] Now, Sibthorpe.

JUNO [*giving her his arm gallantly*] You have called me Sibthorpe! Thank you. I think Lunn's conduct fully justifies me in allowing you to do it.

MRS LUNN. Yes: I think you may let yourself go now.

JUNO. Seraphita: I worship you beyond expression.

MRS LUNN. Sibthorpe: you amuse me beyond description. Come. [*They go in to dinner together*].

THE ADMIRABLE BASHVILLE

OR

CONSTANCY UNREWARDED

BEING THE NOVEL OF CASHEL BYRON'S PROFESSION DONE INTO A STAGE PLAY IN THREE ACTS AND IN BLANK VERSE

The Admirable Bashville was first produced at Covent Garden, London, on 14 December 1902, with the following cast:

LYDIA	*Miss Zimmerman*
CASHEL BYRON	*W. R. Titterton*
MELLISH	*Cecil Chesterton*
LUCIAN	*Duncan Williams*
BASHVILLE	*Gerald Bishop*
CETEWAYO	*Mr. Oddam*
PARADISE	*Not named*
LORD WORTHINGTON	*Not named*
MASTER OF THE REVELS	*Not named*
A POLICEMAN	*John Kirby*
ADELAIDE GISBORNE	*Miss Salom*

PREFACE TO THE ADMIRABLE BASHVILLE

It may be asked why I wrote The Admirable Bashville in blank verse. My answer is that the operation of the copyright law of that time (now happily superseded) left me only a week to write it in. Blank verse is so childishly easy and expeditious (hence, by the way, Shakespear's copious output), that by adopting it I was enabled to do within the week what would have cost me a month in prose.

Besides, I am fond of blank verse. Not nineteenth century blank verse, of course, nor indeed, with a very few exceptions, any post-Shakespearean blank verse. Nay, not Shakespearean blank verse itself later than the histories. I am quite sure that any one who is to recover the charm of blank verse must go back frankly to its beginnings, and start a literary pre-Raphaelite Brotherhood. I like the melodious sing-song, the clear simple one-line and two-line sayings, and the occasional rhymed tags, like the half closes in an eighteenth century symphony, in Peele, Kyd, Greene, and the histories of Shakespear. Accordingly, I poetasted The Admirable Bashville in the primitive Elizabethan style. And lest the literary connoisseurs should declare that there was not a single correct line in all my three acts, I stole or paraphrased a few from Marlowe and Shakespear (not to mention Henry Carey); so that if any man dared quote me derisively, he should do so in peril of inadvertently lighting on a purple patch from Hamlet or Faustus.

I also endeavored in this little play to prove that I was not the heartless creature some of my critics took me for. I observed the established laws of stage popularity and probability. I simplified the character of the heroine, and summed up her sweetness in the one sacred word: Love. I gave consistency to the heroism of Cashel. I paid to Morality, in the final scene, the tribute of poetic justice. I restored to Patriotism its usual place on the stage, and gracefully acknowledged The Throne as the fountain of social honor. I paid particular attention to the construction of the play, which will be found equal in this respect to the best contemporary models.

And the result was that the British playgoer, to whom Elizabethan English is a dead language, only half understood nine-tenths of the play, and applauded the other tenth (the big speeches) with a seriousness that was far funnier than any burlesque.

The play, by the way, should be performed on an Elizabethan stage, with traverses for the indoor scenes, and with only one interval after the second act.

* * * * * *

On reading over the above after a lapse of thirty years I am not quite so sure as I was that Elizabethan English may not again become a living language to the ordinary playgoer. To people who never read anything but newspapers and popular magazines, a good deal of Shakespear's more euphuistic blank verse is hardly more intelligible than classical Greek. Even actors may be heard repeating it by rote with an air that persuades the public that they understand what they are saying; but it cannot impose any such illusion on a professionally skilled listener.

Then there are the people who do not go to Protestant churches nor read anything at all, and consequently understand no English except modern vernacular English. This class is by no means a negligible one even in the theatre; for it includes a large body of intelligent manual and open air workers and sportsmen who, though after their day's exertions they fall asleep in less than a minute if they sit down with an open book in their hands, can be kept awake and alert very effectually in the theatre by a play. Only, it must be a play in the vernacular. Otherwise it does not exist for them except as an incomprehensible bore.

There was a time when not only the theatres but the newspapers addressed themselves to the literate alone. Hunt up an old melodrama (say Sweeny Todd the Demon Barber of Fleet Street) or an old newspaper file; and you will at once see that the writers of the play and of the contemporary leading articles, though they may have been the seediest of Bohemians, had learnt Latin grammar and read books written by persons similarly schooled. They had literally the benefit of clergy, and wrote accordingly. With the advent of compulsory education sixty years ago, and the creation thereby of a class which could read and write, but had no Latin and less Greek, newspapers and plays alike soon came to be written by illiterate masters of the vernacular; and I myself welcomed the change and discarded my early very classical style for a vernacular one. Nowadays, when I read typewritten plays by young authors, as I sometimes have occasion to do, I find in them such illiteracies as He exits, She exits, They exit etc. etc. Chapman, who wrote all his stage directions in Latin, or Ben Jonson, who deplored the slenderness of Shakespear's classical education, would have risen up and roared for a birchrod to castigate such execrable solecisms. By the end of the nineteenth century the press and the theatre had lost all their Latinity; and this was why, whenever The Admirable Bashville was performed, men of letters like Maurice Hewlett would chuckle delightedly over it almost line by line, whilst the ordinary playgoers would listen with a puzzled and troubled stare, wondering what on earth it was all about and how they ought to take it, and the unfortunate persons who had been forced to "get up Shakespear" as part of an academic course on English literature, sat with a scowl of malignant hatred that poisoned the atmosphere. When Bashville was followed by a piece in the vernacular the relief of the audience was so great that there was always a burst of applause at the very first sentence.

And yet, whenever the meaning of the words was clear, the listeners shewed unmistakably that they liked hyperbolical rhetoric and deliberately artificial language. My parodies of the Elizabethan mannerism, and funny echoes of pet lines from the Elizabethan playwrights were, as such, quite lost on them; but Ben Webster brought down the house with Cashel Byron's declamatory repudiation of the name of gentleman, and James Hearn's lamentation over the tragedy of Cetewayo came off, not as a mockery, but as genuine tragedy, which indeed it also is. It was the literary fun that proved a mere puzzle, in spite of the acting of casts which included such accomplished comedians as Charles Quatermaine, William Wyes, Lennox Pawle, Henrietta Watson, Marie Lohr, and Fanny Brough.

Another significant fact pointed in the same direction. In no country is the worship of the old authorized version of the Bible carried to greater lengths than in the United States of America. To alter a single word of it was, it was believed, to incur the curse in the last chapter of Revelations. Even in England the very timid official revision of 1885 shocked our native Fundamentalists (a ridiculous but convenient name not then invented). Yet it was in the United States that the ministers of religion first found themselves compelled to produce versions in modern vernacular and journalese under stress of the flat fact that their flocks often could not understand the old authorized version, and always found the style so artificial that though it could produce an unintelligent reverence it brought no intimate conviction to the reader.

Sometimes, however, the simple and direct passages were not sentimental enough to satisfy people whose minds were steeped in modern literary sob stuff. For instance, such bald statements about Barabbas as that he was a robber, or that he had killed a certain man in a sedition, quite failed to interest anyone in him; but when Marie Corelli expanded this concise information into a novel in her own passionate and richly colored style it sold like hot cakes.

I must make a personal confession in this matter. Though I was saturated with the Bible and with Shakespear before I was ten years old, and the only grammar I ever learned was Latin grammar, so that Elizabethan English became a mother tongue to me, yet when I first read such vivid and unaffected modern versions as Dr. James Moffatt's New Translation of the New Testament I at once got from them so many lights on the Bible narratives which I had missed in the authorized version that I said to myself "Some day I will translate Hamlet into modern vernacular English." But indeed if the alienation of our young from Elizabethan English continues it will be necessary to produce revised versions not only of Shakespear but of Sir Walter Scott and even of my own early novels.

Still, a revival of Elizabethan literature may be possible. If I, as an Irish child in the eighteen-sixties, could without enforced study become so familiar with it that I had some difficulty as a journalist later on in getting rid of it, it must be possible for the same thing to occur to an English child in the nineteen-sixties. The Elizabethan style has many charms for imaginative children. It is bloody, bombastic, violent, senselessly pretentious, barbarous and childish in its humor, and full of music. In short, the taste for it, as anyone can observe at the Old Vic or the Stratford Festivals, is essentially half childish, half musical. To acquire it, all that is necessary is access to it. Now the opportunities for such access are enormously wider than they used to be. Of course as long as we persist in stuffing Shakespear and the Bible down our children's throats with threats of condign punishment if they fail to answer silly questions about them, they will continue to be loathed as they very largely are at present. But if our children, when they have been simply taught to read, have plenty of dramatically illustrated Bibles and Shakespears left in their way, with the illustrated passages printed under the pictures, it will soon be possible to find a general audience which can laugh at The Admirable Bashville as heartily as Maurice Hewlett did, and for repertory theatres to amuse themselves and their congregations with occasional performances of Carey's Chrononhotonthologos, Fielding's Tom Thumb, and even Bombastes Furioso.

I shall not here raise the question of whether such a revival is desirable. It would carry me too far and plunge me too deep for a volume of trifles and tomfooleries. But as the Elizabethan style is unquestionably both musical and powerful, I may at least say that it is better to have a sense of it and a fancy for it than to have no sense of style or literary fancy at all.

THE ADMIRABLE BASHVILLE: OR, CONSTANCY UNREWARDED

ACT I

A glade in Wiltstoken Park

Enter LYDIA

LYDIA. Ye leafy breasts and warm protecting wings
Of mother trees that hatch our tender souls,
And from the well of Nature in our hearts
Thaw the intolerable inch of ice
That bears the weight of all the stamping world,
Hear ye me sing to solitude that I,
Lydia Carew, the owner of these lands,
Albeit most rich, most learned, and most wise,
Am yet most lonely. What are riches worth
When wisdom with them comes to shew the purse bearer
That life remains unpurchasable? Learning
Learns but one lesson: doubt! To excel all
Is, to be lonely. Oh, ye busy birds,
Engrossed with real needs, ye shameless trees
With arms outspread in welcome of the sun,
Your minds, bent singly to enlarge your lives,
Have given you wings and raised your delicate heads
High heavens above us crawlers.

A rook sets up a great cawing; and the other birds chatter loudly as a gust of wind sets the branches swaying. She makes as though she would shew them her sleeves.

Lo, the leaves
That hide my drooping boughs! Mock me—poor maid!—
Deride with joyous comfortable chatter
These stolen feathers. Laugh at me, the clothed one.
Laugh at the mind fed on foul air and books.

Books! Art! And Culture! Oh, I shall go mad.
Give me a mate that never heard of these,
A sylvan god, tree born in heart and sap;
Or else, eternal maidhood be my hap.

Another gust of wind and bird-chatter. She sits on the mossy root of an oak and buries her face in her hands. Cashel Byron, in a white singlet and breeches, comes through the trees.

CASHEL. Whats this? Whom have we here? A woman!
LYDIA [*looking up*] Yes.
CASHEL. You have no business here. I have. Away!
Women distract me. Hence!
LYDIA. Bid you me hence?
I am upon mine own ground. Who are you?
I take you for a god, a sylvan god.
This place is mine: I share it with the birds,
The trees, the sylvan gods, the lovely company
Of haunted solitudes.
CASHEL. A sylvan god!
A goat-eared image! Do your statues speak?
Walk? heave the chest with breath? or like a feather
Lift you—like this? [*He sets her on her feet.*
LYDIA [*panting*] You take away my breath!
Youre strong. Your hands off, please. Thank you. Farewell.
CASHEL. Before you go: when shall we meet again?
LYDIA. Why should we meet again?
CASHEL. Who knows? We shall.
That much I know by instinct. Whats your name?
LYDIA. Lydia Carew.
CASHEL. Lydia's a pretty name.
Where do you live?
LYDIA. I' the castle.
CASHEL [*thunderstruck*] Do not say
You are the lady of this great domain.
LYDIA. I am.
CASHEL. Accursed luck! I took you for
The daughter of some farmer. Well, your pardon.
I came too close: I looked too deep. Farewell.

LYDIA. I pardon that. Now tell me who you are.
CASHEL. Ask me not whence I come, nor what I am.
You are the lady of the castle. I
Have but this hard and blackened hand to live by.
LYDIA. I have felt its strength and envied you. Your name?
I have told you mine.
CASHEL. My name is Cashel Byron.
LYDIA. I never heard the name; and yet you utter it
As men announce a celebrated name.
Forgive my ignorance.
CASHEL. I bless it, Lydia.
I have forgot your other name.
LYDIA. Carew.
Cashel's a pretty name too.
MELLISH [*calling through the wood*] Coo-ee! Byron!
CASHEL. A thousand curses! Oh, I beg you, go.
This is a man you must not meet.
MELLISH [*further off*] Coo-ee!
LYDIA. He's losing us. What does he in my woods?
CASHEL. He is a part of what I am. What that is
You must not know. It would end all between us.
And yet there's no dishonor in't: your lawyer,
Who let your lodge to me, will vouch me honest.
I am ashamed to tell you what I am—
At least, as yet. Some day, perhaps.
MELLISH [*nearer*] Coo-ee!
LYDIA. His voice is nearer. Fare you well, my tenant.
When next your rent falls due, come to the castle.
Pay me in person. Sir: your most obedient.
[*She curtsies and goes.*
CASHEL. Lives in this castle! Owns this park! A lady
Marry a prizefighter! Impossible.
And yet the prizefighter must marry her.

Enter MELLISH

Ensanguined swine, whelped by a doggish dam,
Is this thy park, that thou, with voice obscene,
Fillst it with yodeled yells, and screamst my name

For all the world to know that Cashel Byron
Is training here for combat.

MELLISH. Swine you me?
Ive caught you, have I? You have found a woman.
Let her shew here again, I'll set the dog on her.
I will. I say it. And my name's Bob Mellish.

CASHEL. Change thy initial and be truly hight
Hellish. As for thy dog, why dost thou keep one
And bark thyself? Begone.

MELLISH. I'll not begone.
You shall come back with me and do your duty—
Your duty to your backers, do you hear?
You have not punched the bag this blesséd day.

CASHEL. The putrid bag engirdled by thy belt
Invites my fist.

MELLISH [*weeping*] Ingrate! O wretched lot!
Who would a trainer be? O Mellish, Mellish,
Trainer of heroes, builder-up of brawn,
Vicarious victor, thou createst champions
That quickly turn thy tyrants. But beware:
Without me thou art nothing. Disobey me,
And all thy boasted strength shall fall from thee.
With flaccid muscles and with failing breath
Facing the fist of thy more faithful foe,
I'll see thee on the grass cursing the day
Thou didst forswear thy training.

CASHEL. Noisome quack
That canst not from thine own abhorrent visage
Take one carbuncle, thou contaminat'st
Even with thy presence my untainted blood.
Preach abstinence to rascals like thyself
Rotten with surfeiting. Leave me in peace.
This grove is sacred: thou profanest it.
Hence! I have business that concerns thee not.

MELLISH. Ay, with your woman. You will lose your fight.
Have you forgot your duty to your backers?
Oh, what a sacred thing your duty is!
What makes a man but duty? Where were we

Without our duty? Think of Nelson's words:
England expects that every man—

CASHEL. Shall twaddle
About his duty. Mellish: at no hour
Can I regard thee wholly without loathing;
But when thou playst the moralist, by Heaven,
My soul flies to my fist, my fist to thee;
And never did the Cyclops' hammer fall
On Mars's armor—but enough of that.
It does remind me of my mother.

MELLISH. Ah,
Byron, let it remind thee. Once I heard
An old song: it ran thus. [*He clears his throat*] Ahem, Ahem!
[*Sings*]—They say there is no other
Can take the place of mother—
I am out o' voice: forgive me; but remember:
Thy mother—were that sainted woman here—
Would say, Obey thy trainer.

CASHEL. Now, by Heaven,
Some fate is pushing thee upon thy doom.
Canst thou not hear thy sands as they run out?
They thunder like an avalanche. Old man:
Two things I hate, my duty and my mother.
Why dost thou urge them both upon me now?
Presume not on thine age and on thy nastiness.
Vanish, and promptly.

MELLISH. Can I leave thee here
Thus thinly clad, exposed to vernal dews?
Come back with me, my son, unto our lodge.

CASHEL. Within this breast a fire is newly lit
Whose glow shall sun the dew away, whose radiance
Shall make the orb of night hang in the heavens
Unnoticed, like a glow-worm at high noon.

MELLISH. Ah me, ah me, where wilt thou spend the night?

CASHEL. Wiltstoken's windows wandering beneath,
Wiltstoken's holy bell hearkening,
Wiltstoken's lady loving breathlessly.

MELLISH. The lady of the castle! Thou art mad.

CASHEL. Tis thou art mad to trifle in my path.
Thwart me no more. Begone.

MELLISH. My boy, my son,
I'd give my heart's blood for thy happiness.
Thwart thee, my son! Ah no. I'll go with thee.
I'll brave the dews. I'll sacrifice my sleep.
I am old—no matter: ne'er shall it be said
Mellish deserted thee.

CASHEL. You resolute gods
That will not spare this man, upon your knees
Take the disparity twixt his age and mine.
Now from the ring to the high judgment seat
I step at your behest. Bear you me witness
This is not Victory, but Execution.

He solemnly projects his fist with colossal force against the waistcoat of Mellish, who doubles up like a folded towel, and lies without sense or motion.

And now the night is beautiful again.

[*The castle clock strikes the hour in the distance.*

Hark! Hark! Hark! Hark! Hark! Hark! Hark! Hark! Hark!
Hark!
It strikes in poetry. Tis ten o'clock.
Lydia: to thee!

He steals off towards the castle. Mellish stirs and groans.

ACT II

SCENE I

London. A room in Lydia's house

Enter LYDIA *and* LUCIAN

LYDIA. Welcome, dear cousin, to my London house.
Of late you have been chary of your visits.

LUCIAN. I have been greatly occupied of late.
The minister to whom I act as scribe
In Downing Street was born in Birmingham,

And, like a thoroughbred commercial statesman,
Splits his infinitives, which I, poor slave,
Must reunite, though all the time my heart
Yearns for my gentle coz's company.

LYDIA. Lucian: there is some other reason. Think!
Since England was a nation every mood
Her scribes with adverbs recklessly have split,
But thine avoidance dates from yestermonth.

LUCIAN. There is a man I like not haunts this house.

LYDIA. Thou speakst of Cashel Byron?

LUCIAN. Aye, of him.
Hast thou forgotten that eventful night
When as we gathered were at Hoskyn House
To hear a lecture by Herr Abendgasse,
He placed a single finger on my chest,
And I, ensorceled, would have sunk supine
Had not a chair received my falling form.

LYDIA. Pooh! That was but by way of illustration.

LUCIAN. What right had he to illustrate his point
Upon my person? Was I his assistant
That he should try experiments on me
As Simpson did on his with chloroform?
Now, by the cannon balls of Galileo
He hath unmanned me: all my nerve is gone.
This very morning my official chief,
Tapping with friendly forefinger this button,
Levelled me like a thunderstricken elm
Flat upon the Colonial Office floor.

LYDIA. Fancies, coz.

LUCIAN. Fancies! Fits! the chief said fits!
Delirium tremens! the chlorotic dance
Of Vitus! What could anyone have thought?
Your ruffian friend hath ruined me. By Heaven,
I tremble at a thumbnail. Give me drink.

LYDIA. What ho, without there! Bashville.

BASHVILLE [*without*] Coming, madam.

Enter BASHVILLE

LYDIA. My cousin ails, Bashville. Procure some wet.

[*Exit* BASHVILLE.

LUCIAN. Some wet!!! Where learnt you that atrocious word? This is the language of a flower-girl.

LYDIA. True. It is horrible. Said I "Some wet"?
I meant, some drink. Why did I say "Some wet"?
Am I ensorceled too? "Some wet"! Fie! fie!
I feel as though some hateful thing had stained me.
Oh, Lucian, how could I have said "Some wet"?

LUCIAN. The horrid conversation of this man
Hath numbed thy once unfailing sense of fitness.

LYDIA. Nay, he speaks very well: he's literate:
Shakespear he quotes unconsciously.

LUCIAN. And yet
Anon he talks pure pothouse.

Enter BASHVILLE

BASHVILLE. Sir: your potion.

LUCIAN. Thanks. [*He drinks*]. I am better.

A NEWSBOY [*calling without*] Extra special
Star! Result of the great fight! Name of the winner!

LYDIA. Who calls so loud?

BASHVILLE. The papers, madam.

LYDIA. Why?
Hath ought momentous happened?

BASHVILLE. Madam: yes.

[*He produces a newspaper.*

All England for these thrilling paragraphs
A week has waited breathless.

LYDIA. Read them us.

BASHVILLE [*reading*] "At noon today, unknown to the police,
Within a thousand miles of Wormwood Scrubbs,
Th' Australian Champion and his challenger,
The Flying Dutchman, formerly engaged
I' the mercantile marine, fought to a finish.
Lord Worthington, the well-known sporting peer,
Was early on the scene."

LYDIA. Lord Worthington!

BASHVILLE. "The bold Ned Skene revisited the ropes
To hold the bottle for his quondam novice;
Whilst in the seaman's corner were assembled
Professor Palmer and the Chelsea Snob.
Mellish, whose epigastrium has been hurt,
'Tis said, by accident at Wiltstoken,
Looked none the worse in the Australian's corner.
The Flying Dutchman wore the Union Jack:
His colors freely sold amid the crowd;
But Cashel's well-known spot of white on blue—"

LYDIA. Whose, did you say?

BASHVILLE. Cashel's, my lady.

LYDIA. Lucian:
Your hand—a chair—

BASHVILLE. Madam: youre ill.

LYDIA. Proceed.
What you have read I do not understand;
Yet I will hear it through. Proceed.

LUCIAN. Proceed.

BASHVILLE. "But Cashel's well-known spot of white on blue
Was fairly rushed for. Time was called at twelve,
When, with a smile of confidence upon
His ocean-beaten mug—"

LYDIA. His mug?

LUCIAN [*explaining*] His face.

BASHVILLE [*continuing*] "The Dutchman came undaunted to the scratch,
But found the champion there already. Both
Most heartily shook hands, amid the cheers
Of their encouraged backers. Two to one
Was offered on the Melbourne nonpareil;
And soon, so fit the Flying Dutchman seemed,
Found takers everywhere. No time was lost
In getting to the business of the day.
The Dutchman led at once, and seemed to land
On Byron's dicebox; but the seaman's reach,

Too short for execution at long shots,
Did not get fairly home upon the ivory;
And Byron had the best of the exchange."

LYDIA. I do not understand. What were they doing?

LUCIAN. Fighting with naked fists.

LYDIA. Oh, horrible!
I'll hear no more. Or stay: how did it end?
Was Cashel hurt?

LUCIAN [*to Bashville*] Skip to the final round.

BASHVILLE. "Round Three: the rumors that had gone about
Of a breakdown in Byron's recent training
Seemed quite confirmed. Upon the call of time
He rose, and, looking anything but cheerful,
Proclaimed with every breath Bellows to Mend.
At this point six to one was freely offered
Upon the Dutchman; and Lord Worthington
Plunged at this figure till he stood to lose
A fortune should the Dutchman, as seemed certain,
Take down the number of the Panley boy.
The Dutchman, glutton as we know he is,
Seemed this time likely to go hungry. Cashel
Was clearly groggy as he slipped the sailor,
Who, not to be denied, followed him up,
Forcing the fighting mid tremendous cheers."

LYDIA. Oh stop—no more—or tell the worst at once.
I'll be revenged. Bashville: call the police.
This brutal sailor shall be made to know
There's law in England.

LUCIAN. Do not interrupt him:
Mine ears are thirsting. Finish, man. What next?

BASHVILLE. "Forty to one, the Dutchman's friends exclaimed.
Done, said Lord Worthington, who shewed himself
A sportsman every inch. Barely the bet
Was booked, when, at the reeling champion's jaw
The sailor, bent on winning out of hand,
Sent in his right. The issue seemed a cert,

When Cashel, ducking smartly to his left,
Cross-countered like a hundredweight of brick—"

LUCIAN. Death and damnation!

LYDIA. Oh, what does it mean?

BASHVILLE. "The Dutchman went to grass, a beaten man."

LYDIA. Hurrah! Hurrah! Hurrah! Oh, well done, Cashel!

BASHVILLE. "A scene of indescribable excitement
Ensued; for it was now quite evident
That Byron's grogginess had all along
Been feigned to make the market for his backers.
We trust this sample of colonial smartness
Will not find imitators on this side.
The losers settled up like gentlemen;
But many felt that Byron shewed bad taste
In taking old Ned Skene upon his back,
And, with Bob Mellish tucked beneath his oxter,
Sprinting a hundred yards to show the crowd
The perfect pink of his condition"—[*a knock*].

LYDIA [*turning pale*] Bashville.
Didst hear? A knock.

BASHVILLE. Madam: tis Byron's knock.
Shall I admit him?

LUCIAN. Reeking from the ring!
Oh, monstrous! Say youre out.

LYDIA. Send him away.
I will not see the wretch. How dare he keep
Secrets from ME? I'll punish him. Pray say
I'm not at home. [*Bashville turns to go*]. Yet stay. I am afraid
He will not come again.

LUCIAN. A consummation
Devoutly to be wished by any lady.
Pray, do you wish this man to come again?

LYDIA. No, Lucian. He hath used me very ill.
He should have told me. I will ne'er forgive him.
Say, Not at home.

BASHVILLE. Yes, madam. [*Exit.*

LYDIA. Stay—

LUCIAN [*stopping her*] No, Lydia:
You shall not countermand that proper order.
Oh, would you cast the treasure of your mind,
The thousands at your bank, and, above all,
Your unassailable social position
Before this soulless mass of beef and brawn.

LYDIA. Nay, coz: youre prejudiced.

CASHEL [*without*] Liar and slave!

LYDIA. What words were those?

LUCIAN. The man is drunk with slaughter.

Enter BASHVILLE *running: he shuts the door and locks it*

BASHVILLE. Save yourselves: at the staircase foot the champion
Sprawls on the mat, by trick of wrestler tripped;
But when he rises, woe betide us all!

LYDIA. Who bade you treat my visitor with violence?

BASHVILLE. He would not take my answer; thrust the door
Back in my face; gave me the lie i' th' throat;
Averred he felt your presence in his bones.
I said he should feel mine there too, and felled him;
Then fled to bar your door.

LYDIA. O lover's instinct!
He felt my presence. Well, let him come in.
We must not fail in courage with a fighter.
Unlock the door.

LUCIAN. Stop. Like all women, Lydia,
You have the courage of immunity.
To strike you were against his code of honor;
But me, above the belt, he may perform on
T' th' height of his profession. Also Bashville.

BASHVILLE. Think not of me, sir. Let him do his worst.
Oh, if the valor of my heart could weigh
The fatal difference twixt his weight and mine,
A second battle should he do this day:
Nay, though outmatched I be, let but my mistress
Give me the word: instant I'll take him on

Here—now—at catchweight. Better bite the carpet
A man, than fly, a coward.

LUCIAN. Bravely said:
I will assist you with the poker.

LYDIA. No:
I will not have him touched. Open the door.

BASHVILLE. Destruction knocks thereat. I smile, and open.

Bashville opens the door. Dead silence. Cashel enters, in tears. A solemn pause.

CASHEL. You know my secret?

LYDIA. Yes.

CASHEL. And thereupon
You bade your servant fling me from your door.

LYDIA. I bade my servant say I was not here.

CASHEL [*to Bashville*] Why didst thou better thy instruction, man?
Hadst thou but said, "She bade me tell thee this,"
Thoudst burst my heart. I thank thee for thy mercy.

LYDIA. Oh, Lucian, didst thou call him "drunk with slaughter"?
Canst thou refrain from weeping at his woe?

CASHEL [*to Lucian*] The unwritten law that shields the amateur
Against professional resentment, saves thee.
O coward, to traduce behind their backs
Defenceless prizefighters!

LUCIAN. Thou dost avow
Thou art a prizefighter.

CASHEL. It was my glory.
I had hoped to offer to my lady there
My belts, my championships, my heaped-up stakes,
My undefeated record; but I knew
Behind their blaze a hateful secret lurked.

LYDIA. Another secret?

LUCIAN. Is there worse to come?

CASHEL. Know ye not then my mother is an actress?

LUCIAN. How horrible!

LYDIA. Nay, nay: how interesting!

CASHEL. A thousand victories cannot wipe out
That birthstain. Oh, my speech bewrayeth it:
My earliest lesson was the player's speech
In Hamlet; and to this day I express myself
More like a mobled queen than like a man
Of flesh and blood. Well may your cousin sneer!
What's Hecuba to him or he to Hecuba?

LUCIAN. Injurious upstart: if by Hecuba
Thou pointest darkly at my lovely cousin,
Know that she is to me, and I to her,
What never canst thou be. I do defy thee;
And maugre all the odds thy skill doth give,
Outside I will await thee.

LYDIA. I forbid
Expressly any such duello. Bashville:
The door. Put Mr Webber in a hansom,
And bid the driver hie to Downing Street.
No answer: tis my will. [*Exeunt* LUCIAN *and* BASHVILLE.
And now, farewell.
You must not come again, unless indeed
You can some day look in my eyes and say:
Lydia: my occupation's gone.

CASHEL. Ah no:
It would remind you of my wretched mother.
O God, let me be natural a moment!
What other occupation can I try?
What would you have me be?

LYDIA. A gentleman.

CASHEL. A gentleman! Cashel Byron, stoop
To be the thing that bets on me! the fool
I flatter at so many coins a lesson!
The screaming creature who beside the ring
Gambles with basest wretches for my blood,
And pays with money that he never earned!
Let me die broken hearted rather!

LYDIA. But
You need not be an idle gentleman.

I call you one of Nature's gentlemen.
CASHEL. Thats the collection for the loser, Lydia.
I am not wont to need it. When your friends
Contest elections, and at foot o' th' poll
Rue their presumption, tis their wont to claim
A moral victory. In a sort they are
Nature's M.P.s. I am not yet so threadbare
As to accept these consolation stakes.
LYDIA. You are offended with me.
CASHEL. Yes I am.
I can put up with much; but—"Nature's gentleman"!
I thank your ladyship of Lyons, but
Must beg to be excused.
LYDIA. But surely, surely,
To be a prizefighter, and maul poor mariners
With naked knuckles, is no work for you.
CASHEL. Thou dost arraign the inattentive Fates
That weave my thread of life in ruder patterns
Than these that lie, antimacassarly,
Asprent thy drawing room. As well demand
Why I at birth chose to begin my life
A speechless babe, hairless, incontinent,
Hobbling upon all fours, a nurse's nuisance?
Or why I do propose to lose my strength,
To blanch my hair, to let the gums recede
Far up my yellowing teeth, and finally
Lie down and moulder in a rotten grave?
Only one thing more foolish could have been,
And that was to be born, not man, but woman.
This was thy folly, why rebuk'st thou mine?
LYDIA. These are not things of choice.
CASHEL. And did I choose
My quick divining eye, my lightning hand,
My springing muscle and untiring heart?
Did I implant the instinct in the race
That found a use for these, and said to me,
Fight for us, and be fame and fortune thine?
LYDIA. But there are other callings in the world.

CASHEL. Go tell thy painters to turn stockbrokers,
Thy poet friends to stoop oer merchants' desks
And pen prose records of the gains of greed.
Tell bishops that religion is outworn,
And that the Pampa to the horsebreaker
Opes new careers. Bid the professor quit
His fraudulent pedantries, and do i' the world
The thing he would teach others. Then return
To me and say: Cashel: they have obeyed;
And on that pyre of sacrifice I, too,
Will throw my championship.

LYDIA. But tis so cruel.

CASHEL. Is it so? I have hardly noticed that,
So cruel are all callings. Yet this hand,
That many a two days bruise hath ruthless given,
Hath kept no dungeon locked for twenty years,
Hath slain no sentient creature for my sport.
I am too squeamish for your dainty world,
That cowers behind the gallows and the lash,
The world that robs the poor, and with their spoil
Does what its tradesmen tell it. Oh, your ladies!
Sealskinned and egret-feathered; all defiance
To Nature; cowering if one say to them
"What will the servants think?" Your gentlemen!
Your tailor-tyrannized visitors of whom
Flutter of wing and singing in the wood
Make chickenbutchers. And your medicine men!
Groping for cures in the tormented entrails
Of friendly dogs. Pray have you asked all these
To change their occupations? Find you mine
So grimly crueller? I cannot breathe
An air so petty and so poisonous.

LYDIA. But find you not their manners very nice?

CASHEL. To me, perfection. Oh, they condescend
With a rare grace. Your duke, who condescends
Almost to the whole world, might for a Man
Pass in the eyes of those who never saw
The duke capped with a prince. See then, ye gods,
The duke turn footman, and his eager dame

Sink the great lady in the obsequious housemaid!
Oh, at such moments I could wish the Court
Had but one breadbasket, that with my fist
I could make all its windy vanity
Gasp itself out on the gravel. Fare you well.
I did not choose my calling; but at least
I can refrain from being a gentleman.

LYDIA. You say farewell to me without a pang.

CASHEL. My calling hath apprenticed me to pangs.
This is a rib-bender; but I can bear it.
It is a lonely thing to be a champion.

LYDIA. It is a lonelier thing to be a woman.

CASHEL. Be lonely then. Shall it be said of thee
That for his brawn thou misalliance mad'st
Wi' the Prince of Ruffians? Never. Go thy ways;
Or, if thou hast nostalgia of the mud,
Wed some bedoggéd wretch that on the slot
Of gilded snobbery, *ventre à terre,*
Will hunt through life with eager nose on earth
And hang thee thick with diamonds. I am rich;
But all my gold was fought for with my hands.

LYDIA. What dost thou mean by rich?

CASHEL. There is a man,
Hight Paradise, vaunted unconquerable,
Hath dared to say he will be glad to hear from me.
I have replied that none can hear from me
Until a thousand solid pounds be staked.
His friends have confidently found the money.
Ere fall of leaf that money shall be mine;
And then I shall posses ten thousand pounds.
I had hoped to tempt thee with that monstrous sum.

LYDIA. Thou silly Cashel, tis but a week's income.
I did propose to give thee three times that
For pocket money when we two were wed.

CASHEL. Give me my hat. I have been fooling here.
Now, by the Hebrew lawgiver, I thought
That only in America such revenues
Were decent deemed. Enough. My dream is dreamed.

Your gold weighs like a mountain on my chest.
Farewell.

LYDIA. The golden mountain shall be thine
The day thou quitst thy horrible profession.

CASHEL. Tempt me not, woman. It is honor calls.
Slave to the Ring I rest until the face
Of Paradise be changed.

Enter BASHVILLE

BASHVILLE. Madam, your carriage,
Ordered by you at two. Tis now half-past.

CASHEL. Sdeath! is it half-past two? The king! the king!

LYDIA. The king! What mean you?

CASHEL. I must meet a monarch
This very afternoon at Islington.

LYDIA. At Islington! You must be mad.

CASHEL. A cab!
Go call a cab; and let a cab be called;
And let the man that calls it be thy footman.

LYDIA. You are not well. You shall not go alone.
My carriage waits. I must accompany you.
I go to find my hat. [*Exit.*

CASHEL. Like Paracelsus,
Who went to find his soul. [*To Bashville*] And now, young man,
How comes it that a fellow of your inches,
So deft a wrestler and so bold a spirit,
Can stoop to be a flunkey? Call on me
On your next evening out. I'll make a man of you.
Surely you are ambitious and aspire—

BASHVILLE. To be a butler and draw corks; wherefore,
By Heaven, I will draw yours.

[*He hits Cashel on the nose, and runs out.*

CASHEL [*thoughtfully putting the side of his forefinger to his nose, and studying the blood on it*] Too quick for me!
There's money in this youth.

Re-enter LYDIA, *hatted and gloved*

LYDIA. O Heaven! you bleed.

CASHEL. Lend me a key or other frigid object,
That I may put it down my back, and staunch
The welling life stream.

LYDIA [*giving him her keys*] Oh, what have you done?

CASHEL. Flush on the boko napped your footman's left.

LYDIA. I do not understand.

CASHEL. True. Pardon me.
I have received a blow upon the nose
In sport from Bashville. Next, ablution; else
I shall be total gules. [*He hurries out.*

LYDIA. How well he speaks!
There is a silver trumpet in his lips
That stirs me to the finger ends. His nose
Dropt lovely color: tis a perfect blood.
I would twere mingled with mine own!

Enter BASHVILLE

What now?

BASHVILLE. Madam, the coachman can no longer wait:
The horses will take cold.

LYDIA. I do beseech him
A moment's grace. Oh, mockery of wealth!
The third class passenger unchidden rides
Whither and when he will: obsequious trams
Await him hourly: subterranean tubes
With tireless coursers whisk him through the town;
But we, the rich, are slaves to Houyhnhnms:
We wait upon their colds, and frowst all day
Indoors, if they but cough or spurn their hay.

BASHVILLE. Madam, an omnibus to Euston Road,
And thence t' th' Angel—

Enter CASHEL

LYDIA. Let us haste, my love:
The coachman is impatient.

CASHEL. Did he guess
He stays for Cashel Byron, he'd outwait

Pompei's sentinel. Let us away.
This day of deeds, as yet but half begun,
Must ended be in merrie Islington.
[*Exeunt* LYDIA *and* CASHEL.

BASHVILLE. Gods! how she hangs on's arm! I am alone.
Now let me lift the cover from my soul.
O wasted humbleness! Deluded diffidence!
How often have I said, Lie down, poor footman:
She'll never stoop to thee, rear as thou wilt
Thy powder to the sky. And now, by Heaven,
She stoops below me; condescends upon
This hero of the pothouse, whose exploits,
Writ in my character from my last place,
Would damn me into ostlerdom. And yet
Theres an eternal justice in it; for
By so much as the ne'er subduéd Indian
Excels the servile negro, doth this ruffian
Precedence take of me. *"Ich dien."* Damnation!
I serve. My motto should have been, "I scalp."
And yet I do not bear the yoke for gold.
Because I love her I have blacked her boots;
Because I love her I have cleaned her knives,
Doing in this the office of a boy,
Whilst, like the celebrated maid that milks
And does the meanest chares, Ive shared the passions
Of Cleopatra. It has been my pride
To give her place the greater altitude
By lowering mine, and of her dignity
To be so jealous that my cheek has flamed
Even at the thought of such a deep disgrace
As love for such a one as I would be
For such a one as she; and now! and now!
A prizefighter! O irony! O bathos!
To have made way for this! Oh, Bashville, Bashville:
Why hast thou thought so lowly of thyself,
So heavenly high of her? Let what will come,
My love must speak: twas my respect was dumb.

SCENE II

The Agricultural Hall in Islington, crowded with spectators. In the arena a throne, with a boxing ring before it. A balcony above on the right, occupied by persons of fashion: among others, Lydia and Lord Worthington.

Flourish. Enter LUCIAN *and* CETEWAYO, *with Chiefs in attendance*

CETEWAYO. Is this the Hall of Husbandmen?
LUCIAN. It is.
CETEWAYO. Are these anæmic dogs the English people?
LUCIAN. Mislike us not for our complexions,
The pallied liveries of the pall of smoke
Belched by the mighty chimneys of our factories,
And by the million patent kitchen ranges
Of happy English homes.
CETEWAYO. When first I came
I deemed those chimneys the fuliginous altars
Of some infernal god. I now perceive
The English dare not look upon the sky.
They are moles and owls: they call upon the soot
To cover them.
LUCIAN. You cannot understand
The greatness of this people, Cetewayo.
You are a savage, reasoning like a child.
Each pallid English face conceals a brain
Whose powers are proven in the works of Newton
And in the plays of the immortal Shakespear.
There is not one of all the thousands here
But, if you placed him naked in the desert,
Would presently construct a steam engine,
And lay a cable t' th' Antipodes.
CETEWAYO. Have I been brought a million miles by sea
To learn how men can lie! Know, Father Webber,
Men become civilized through twin diseases,
Terror and Greed to wit: these two conjoined
Become the grisly parents of Invention.

Why does the trembling white with frantic toil
Of hand and brain produce the magic gun
That slays a mile off, whilst the manly Zulu
Dares look his foe i' the face; fights foot to foot;
Lives in the present; drains the Here and Now;
Makes life a long reality, and death
A moment only; whilst your Englishman
Glares on his burning candle's winding-sheets,
Counting the steps of his approaching doom,
And in the murky corners ever sees
Two horrid shadows, Death and Poverty:
In the which anguish an unnatural edge
Comes on his frighted brain, which straight devises
Strange frauds by which to filch unearnéd gold,
Mad crafts by which to slay unfacéd foes,
Until at last his agonized desire
Makes possibility its slave. And then—
Horrible climax! All-undoing spite!—
Th' importunate clutching of the coward's hand
From wearied Nature Devastation's secrets
Doth wrest; when straight the brave black-livered man
Is blown explosively from off the globe;
And Death and Dread, with their white-livered slaves,
Oer-run the earth, and through their chattering teeth
Stammer the words "Survival of the Fittest."
Enough of this: I came not here to talk.
Thou sayest thou hast two white-faced ones who dare
Fight without guns, and spearless, to the death.
Let them be brought.

LUCIAN. They fight not to the death,
But under strictest rules: as, for example,
Half of their persons shall not be attacked;
Nor shall they suffer blows when they fall down,
Nor stroke of foot at any time. And, further,
That frequent opportunities of rest
With succor and refreshment be secured them.

CETEWAYO. Ye gods, what cowards! Zululand, my Zululand:

Personified Pusillanimity
Hath taen thee from the bravest of the brave!

LUCIAN. Lo the rude savage whose untutored mind
Cannot perceive self-evidence, and doubts
That Brave and English mean the self-same thing!

CETEWAYO. Well, well, produce these heroes. I surmise
They will be carried by their nurses, lest
Some barking dog or bumbling bee should scare them.

CETEWAYO *takes his state. Enter* PARADISE

LYDIA. What hateful wretch is this whose mighty thews
Presage destruction to his adversaries.

LORD WORTHINGTON. Tis Paradise.

LYDIA. He of whom Cashel spoke?
A dreadful thought ices my heart. Oh, why
Did Cashel leave us at the door?

Enter CASHEL

LORD WORTHINGTON. Behold!
The champion comes.

LYDIA. Oh, I could kiss him now
Here, before all the world. His boxing things
Render him most attractive. But I fear
Yon villain's fists may maul him.

WORTHINGTON. Have no fear.
Hark! the king speaks.

CETEWAYO. Ye sons of the white queen:
Tell me your names and deeds ere ye fall to.

PARADISE. Your royal highness, you beholds a bloke
What gets his living honest by his fists.
I may not have the polish of some toffs
As I could mention on; but up to now
No man has took my number down. I scale
Close on twelve stun; my age is twenty-three;
And at Bill Richardson's Blue Anchor pub
Am to be heard of any day by such
As likes the job. I dont know, governor,
As ennythink remains for me to say.

CETEWAYO. Six wives and thirty oxen shalt thou have
If on the sand thou leave thy foeman dead.
Methinks he looks full scornfully on thee.
[*To Cashel*] Ha! dost thou not so?

CASHEL. Sir, I do beseech you
To name the bone, or limb, or special place
Where you would have me hit him with this fist.

CETEWAYO. Thou hast a noble brow; but much I fear
Thine adversary will disfigure it.

CASHEL. Theres a divinity that shapes our ends
Rough hew them how we will. Give me the gloves.

THE MASTER OF THE REVELS. Paradise, a professor. Cashel Byron,
Also professor. Time! [*They spar.*

LYDIA. Eternity
It seems to me until this fight be done.

CASHEL. Dread monarch: this is called the upper cut,
And this is a hook-hit of mine own invention.
The hollow region where I plant this blow
Is called the mark. My left, you will observe,
I chiefly use for long shots: with my right
Aiming beside the angle of the jaw
And landing with a certain delicate screw
I without violence knock my foeman out.
Mark how he falls forward upon his face!
The rules allow ten seconds to get up;
And as the man is still quite silly, I
Might safely finish him; but my respect
For your most gracious majesty's desire
To see some further triumphs of the science
Of self-defence postpones awhile his doom.

PARADISE. How can a bloke do hisself proper justice
With pillows on his fists?

[*He tears off his gloves and attacks Cashel with his bare knuckles.*

THE CROWD. Unfair! The rules!

CETEWAYO. The joy of battle surges boiling up

And bids me join the mellay. Isandhlana
And Victory! [*He falls on the bystanders.*

THE CHIEFS. Victory and Isandhlana!

[*They run amok. General panic and stampede. The ring is swept away.*

LUCIAN. Forbear these most irregular proceedings.
Police! Police!

[*He engages Cetewayo with his umbrella. The balcony comes down with a crash. Screams from its occupants. Indescribable confusion.*

CASHEL [*dragging Lydia from the struggling heap*] My love, my love, art hurt?

LYDIA. No, no; but save my sore oermatchéd cousin.

A POLICEMAN. Give us a lead, sir. Save the English flag.
Africa tramples on it.

CASHEL. Africa!
Not all the continents whose mighty shoulders
The dancing diamonds of the seas bedeck
Shall trample on the blue with spots of white.
Now, Lydia, mark thy lover. [*He charges the Zulus.*

LYDIA. Hercules
Cannot withstand him. See: the king is down;
The tallest chief is up, heels over head,
Tossed corklike oer my Cashel's sinewy back;
And his lieutenant all deflated gasps
For breath upon the sand. The others fly.
In vain: his fist oer magic distances
Like a chameleon's tongue shoots to its mark;
And the last African upon his knees
Sues piteously for quarter. [*Rushing into Cashel's arms*]
Oh, my hero:
Thoust saved us all this day.

CASHEL. Twas all for thee.

CETEWAYO [*trying to rise*] Have I been struck by lightning?

LUCIAN. Sir, your conduct
Can only be described as most ungentlemanly.

POLICEMAN. One of the prone is white.

CASHEL. Tis Paradise.
POLICEMAN. He's choking: he has something in his mouth.
LYDIA [*to Cashel*] Oh Heaven! there is blood upon your hip.
Youre hurt.
CASHEL. The morsel in yon wretch's mouth
Was bitten out of me.
[*Sensation. Lydia screams and swoons in Cashel's arms.*

ACT III

Wiltstoken. A room in the Warren Lodge
Lydia at her writing-table

LYDIA. O Past and Present, how ye do conflict
As here I sit writing my father's life!
The autumn woodland woos me from without
With whispering of leaves and dainty airs
To leaves this fruitless haunting of the past.
My father was a very learnéd man.
I sometimes think I shall oldmaided be
Ere I unlearn the things he taught to me.

Enter POLICEMAN

POLICEMAN. Asking your ladyship to pardon me
For this intrusion, might I be so bold
As ask a question of your people here
Concerning the Queen's peace?
LYDIA. My people here
Are but a footman and a simple maid;
And both have craved a holiday to join
Some local festival. But, sir, your helmet
Proclaims the Metropolitan Police.
POLICEMAN. Madam, it does; and I may now inform you
That what you term a local festival
Is a most hideous outrage gainst the law,
Which we to quell from London have come down:
In short, a prizefight. My sole purpose here

Is to inquire whether your ladyship
Any bad characters this afternoon
Has noted in the neighborhood.

LYDIA. No, none, sir.
I had not let my maid go forth today
Thought I the roads unsafe.

POLICEMAN. Fear nothing, madam:
The force protects the fair. My mission here
Is to wreak ultion for the broken law.
I wish your ladyship good afternoon.

LYDIA. Good afternoon. [*Exit* POLICEMAN.
A prizefight! O my heart!
Cashel: hast thou deceived me? Can it be
Thou hast backslidden to the hateful calling
I asked thee to eschew?
O wretched maid,
Why didst thou flee from London to this place
To write thy father's life, whenas in town
Thou mightst have kept a guardian eye on him—
Whats that? A flying footstep—

Enter CASHEL

CASHEL. Sanctuary!
The law is on my track. What! Lydia here!

LYDIA. Ay: Lydia here. Hast thou done murder, then,
That in so horrible a guise thou comest?

CASHEL. Murder! I would I had. Yon cannibal
Hath forty thousand lives; and I have taen
But thousands thirty-nine. I tell thee, Lydia,
On the impenetrable sarcolobe
That holds his seedling brain these fists have pounded
By Shrewsb'ry clock an hour. This bruiséd grass
And cakéd mud adhering to my form
I have acquired in rolling on the sod
Clinched in his grip. This scanty reefer coat
For decency snatched up as fast I fled
When the police arrived, belongs to Mellish.
Tis all too short; hence my display of rib

And forearm mother-naked. Be not wroth
Because I seem to wink at you: by Heaven,
Twas Paradise that plugged me in the eye
Which I perforce keep closing. Pity me,
My training wasted and my blows unpaid.
Sans stakes, sans victory, sans everything
I had hoped to win. Oh, I could sit me down
And weep for bitterness.

LYDIA. Thou wretch, begone.

CASHEL. Begone!

LYDIA. I say begone. Oh, tiger's heart
Wrapped in a young man's hide, canst thou not live
In love with Nature and at peace with Man?
Must thou, although thy hands were never made
To blacken other's eyes, still batter at
The image of Divinity? I loathe thee.
Hence from my house and never see me more.

CASHEL. I go. The meanest lad on thy estate
Would not betray me thus. But tis no matter.

[He opens the door.

Ha! the police. I'm lost. *[He shuts the door again.*
Now shalt thou see
My last fight fought. Exhausted as I am,
To capture me will cost the coppers dear.
Come one, come all!

LYDIA. Oh, hide thee, I implore:
I cannot see thee hunted down like this.
There is my room. Conceal thyself therein.
Quick, I command. *[He goes into the room.*
With horror I foresee,
Lydia, that never lied, must lie for thee.

Enter POLICEMAN, *with* PARADISE *and* MELLISH *in custody,* BASHVILLE, constables, and others

POLICEMAN. Keep back your bruiséd prisoner lest he shock
This wellbred lady's nerves. Your pardon, maam;
But have you seen by chance the other one?
In this direction he was seen to run.

LYDIA. A man came here anon with bloody hands
And aspect that did turn my soul to snow.

POLICEMAN. Twas he. What said he?

LYDIA. Begged for sanctuary.
I bade the man begone.

POLICEMAN. Most properly.
Saw you which way he went?

LYDIA. I cannot tell.

PARADISE. He seen me coming; and he done a bunk.

POLICEMAN. Peace, there. Excuse his damaged features, lady:
He's Paradise; and this one's Byron's trainer,
Mellish.

MELLISH. Injurious copper, in thy teeth
I hurl the lie. I am no trainer, I.
My father, a respected missionary,
Apprenticed me at fourteen years of age
T' the poetry writing. To these woods I came
With Nature to commune. My revery
Was by a sound of blows rudely dispelled.
Mindful of what my sainted parent taught
I rushed to play the peacemaker, when lo!
These minions of the law laid hands on me.

BASHVILLE. A lovely woman, with distracted cries,
In most resplendent fashionable frock,
Approaches like a wounded antelope.

Enter ADELAIDE GISBORNE

ADELAIDE. Where is my Cashel? Hath he been arrested?

POLICEMAN. I would I had thy Cashel by the collar:
He hath escaped me.

ADELAIDE. Praises be for ever!

LYDIA. Why dost thou call the missing man thy Cashel?

ADELAIDE. He is mine only son.

ALL. Thy son!

ADELAIDE. My son.

LYDIA. I thought his mother hardly would have known him,
So crushed his countenance.

ADELAIDE. A ribald peer,
Lord Worthington by name, this morning came
With honeyed words beseeching me to mount
His four-in-hand, and to the country hie
To see some English sport. Being by nature
Frank as a child, I fell into the snare,
But took so long to dress that the design
Failed of its full effect; for not until
The final round we reached the horrid scene.
Be silent all; for now I do approach
My tragedy's catastrophe. Know, then,
That Heaven did bless me with an only son,
A boy devoted to his doting mother—

POLICEMAN. Hark! did you hear an oath from yonder room?

ADELAIDE. Respect a broken-hearted mother's grief,
And do not interrupt me in my scene.
Ten years ago my darling disappeared
(Ten dreary twelvemonths of continuous tears,
Tears that have left me prematurely aged;
For I am younger far than I appear).
Judge of my anguish when today I saw
Stripped to the waist, and fighting like a demon
With one who, whatsoe'er his humble virtues,
Was clearly not a gentleman, my son!

ALL. O strange event! O passing tearful tale!

ADELAIDE. I thank you from the bottom of my heart
For the reception you have given my woe;
And now I ask, where is my wretched son?
He must at once come home with me, and quit
A course of life that cannot be allowed.

Enter CASHEL

CASHEL. Policeman: I do yield me to the law.

LYDIA. Oh no.

ADELAIDE. My son!

CASHEL. My mother! Do not kiss me.
My visage is too sore.

POLICEMAN. The lady hid him.
This is a regular plant. You cannot be
Up to that sex. [*To Cashel*] You come along with me.

LYDIA. Fear not, my Cashel: I will bail thee out.

CASHEL. Never. I do embrace my doom with joy.
With Paradise in Pentonville or Portland
I shall feel safe: there are no mothers there.

ADELAIDE. Ungracious boy—

CASHEL. Constable: bear me hence.

MELLISH. Oh, let me sweetest reconcilement make
By calling to thy mind that moving song:—
[*Sings*] They say there is no other—

CASHEL. Forbear at once, or the next note of music
That falls upon thine ear shall clang in thunder
From the last trumpet.

ADELAIDE. A disgraceful threat
To level at this virtuous old man.

LYDIA. Oh, Cashel, if thou scornst thy mother thus,
How wilt thou treat thy wife?

CASHEL. There spake my fate:
I knew you would say that. Oh, mothers, mothers,
Would you but let your wretched sons alone
Life were worth living! Had I any choice
In this importunate relationship?
None. And until that high auspicious day
When the millennium on an orphaned world
Shall dawn, and man upon his fellow look,
Reckless of consanguinity, my mother
And I within the self-same hemisphere
Conjointly may not dwell.

ADELAIDE. Ungentlemanly!

CASHEL. I am no gentleman. I am a criminal,
Redhanded, baseborn—

ADELAIDE. Baseborn! Who dares say it?
Thou art the son and heir of Bingley Bumpkin
FitzAlgernon de Courcy Cashel Byron,
Sieur of Park Lane and Overlord of Dorset,
Who after three months wedded happiness

Rashly fordid himself with prussic acid,
Leaving a tearstained note to testify
That having sweetly honeymooned with me,
He now could say, O Death, where is thy sting?

POLICEMAN. Sir: had I known your quality, this cop
I had averted; but it is too late.
The law's above us both.

Enter LUCIAN, *with an Order in Council*

LUCIAN. Not so, policeman.
I bear a message from The Throne itself
Of fullest amnesty for Byron's past.
Nay, more: of Dorset deputy lieutenant
He is proclaimed. Further, it is decreed,
In memory of his glorious victory
Over our country's foes at Islington,
The flag of England shall for ever bear
On azure field twelve swanlike spots of white;
And by an exercise of feudal right
Too long disused in this anarchic age
Our sovereign doth confer on him the hand
Of Miss Carew, Wiltstoken's wealthy heiress.

[*General acclamation.*

POLICEMAN. Was anything, sir, said about me?

LUCIAN. Thy faithful services are not forgot:
In future call thyself Inspector Smith.

[*Renewed acclamation.*

POLICEMAN. I thank you, sir. I thank you, gentlemen.

LUCIAN. My former opposition, valiant champion,
Was based on the supposed discrepancy
Betwixt your rank and Lydia's. Heres my hand.

BASHVILLE. And I do here unselfishly renounce
All my pretensions to my lady's favor. [*Sensation.*

LYDIA. What, Bashville! didst thou love me?

BASHVILLE. Madam: yes.
Tis said: now let me leave immediately.

LYDIA. In taking, Bashville, this most tasteful course
You are but acting as a gentleman
In the like case would act. I fully grant

Your perfect right to make a declaration
Which flatters me and honors your ambition.
Prior attachment bids me firmly say
That whilst my Cashel lives, and polyandry
Rests foreign to the British social scheme,
Your love is hopeless; still, your services,
Made zealous by disinterested passion,
Would greatly add to my domestic comfort;
And if—

CASHEL. Excuse me. I have other views.
Ive noted in this man such aptitude
For art and exercise in his defence
That I prognosticate for him a future
More glorious than my past. Henceforth I dub him
The Admirable Bashville, Byron's Novice;
And to the utmost of my mended fortunes
Will back him gainst the world at ten stone six.

ALL. Hail, Byron's Novice, champion that shall be!

BASHVILLE. Must I renounce my lovely lady's service,
And mar the face of man?

CASHEL. Tis Fate's decree.
For know, rash youth, that in this star crost world
Fate drives us all to find our chiefest good
In what we can, and not in what we would.

POLICEMAN. A post-horn—hark!

CASHEL. What noise of wheels is this?

Lord Worthington drives upon the scene in his four-in-hand, and descends.

ADELAIDE. Perfidious peer!

LORD WORTHINGTON. Sweet Adelaide—

ADELAIDE. Forbear,
Audacious one: my name is Mrs Byron.

LORD WORTHINGTON. Oh, change that title for the sweeter one
Of Lady Worthington.

CASHEL. Unhappy man,
You know not what you do.

LYDIA. Nay, tis a match
Of most auspicious promise. Dear Lord Worthington,
You tear from us our mother-in-law—

CASHEL. Ha! True.

LYDIA. —but we will make the sacrifice. She blushes:
At least she very prettily produces
Blushing's effect.

ADELAIDE. My lord: I do accept you.

[*They embrace. Rejoicings.*

CASHEL [*aside*] It wrings my heart to see my noble backer
Lay waste his future thus. The world's a chessboard,
And we the merest pawns in fist of Fate.
[*Aloud*] And now, my friends, gentle and simple both,
Our scene draws to a close. In lawful course
As Dorset's deputy lieutenant I
Do pardon all concerned this afternoon
In the late gross and brutal exhibition
Of miscalled sport.

LYDIA [*throwing herself into his arms*] Your boats are burnt at last.

CASHEL. This is the face that burnt a thousand boats,
And ravished Cashel Byron from the ring.
But to conclude. Let William Paradise
Devote himself to science, and acquire,
By studying the player's speech in Hamlet,
A more refined address. You, Robert Mellish,
To the Blue Anchor hostelry attend him;
Assuage his hurts, and bid Bill Richardson
Limit his access to the fatal tap.
Now mount we on my backer's four-in-hand,
And to St George's Church, whose portico
Hanover Square shuts off from Conduit Street,
Repair we all. Strike up the wedding march;
And, Mellish, let thy melodies trill forth
Broad oer the wold as fast we bowl along.
Give me the post-horn. Loose the flowing rein;
And up to London drive with might and main.

[*Exeunt.*

VILLAGE WOOING

A COMEDIETTINA FOR TWO VOICES

Village Wooing was first produced at the Little Theatre, Dallas, on 16 April 1934, with the following cast:

THE DECK STEWARD	*Not named*
A PASSENGER, 'Z'	*Keith Woolley*
AN AUTHOR, 'A'	*Charles Meredith*

VILLAGE WOOING

FIRST CONVERSATION

The lounge deck of the Empress of Patagonia, a pleasure ship. Two of the deck chairs are occupied by A, *a literary looking pale gentleman under forty in green spectacles, a limp black beard, and a tropical suit of white silk, who is writing and does not wish to be disturbed, and* Z, *a young woman, presentable but not aristocratic, who is bored with her book. She is undressed for bathing, but is very modestly covered up with a not too flamboyant wrap.*

Z. Excuse me. Could you tell me the time?

A. [*curtly*] Eleven.

Z. My watch makes it half past ten.

A. The clocks were put on half an hour last night. We are going east.

Z. I always think it adds to the interest of a voyage having to put on your watch.

A. I am glad you are so easily interested. [*He resumes his writing pointedly*].

Z. The steward will be round with the soup in half an hour. I thought we should have to wait an hour.

A. I never take it. It interrupts my work.

Z. Why do you work all the time? It's not what one comes on a pleasure cruise for, is it?

A. Work is my only pleasure.

Z. Oh, thats not good sense, is it? It gives me the pip to see you always sitting there over your writing, and never enjoying yourself, nor even taking a drop of soup. You should get up and have a game of deck quoits: you will feel ever so much better after it.

A. I feel perfectly well, thank you. And I loathe deck games, especially deck quoits. The slapping of those silly things on the deck destroys the quiet of the ship.

Z. Oh, I see. That is why you select this end of the deck. I often wondered why.

A. Within the last fortnight you have inspected the priceless antiquities of Naples, Athens, Egypt, and the Holy Land. Please occupy your mind with them until the soup comes.

Z. I never cared much for geography. Where are we now?

A. We are on the Red Sea.

Z. But it's blue.

A. What did you expect it to be?

Z. Well, I didnt know what color the sea might be in these parts. I always thought the Red Sea would be red.

A. Well, it isnt.

Z. And isnt the Black Sea black?

A. It is precisely the color of the sea at Margate.

Z. [*eagerly*] Oh, I am so glad you know Margate. Theres no place like it in the season, is there?

A. I dont know: I have never been there.

Z. [*disappointed*] Oh, you ought to go. You could write a book about it.

A. [*shudders, sighs, and pretends to write very hard*]!

A pause.

Z. I wonder why they call it the Red Sea.

A. Because their fathers did. Why do you call America America?

Z. Well, because it is America. What else would you call it?

A. Oh, call it what you like, dear lady; but I have five hundred words to write before lunch; and I cannot do that if I talk to you.

Z. [*sympathetically*] Yes: it is awful to have to talk to people, isnt it? Oh, that reminds me: I have something really interesting to tell you. I believe the man in the cabin next mine beats his wife.

A. I feel a little like him myself. Some women would provoke any men to beat them.

Z. I will say this for him, that she always begins it.

A. No doubt.

Z. I hate a nagger: dont you?

A. It is your privilege as a woman to have the last word. Please take it and dont end all your remarks with a question.

Z. You are funny.

A. Am I? I never felt less funny in my life.

Z. I cant make you out at all. I am rather good at making out people as a rule; but I cant make head or tail of you.

A. I am not here to be made out. You are not here to make people out, but to revel in the enjoyments you have paid for. Deck tennis, deck quoits, shuffleboard, golf, squash rackets, the swimming pool, the gymnasium all invite you.

Z. I am no good at games: besides, theyre silly. I'd rather sit and talk.

A. Then for heaven's sake talk to somebody else. I have no time for talk. I have to work my passage.

Z. What do you mean: work your passage? You are not a sailor.

A. No. I make a precarious living on board ship by writing the Marco Polo Series of Chatty Guide Books. Unless I complete two thousand words a day I am bankrupt. I cannot complete them if you persist in talking to me.

Z. Do you mean you are writing a book about this cruise?

A. I am trying to—under great difficulties.

Z. Will I be in it?

A. [*grimly*] You will.

Z. How thrilling! I have never been put in a book before. You will read me what you have written about me, wont you?

A. When the book is published you can read it to your heart's content.

Z. But I should like you to get me right. After all, what do you know about me? I will tell you the whole of my life if you like.

A. Great heavens, NO. Please dont.

Z. Oh, I dont care who knows it.

A. Evidently. You would hardly offer to tell it to a perfect stranger if you cared, or if it was of the smallest interest.

Z. Oh, I'd never think of you as a stranger. Here we are on

the same ship, arnt we? And most people would think my life quite a romance. Wouldnt you really like to hear it?

A. No, I tell you. When I want romances I invent them for myself.

Z. Oh, well, perhaps you wouldnt think it very wonderful. But it was a regular treat for me. You may think because I am well dressed and travelling de lucks and all that, that I am an educated lady. But I'm not.

A. I never supposed for a moment that you were.

Z. But how could you know? How did you find out?

A. I didnt find out. I knew.

Z. Who told you?

A. Nobody told me.

Z. Then how did you know?

A. [*exasperated*] How do I know that a parrot isnt a bird of paradise?

Z. Theyre different.

A. Precisely.

Z. There you are, you see. But what would you take me for if you met me in a third class carriage?

A. I should not notice you.

Z. I bet you would. I maynt be a beauty; but when I get into a railway carriage every man in it has a look at me.

A. I am not Everyman. Everyman thinks that every woman that steps into a railway carriage may be the right woman. But she is always a disappointment.

Z. Same with the women, isnt it? If you were a woman youd know.

A. I am a woman; and you are a man, with a slight difference that doesnt matter except on special occasions.

Z. Oh, what a thing to say! I never could bring myself to believe that. I know, of course, that men have their weaknesses and their tempers; but all the same there is something wonderful you can get from a man that you never could get from a woman. Dont you think so?

A. Inexperienced men think there is something wonderful you can get from a woman that you never could get from a man. Hence many unhappy marriages.

Z. Are you married?

A. Widower. Are you?

Z. Oh, thats the first time youve asked me a question. We're getting on, arnt we?

A. No. I am not getting on with my work.

Z. Youre an intellectual, arnt you?

A. What do you think you mean by an intellectual?

Z. Only that you consider me no better than an idiot, and that you were a bad husband, most likely.

A. You are quite right on both points.

Z. I thought so.

A. And now, please, may I go on with my work?

Z. Please yourself. I'm not hindering you.

A. Thank you. [*He resumes his writing*].

A pause.

Z. What books would you recommend me to read to improve my mind?

A. [*shouting furiously*] Steward.

Z. Oh, you shouldnt trouble the steward now. He's busy getting the soup.

A. I want him to remove my chair to the very furthest extremity of this ship.

Z. I always say it's fresher under the awning at the end. You dont mind if I move too, do you?

A. If you persecute me any more I shall go overboard. Dont you see that I want to be left alone to work, and that your chatter is preventing me from working?

Z. [*sympathetically*] It is annoying to have somebody talking to you all the time when you dont want to. But it's just as bad when you want to talk, and the other person wont, isnt it?

A. There are three or four hundred persons on this ship. Cannot you find one of them with the same insatiable thirst for conversation as yourself?

Z. Well; but we all have to make ourselves agreeable, havnt we?

A. Not at oneanother's expense. You are not making yourself agreeable to me at present: you are driving me mad.

Z. My father used to say that men and women are always driving oneanother mad.

A. That sounds literary. Was your father a man of letters?

Z. Yes: I should think he was. A postman.

A. A what?

Z. A postman. A village postman.

A. Ha ha! Ha ha ha!

Z. What is there funny in that?

A. I dont know. Ha ha! The postman's daughter hath ripe red lips: butter and eggs and a pound of cheese! Ha ha ha!

Z. Well, I'm glad Ive amused you. But I dont think it's very polite of you to laugh at my father.

A. [*punctiliously—recovering himself*] You are right. I was rude. But a good laugh is worth a hundred pounds to me. I feel a different man. Forgive me. You see, you quoted a remark of your father's—almost an epigram—which suggested that he must have been a man of genius.

Z. Well, so he was. He had a genius for walking.

A. For what?

Z. For walking. When he was a child, he won a prize as The Infant Pedestrian. And would you believe it, my mother was that indoory that she grudged having to go out and do her marketing. After we had a telephone put in she never went out at all.

A. Thats strange. As she was never out and he was never in, the household should have been a quiet one; but that remark of his about men and women driving oneanother mad rather suggests the opposite.

Z. So it was the opposite. She was always complaining of being lonely; and he was always at her to take more exercise. When they were not quarrelling about that, they were quarrelling about me. You see, they had great ambitions for me. She wanted me to be a parlormaid in a great house. He wanted me to be a telephone operator. He said there is no future for the great houses and a great future for telephones.

A. And you? Had you no ambition for yourself?

Z. Oh, I wanted to be something romantic, like an acrobat in a circus.

A. And what actually happened?

Z. I became shop assistant and telephone operator in the village shop.

A. Do village shop assistants and telephone girls—

Z. Operators.

A. Pardon: operators. Do they earn enough to take cruises round the world in pleasure ships?

Z. Not they. I won the first prize in a newspaper competition. My mother wanted me to save it: she said it would help me to get a thrifty husband. My father told me to blue it all in a lump while I had the chance. "You will be poor all your life," he said; "but now you have the chance of living at the rate of five thousand a year for four months. Dont miss it," he said: "see what it's like. Have your fling," he said; "for they never can take that away from you once youve had it." His idea was a walking tour, spending the nights in the best hotels; but I chose the ship because it's more dressy and more people to look at. Besides, I can get all the walking I want round the deck. At the end of the cruise back I go to the village shop without a penny.

A. Have they found out here that you are not a lady?

Z. The Americans dont know the difference: they think my telephone talk is aristocratic; and the English wont speak to anyone anyhow. And lots of them are just like me.

A. Well, how do you like living at the rate of five thousand a year? Is it worth it?

Z. It is while the novelty lasts. You see, when youre at home you get tired of doing the same thing every day: the same places! the same faces! the same old round. When you get a holiday you go off in a crowded hot excursion train to the seaside and make yourself tired and miserable just because it's a change; and youd do anything for a change. But here it's change all the time until you begin to realize what it is to have a settled home and belong somewhere. I shant be sorry to get home to the shop and the telephone. I get such a dreadful lost dog feeling sometimes. Other times it seems such a foolish waste of money. And I hate wasting money.

A. Thats an extremely attractive point in your character. My wife used to waste my money. Stick to that and you will get married in no time.

Z. Oh, I have had plenty of offers. But you know it's a terrible thing to be a poor man's wife when you have been accustomed to a clean decent job. I have seen so many bright jolly girls turn into dirty old drudges through getting married.

A. Dont be afraid of dirt. Mine is a clean job; but I often wish I had a dirty one to exercise me and keep me in health. Women are so set on clean collars that they make their sons clerks when they would be stronger and earn more money as navvies. I wish I was a navvy instead of writing guide books.

Z. Well, whats to prevent you?

A. I am not trained to manual work. Half an hour of it would make me wish myself dead. And five minutes of my work would produce a strike among the navvies. I am only a writing machine, just as a navvy is a digging machine.

Z. I dont think the world is rightly arranged: do you?

A. We must take the world as we find it. It's we that are not rightly arranged.

Z. Thats what I mean. Well, I suppose I mustnt interrupt your work.

A. You mean that the steward is coming round with the soup at last.

Z. Well, it's half past eleven, isnt it?

The steward appears with the soup and offers it to Z, *who seizes it eagerly; then to* A.

A. No, thank you. No soup.

He buries himself in his work, unmolested.

She buries herself in the soup.

SECOND CONVERSATION

In a village shop and post office on the Wiltshire Downs on a fine summer morning. The counter is for general shopping for most of its length; but one end is reserved and railed in for postal business. A couple of chairs are available for customers. The goods for sale include ginger beer in stone bottles, tablets of milk chocolate, glass jars of sweets containing (inter alia) sugared almonds, all on the counter; cheese, butter, and Hovis bread handy to the scales; and, in front of the counter, a sack of apples on the floor and some string bags hanging from the rafters.

Z. [*invisible*] Th-reee ni-nnn. Sorry: no such number. Whoo-mmm do you want? Doctor Byles? One fi-fff. You are through.

A *comes in. He is in hiking costume, with stick and rucksack, but wears well cut breeches (not plus fours) instead of shorts. Seeing nobody to attend to him he raps loudly on the counter with his stick.* Z *emerges.*

A. I want a packet of milk chocolate—

Z. Thanks very much.

A. [*continuing*]—a couple of hard apples—

Z. Thanks very much. [*She comes out through the counter to get them from the sack*].

A. [*continuing*]—quarter of a pound of Cheddar cheese—

Z. Thanks very much.

A. Dont interrupt me. You can express your gratitude for the order when I have finished. Quarter of a pound of your best butter, a small loaf of Hovis, and twopennyworth of sugared almonds.

Z. Anything else?

A. No, thank you.

Z. Thanks very much. [*She goes back through the counter to cut and weigh the butter and cheese*].

He sits down watching her deft but leisurely proceedings.

A. Do you sell baskets?

Z. We sell everything. Hadnt you better have a string bag? It's handier; and it packs away almost to nothing when it's empty.

A. What is a string bag? Shew me one.

Z. [*coming out and taking one down*] This is the cheapest. Or would you like a better quality with a Zip fastening?

A. Certainly not. I should have the trouble of opening and shutting it, and the worry of wondering whether it would open or shut, with no compensatory advantage whatever.

Z. Thats just like you. Youre not a bit changed.

A. What do you mean? I have been in this shop for less than two minutes. Why should I have changed in that time?

Z. Excuse me: I shouldnt have mentioned it. Will you take a string bag?

A. Yes.

Z. Thanks very much. Shall I put the rest of the order into it?

A. Of course. What else do you suppose I am buying it for? Have you any buttermilk?

Z. Sorry. We dont stock it.

A. Any ginger beer?

Z. Yes. We have a very good local brew.

A. Shove a bottle into the string bag.

Z. Thanks very much.

A. How many times a day do you say thanks very much?

Z. Depends on the number of orders.

A. Dont say it to me again, if you dont mind. It gets on my nerves.

Z. It used to get on mine, at first. But I am used to it.

A. Have you a guide book of this village?

Z. Sorry. Theres a leaflet in the church, written by the vicar. You are expected to put tuppence in the box for it. Excuse me; but the chocolates are tuppence, sixpence, and a shilling. Which size would you run to?

A. It is a poor heart that never rejoices. I will have a shilling one.

Z. Thanks very much.

A. Dont.

Z. Excuse me: I cant help it. I say it without thinking: same as if you touched a button.

The telephone rings.

A. Someone has touched the button.

Z. [*vanishing into the post office section*] What number please? Whitehall on-n-ne two on-n-e two. I will ring you. Whitehall one two one two. Yes. [*She reappears*] Thats a police call.

A. You need not point the information at me. I am not the criminal.

Z. Oh, it isnt a criminal. Somebody thats been broadcasted on the wireless as lost. You know the sort of thing. Missing from his home since January the first. Last seen in a deck chair on the Empress of Patagonia talking to a female. Suffering from loss of memory.

A. How extraor—[*the telephone rings again*].

Z. Excuse me. [*She vanishes*]. You are through to Whitehall. [*She reappears*].

A. You have hit on an extraordinary coincidence. I wonder whether you will believe me when I tell you that in January last I was sitting on the deck of a ship named the Empress of Patagonia, and that I was talking to a female—or rather she was talking to me. How that woman did talk!

Z. And are you suffering from loss of memory?

A. Certainly not. I never forget anything.

Z. Oh, then it cant be you, can it?

A. There! Can it? That woman always finished up with can it? wont it? isnt it? so that you had to answer her out of common politeness. Take care never to pick up that trick or you will be murdered some day.

Z. Some people are like that. It often goes with orange colored eyes [*or whatever color her eyes happen to be*]. Did you notice the color of her eyes?

A. No: I never notice things like that. I am not a detective. It is people's characters that impress me; I cant tell you the color of her hair or the shape of her nose; but I can tell you that she was a most fearful nuisance. How much does all that come to?

Z. The string bag sixpence, chocolates a shilling: one and sixpence. The ginger beer is—

A. Spare me the details. Will ten shillings cover it?

Z. Oh yes, of course. You shouldnt be so careless about money.

A. [*presenting a Treasury note*] Cease preaching. Take it; and give me the change.

Z. Let me see. Eighteenpence, and fourpence for the ginger beer is one and tenpence, isnt it?

A. Have I denied it?

Z. Cheese threepence: two and a penny; butter sixpence: two and sevenpence; apples we sell by the pound. Hadnt you better have a pound?

A. How many to the pound?

Z. Three.

A. I cannot eat more than two apples at a time. Charge me for a pound; and eat the odd one yourself.

Z. Oh well, say threepence for two: thats two and tenpence, isnt it?

A. I dont know.

Z. Hovis, tuppence halfpenny. Three shillings and a halfpenny. Do you happen to have a halfpenny to save having to take fippence halfpenny in coppers?

A. I hate halfpennies: I always throw them away. Stop. I have one. Here.

Z. Thanks very much. [*Handing him his change coin by coin*] Three, four, five, seven and six, ten. Thanks very much.

A. [*pocketing his change, but remaining comfortably seated*] Dont you find it rather dull in this village shop saying thanks very much all day?

Z. Well, no matter where you are you are doing the same thing all day and every day, arnt you? The only way to get it off your mind is to live in the same place and stick at the same job. Then you never have to think about it. Thats the way the people live here; and they live for ever so long: eighty's no age here. Grandfather will be a hundred and two in August. Thats because he's never had to worry about what he'll do or where he'll go. He just imagines and imagines. It's the only way to be happy and longlived.

A. But if your imagination has only one village in it it must be pretty bare. How would you like to live in a room with only one chair in it.

Z. Well, if you have only one seat what more do you want than one chair? Up at the castle there are thirtysix chairs of one sort or another in the big drawing room, but Lady Flopping cant flop on more than one, can she?

A. [*pointing to the vacant chair*] May I suggest that you flop on that one while we talk?

Z. [*sitting down*] Thanks very much.

A. I am not interrupting your work, I hope. There is nothing so maddening as to be talked to when you want to work.

Z. Talking is part of the work in a village shop.

A. Tell me: do you ever read?

Z. I used to read travels and guide books. We used to stock the Marco Polo series. I was mad about travelling. I had daydreams about the glory that was Greece, the grandeur that was Rome, and all that flapdoodle.

A. Flapdoodle!

Z. Well, I suppose I shouldnt call it that; but it ended in my going to Rome and Athens. They were all right; but the old parts were half knocked down; and I couldnt see any glory or grandeur different to Cheltenham. I was glad to be home again. And I had so wanted to meet the Marco Polo man and walk about with him in the ruins by moonlight and hear him go on about them!

A. The Marco Polo man! The milkman! the postman! the muffin man! the Marco Polo man! Some frustrated poet, earning his crust by quoting scraps of verse to bring the Call of the East to dreaming telephone girls.

Z. Operators.

A. Operators dont dream. Girls! girls of the golden west. Did that poor devil never bring you the Call of the East?

Z. I'd read about it in novels and seen it on the films. They were all about moony drunkards and sheeks and the sort of girls that go dotty about them. I went right round the world to see the reality. Pretty places, of course; but the heat! and the mosquitoes! and the smells!! Travelling just destroyed the world for me as I imagined it. Give me this village all the time.

A. Had you no thrill when you stood somewhere where a poet had said "Stop; for thy tread is on an empire's dust"?

Z. A guide, you mean. Theyd take the poetry out of anything; and all the time youre thinking what you ought to give them. If you fancy empires' dusts and all that sort of thing you should meet our vicar and start him talking about our standing stones, and the barrows on the downs, and the Mound. Every grain of our dust, he says, is full of history. Same everywhere, I expect.

A. Are you married?

Z. No. Why? Have you any intentions?

A. Dont be in a hurry. Weve known each other less than ten minutes.

Z. How much better do you think you will know me when we have talked for twenty years?

A. That is profoundly true. Still, I must think it over.

Z. Nobody would ever marry if they thought it over. Youve got to take your chance, no matter how long you think.

A. You are in a hurry.

Z. Well, I am past the age at which girls marry here, though I'm the pick of this village. Thats because I thought all my offers over. So I have made up my mind to take the next man that asks me, provided he's reasonably suitable.

A. Do I strike you as being reasonably suitable?

Z. Well, I think I have the sort of commonsense you need to keep you straight. And you being a widower know what to expect from a woman. An inexperienced man expects the earth.

A. How do you know that I am a widower?

Z. You told me.

A. Did I? When did I tell you?

Z. Never mind. You did. I have noticed you have a bad memory; but I have a very good one; so it wont matter.

A. Steady. Steady. I have not yet made myself liable to an action for breach of promise.

Z. Dont be afraid. I'm not that sort. We dont consider it respectable here.

A. Should I get any money with you? Do you own the shop?

Z. No. All the money I ever had I blued on a trip round the world. But Mrs Ward is getting too old for the business: she couldnt run it now without me. If you could afford to buy her an annuity she'd sell it.

A. I dont know how much annuities cost.

Z. You will find it in Whitaker's almanac.

A. This is rather upsetting. Somehow I have always taken it for granted that when I married again I'd marry a woman with money.

Z. Oh, that wouldnt suit you at all. She'd want to spend it going into society and travelling about. How could you bear that sort of life? you that never spoke to anyone on the ship and wouldnt take any part in their games and dances! When it got about that you were the Marco Polo man—the man of all our dreams as you might say—I made a bet that I'd get you to talk to me; and I had all the trouble in the world to win it.

A. Do you mean to say that we have met before? That you were on that trip round the world?

Z. Of course I do. But you never notice anything. Youre always reading or writing. The world doesnt exist for you. You never looked at me really. Youre shy with strangers, arnt you?

A. I am absolutely certain I never spoke to any woman on that ship. If I talk to women they always want to marry me.

Z. Well, there you are, you see! The moment I set eyes on you I said to myself, "Now thats the sort of man that would suit me as a husband." I'd have said it even if you hadnt been the Marco Polo man.

A. Love at first sight: what?

Z. Oh no. You know, if I fell in love with a man I'd never marry him: he could make me so miserable. But there was something about you: I dont exactly know what; but it made me feel that I could do with you in the house; and then I could fall in love with anyone I liked without any fear of making a fool of myself. I suppose it was because you are one of the quiet sort and dont run after women.

A. How do you know I dont run after women?

Z. Well, if you want to know, it's because you didnt run after me. You mightnt believe it; but men do run after me.

A. Why?

Z. Oh, how do I know? They dont know, themselves. But the lot of money they spend on things they dont want merely to come in and have a look at me and a word with me, you wouldnt believe. It's worth at least twenty pounds a year to the business.

A. [*putting on his glasses and looking at her attentively for the first time*] I shouldnt call you a pretty woman.

Z. Oh, I'm not pretty. But what you might call desirable, dont you think?

A. [*alarmed*] No I dont think. May I explain? I am a man of letters and a gentleman. I am accustomed to associate with ladies. That means that I am accustomed to speak under certain well understood reserves which act as a necessary protection to both parties. You are not a lady: you are a villager; but somebody has educated you—probably the Church or the local authority—to a point at which you can impose on unobservant and unwary travellers. You have had finishing lessons on the telephone which give you a distinguished articulation: you can say Th-reee fiv-v-v-v-e ni-n-n-n instead of theree fauv nawn. But you have not acquired any of the reserves. You say what you think. You announce all the plans that wellbred women conceal. You play with your cards on the table instead of keeping them where a lady should keep them: up your sleeve.

Z. Well, wheres the harm?

A. Oh, no harm. Quite the contrary. But I feel rushed.

Z. What do you mean? rushed?

A. Rushed. Precipitated. Carried to lengths I had no intention of going to.

Z. Well, it gets you somewhere: doesnt it?

A. Yes; but where?

Z. Here. Theres no mystery about it. Here, in a good business in a village shop in a quiet place, with me to keep it straight and look after you.

A. May I ask how much that expression "looking after me" includes? Let me be clear on the point. As a matter of fact I possess a small property which I could sell for enough to purchase an annuity for old Mrs Williams—

Z. Ward.

A. I believe I have enough to purchase annuities for both Mrs Ward and Mrs Williams, as they are presumably both centenarians. But why on earth should I complicate the transaction by marrying you? I could pay you your present wages—

Z. Salary.

A. I beg your pardon: salary. You will retain your present position as my shopgirl.

Z. Shop assistant.

A. I beg your pardon: shop assistant. You can then make your own matrimonial arrangements, and leave me to make mine.

Z. Oh, I'll make my own matrimonial arrangements all right enough. You may depend on that.

A. Excuse me: I added "and leave me to make mine." Can I depend on you for that also?

Z. Well, we'll see.

A. [*angrily firm*] No: you will not see.

Z. Well, what?

A. I dont know what. I will not commit myself. We'll see.

Z. Just so: we'll see. It's a bargain then?

A. No: it most certainly is not a bargain. When I entered this shop half an hour ago I had not the faintest notion of buying a village shop or marrying a village maiden or any of the things you have put into my head. Have you ever read the fable of the spider and the fly?

Z. No; but I used to sing a song called the honeysuckle and the bee.

A. [*resolutely*] Goodmorning. [*He makes for the door*].

Z. [*following him with the string bag*] You are forgetting your things.

A. [*taking it*] Thank you.

Z. Thanks very much.

She tempts him to kiss her.

A. No!!! [*he strides out*].

THIRD CONVERSATION

A is now the proprietor of the shop with Z as his hired assistant. The counter has been fitted with a desk at the opposite end to the post office section. At this A sits writing. He wears pepper-and-salt trousers of country cut, with an apron. He is in his shirtsleeves, and looks every inch a shopkeeper. Z comes in through the post office, very fresh and matutinal.

Z. Morning, boss.

A. Good morning, slave.

Z. I havnt begun slaving yet. You have been at it for half an hour. Whatever on earth are you working at so hard?

A. I am making out my balance sheet.

Z. Oh, you neednt do that. The accountant's clerk from Salisbury does all that when he makes out the income tax return. Youre not expected to do figures in this village. Fancy old Mrs Ward doing such a thing!

A. When I bought this shop from Mrs Ward for an annuity I found she was much cleverer at figures than I was. She should have been a moneylender.

Z. She was. She lent a shilling for a penny a week.

A. That must have been between four and five hundred per cent per annum. Shylock would have blushed.

Z. Whats the good of it when you have to give credit at the shop, and then lend the customers the money to pay you?

A. Mrs Ward should have gone to Geneva. International finance would have come naturally to her.

Z. Thats too clever for me. Anyhow, you neednt worry over a balance sheet. The accountant will do all that for you.

A. [*rising and waving the balance sheet proudly as he comes through the counter into the public part of the shop*] This is not an accountant's balance sheet. It is a Robinson Crusoe balance sheet.

Z. [*following him*] Whatever's that?

A. Crusoe drew up a balance sheet of the advantages and disadvantages of being cast away on a desert island. I am cast away in a village on the Wiltshire Downs. I am drawing up a similar balance sheet. I propose to read it to you as far as I have got. [*He takes one of the customer's chairs*]. You can remind me of anything I have forgotten.

Z. Lets have it. [*She takes the other chair*].

A. I begin with the credit entries.

Z. Things to your own credit, you mean?

A. No, to the credit of village shopkeeping as a way of life.

Z. Oh, you are silly, boss.

A. That is a disrespectful remark. As such, it should not be made to a boss by his slave. The understanding on which I raised your salary when I engaged you as my assistant was that our relations should be completely conventional and businesslike on your side, however I might occasionally forget myself.

Z. [*rising*] Very well: you can keep your balance sheet to yourself. I will go on with the telephone call book.

A. You will do nothing of the sort. You will do what I tell you to do. That is what I pay you for. Sit down again. [*She does so*]. Now listen. [*He takes up his manuscript and reads*]. Item: I have sharpened my faculties, and greatly improved in observation and mathematics.

Z. Couldnt you put it into shorter words? What does it mean?

A. It means that formerly I always took what money was given me without condescending to count it or attempting to calculate it. I can now both calculate and count quite rapidly. Formerly I made no distinctions between grades of butter and eggs. To me an egg was an egg: butter was butter. I now make critical distinctions of the greatest subtlety, and value them in terms of money. I am forced to admit that the shopkeeper is enormously superior to the Marco Polo man, and that I have learnt more in three months in this shop than I learnt in three years in Oxford.

Z. I cant believe that about the learning. But see how your manners have improved!

A. My manners!!

Z. Yes. Why, on that ship you hadnt a word to throw to a dog; and if anyone came near you you shrank up into yourself like a hedgehog, afraid that they didnt belong to your class and wanted to speak to you without an introduction. Now it's a pleasure to hear you say "Good morning; and what can I do for you today, Mrs Burrel?" and "Have you noticed the cauliflowers today, maam? Not a touch of frost on them!" and "Sparrowgrass very good today, my lady, if you would be wanting some."

A. I positively deny that I have ever in my life called asparagus sparrowgrass to an educated customer. Of course, when people are too ignorant to know the names of what they eat, that is another matter.

Z. Well, anyhow, your manners have improved, havnt they?

A. I dont know. I know that they are no longer disinterested and sincere.

Z. No more they never used to be. Never easy with anybody. Now you are hail fellow well met, as you might say, with everybody.

A. The world has become a world of customers. Let me write that down. [*He pencils on the back of his balance sheet*] "Manners will never be universally good until every person is every other person's customer."

Z. Youre not a real shopkeeper yet, boss. All you want is to find something clever to write.

A. Well, why not? Find enough clever things to say, and you are a Prime Minister. Write them down, and you are a Shakespear.

Z. Yes; but who wants to be a Prime Minister or a Shakespear? Youve got to make a living.

A. Well, am I not making a living? I am no poorer than when I bought the shop.

Z. But if the money goes as fast as it comes you cant save anything.

A. I loathe saving. It turns human nature sour. "Cast your

bread upon the waters; and it will return to you after many days."

Z. And how are you to live for the many days with nothing to eat?

A. I dont know. One does, somehow. Stop asking questions; and let us get on with the balance sheet.

Z. I speak for your good.

A. [*rising wrathfully*] The most offensive liberty one human being can possibly take with another. What business is it of yours?

Z. [*rising and facing him*] If you wont think for yourself somebody else must think for you. It's my business as much as yours.

A. Oh, indeed! Who does this shop belong to? I mean to whom does this shop belong?

Z. I get my living out of it, dont I. If it shuts up what becomes of me?

A. Well, if you come to that, what becomes of me? You can get another job. I very greatly doubt whether anyone would give me one. [*Calming down*] Can you not be content with the fact that the shop is making enough to support two people? [*He resumes his seat*].

Z. Aye; but suppose it had to support three people!

A. Why suppose? It hasnt: thats all.

Z. It's not all. If you marry a stranger there will be three. And what about the children?

A. The remedy is simple. I shall not marry.

Z. You dont know.

A. Neither do you.

Z. Yes I do. You have married once; and you will marry twice. Somebody will snap you up. You are that sort of man.

A. If a woman snaps me up she must take the consequences. She must assist in the shop. And you will get the sack.

Z. Oh, you are tiresome. [*She sits down, discouraged*]. But you see my point, at all events.

A. No. What point?

Z. Well, that it's really cheaper to keep a wife than to pay an assistant. Let alone that you dont have to live a single life.

A. You can get rid of an assistant if she doesnt suit. You cant get rid of a wife.

Z. If people thought that way, theyd never get married.

A. Precisely.

Z. In this life you have to take chances.

A. I have taken them, and escaped.

Z. You wont escape here. We dont hold with bachelors here.

A. You cant do without a general shop here, nor a post office. While I command both I am in an impregnable strategic position.

Z. Well, I dont like to say it; but people are beginning to talk.

A. Beginning! When did they ever stop?

Z. Oh, theres no use talking to you.

A. Not the slightest.

Z. Oh well then, take a month's notice. [*She rises*].

A. A month's notice!

Z. Yes: a month's notice.

A. A month's notice because I refuse to marry some ridiculous village maiden or illiterate widow with whom I could not hold a moment's conversation!

Z. Wives are not for conversation: thats for visitors. Youve had plenty of conversation with me.

A. Leave yourself out of this conversation, please.

Z. Oh, very well. A month's notice.

A. Dont say that again. Utter nonsense. What have you to complain of? You are quite well off here. I purposely pay you ten pounds a year more than you could get anywhere else.

Z. Why?

A. What do you mean, why?

Z. Why do you pay me ten pounds more than you could get another assistant for?

A. Heaven only knows!

Z. [*in a fury*] I'll go this very day. I'll go this very minute. You can keep my month. You dont know when youre well off. Youre selfish. I dont wonder your wife died. Did she die mad?

A. [*gravely*] As a matter of fact, she did. I am one of those unlucky men who draw the black chances in the lottery of marriage.

Z. [*remorsefully*] Oh, I didnt know: I didnt indeed. I was only joking. [*She sits again*] I wouldnt have said it for the world if I'd known.

A. Never mind: I know you didnt mean it. By the way, I made an inconsiderate remark which hurt you. I did not intend that. I should have told you seriously that I pay you ten pounds more than the market rate because I value your services in the shop, and wish to offer you every inducement to stay here permanently.

Z. Ten pounds extra, to stay all my life here as a single woman!

A. Not necessarily. You can get married if you wish.

Z. Who to?

A. To whom? Oh, anyone.

Z. Anyone in the village is good enough for me; but nobody in the village is good enough for you: is that it?

A. Dont lose your temper again.

Z. I will if I like. And if you knew how near I was to putting a couple of extra words in, youd perhaps realize that a woman wants something more in life than a job and a salary.

A. I know that perfectly well. There is one thing we are all out for when we are young.

Z. And what is that, pray?

A. Trouble, adventure, hardship, care, disappointment, doubt, misery, danger, and death.

Z. Not me, thank you. All I want is a husband and the usual consequences.

A. The same thing. Marriage is the village form of all these adventures.

Z. Oh, why dont you take a more cheerful view of life?

A. I have learnt not to expect too much from life. That is the secret of real cheerfulness, because I am always getting agreeable surprises instead of desolating disappointments.

Z. Well, your second marriage may be an agreeable surprise, maynt it?

A. What, exactly, do you mean by my second marriage? I have only been married once. I mean I have been married only once.

Z. Well, look here? Straight, now? Is there any man in this village that would be suitable to me now that I have got used to you?

A. My dear: men are all alike.

Z. You mean it will make no difference to me who I marry.

A. Very little, I am afraid.

Z. And women are all alike too, arnt they?

A. [*suspicious*] What are you getting at?

Z. If it doesnt matter who anybody marries, then it doesnt matter who I marry and it doesnt who you marry.

A. Whom, not who.

Z. Oh, speak English: youre not on the telephone now. What I mean is that if it doesnt matter to me it doesnt matter to you either.

A. You admit, then, that it doesnt matter?

Z. No I dont. It's a lie.

A. Oh!

Z. Dont "oh" me. All men are not alike to me. There are men —and good nice men, too—that I wouldnt let touch me. But when I saw you on the ship I said to myself "I could put up with him."

A. Not at all. You told me just now that you said something quite different. I believe you really said something much more rapturous. Being rather a futile sort of person I attract vigorous women like you.

Z. When you looked at me out of the corner of your eye— you looked at all the women out of the corner of your eye in spite of your keeping yourself so much to yourself— did you never say "I could put up with her"?

A. No. I said "Damn that woman: she wont stop talking to me and interrupting my work."

Z. Well, I tell you we were made for oneanother. It maynt be as plain to you as to me yet; but if it's plain to me there must be something in it; for I'm never wrong when I see a thing quite plain. I dont believe youd ever have bought this shop and given up being a gentleman if I hadnt been here.

A. Now that you mention it I believe that is true. You were one of the amenities of the estate.

Z. Well, I might be one of the amenities of the estate of holy matrimony, mightnt I?

A. Take care. You may find what you are trying to do easier than you think. About five per cent of the human race consists of positive masterful acquisitive people like you, obsessed with some passion which they must gratify at all hazards. The rest let them have their own way because they have neither the strength nor the courage to resist, or because the things the masterful ones want seem trifling beside the starry heavens and the destiny of Man. I am not one of the masterful ones. I am not worth marrying. Any woman could marry me if she took trouble enough.

Z. Thats just what I'm afraid of. If I let you out of my sight for a month I might find you married to someone else at the end of it. Well, I'm taking no chances. I dont set up to be masterful: I dont like selfish uppish domineering people any more than you do; but I must and will have you; and thats all about it.

A. Well, you already have me—as an employer. And you are independent of me, and can leave me if you are not satisfied.

Z. How can I be satisfied when I cant lay my hands on you? I work for you like a slave for a month on end; and I would have to work harder as your wife than I do now; but there come times when I want to get hold of you in my arms, every bit of you; and when I do I'll give you something better to think about than the starry heavens, as you call them. Youll find that you have senses to gratify as well as fine things to say.

A. Senses! You dont know what youre talking about. Look around you. Here in this shop I have everything that can gratify the senses: apples, onions, and acid drops; pepper and mustard; cosy comforters and hot water bottles. Through the window I delight my eyes with the old church and market place, built in the days when beauty came naturally from the hands of mediæval craftsmen. My ears are filled with delightful sounds, from the cooing of doves and the humming of bees to the wireless echoes of Beethoven and Elgar. My nose can gloat over our sack of fresh lavender or our special sixpenny Eau de Cologne when the smell of rain on dry earth is denied me. My senses are saturated with satisfactions of all sorts. But when I am full to the neck with onions and acid drops; when I am so fed up with mediæval architecture that I had rather die than look at another cathedral; when all I desire is rest from sensation, not more of it, what use will my senses be to me if the starry heavens still seem no more than a senseless avalanche of lumps of stone and wisps of gas— if the destiny of Man holds out no higher hope for him than the final extinction and annihilation of so mischievous and miserable a creature?

Z. We dont bother about all that in the village.

A. Yes you do. Our best seller here is Old Moore's Almanack; and next to it comes Napoleon's Book of Fate. Old Mrs Ward would never have sold the shop to me if she had not become persuaded that the Day of Judgment is fixed for the seventh of August next.

Z. I dont believe such nonsense. Whats it all got to do with you and me?

A. You are inexperienced. You dont know. You are the dupe of thoughtless words like sensuality, sensuousness, and all the rest of the twaddle of the Materialists. I am not a Materialist: I am a poet; and I know that to be in your arms will not gratify my senses at all. As a matter of mere physical sensation you will find the bodily contacts to which you are looking forward neither convenient nor decorous.

Z. Oh, dont talk like that. You mustnt let yourself think about it like that.

A. You must always let yourself think about everything. And you must think about everything as it is, not as it is talked about. Your secondhand gabble about gratifying my senses is only your virgin innocence. We shall get quite away from the world of sense. We shall light up for oneanother a lamp in the holy of holies in the temple of life; and the lamp will make its veil transparent. Aimless lumps of stone blundering through space will become stars singing in their spheres. Our dull purposeless village existence will become one irresistible purpose and nothing else. An extraordinary delight and an intense love will seize us. It will last hardly longer than the lightning flash which turns the black night into infinite radiance. It will be dark again before you can clear the light out of your eyes; but you will have seen; and for ever after you will think about what you have seen and not gabble catchwords invented by the wasted virgins that walk in darkness. It is to give ourselves this magic moment that we feel that we must and shall hold one-another in our arms; and when the moment comes, the world of the senses will vanish; and for us there will be nothing ridiculous, nothing uncomfortable, nothing unclean, nothing but pure paradise.

Z. Well, I am glad you take a nice view of it; for now I come to think of it I never could bear to be nothing more to a man than a lollipop. But you mustnt expect too much.

A. I shall expect more than you have ever dreamt of giving, in spite of the boundless audacity of women. What great men would ever have been married if the female nobodies who snapped them up had known the enormity of their own presumption? I believe they all thought they were going to refine, to educate, to make real gentlemen of their husbands. What do you intend to make of me, I wonder?

Z. Well, I have made a decent shopkeeper of you already, havnt I? But you neednt be afraid of my not appreciating you. I want a fancy sort of husband, not a common villager that any woman could pick up. I shall be proud of you. And now Ive nailed you, I wonder at my own nerve.

A. So do I.

Z. I'm not a bit like that, you know, really. Something above me and beyond me drove me on. Thats why I know it will be all right. Dont be afraid. I cant make a fine speech about it like you; but it will be all right. I promise you that.

A. Very well. Go round to the rectory; and put up the banns.

And tell the rector's wife that we got in some prime artichokes this morning. She's fond of artichokes.

Z. You are sure you feel happy about it?

A. I dont know what I feel about it. Go and do as you are told; and dont ask ridiculous questions.

The telephone rings. She hastens to answer it.

Z. Number, please? . . . Oh, an order. Thanks very much. . . . Yes: we have some very fine artichokes just in this morning. . . . Thanks very much: they shall be sent round directly. Oh; and theres something else—are you there? . . . Sorry to detain you: could I speak to the rector? . . . Yes: it's rather particular. It's about banns . . . banns . . . BANNS: b for beauty, a for audacity, two enns for nonsense, and s for singing. . . . Yes, banns: thats right. . . . Who are the what? . . . Oh, the parties! Of course. Well, it's—

The curtain falls

In the Sunda Strait,
27th January 1933